The Grandmother of Time

The Grandmother of Time

A Woman's Book of Celebrations, Spells, and Sacred Objects for Every Month of the Year

ZSUZSANNA E. BUDAPEST

HarperSanFrancisco
A Division of HarperCollinsPublishers

Artwork for chapter openers by Judith Mitchell.
Other art by Robin Dorn.
Book Design by Irene Imfeld.

Library of Congress Cataloging-in-Publication Data

Budapest, Zsuzsanna Emese, 1940–
    The grandmother of time: a woman's book of celebrations, spells,
and sacred objects for every month of the year / Zsuzsanna Budapest.
    —1st ed.
        p.   cm.
    Bibliography: p.
    Includes index.
    ISBN 0-06-250109-7
    1. Women—Prayer-books and devotions—English.   2. Devotional
calendars.   I. Title.
BL625.7.B83   1989
291.4'46'024042—dc19   88-45994
                                                            CIP

98 97 96 95   RRD(H) 10 9

What is remembered lives. I dedicate this work to the Goddess of Celebrations, Habondia; may she lead us back to her paradise.

On the human side, I dedicate this book to my beloved sons, László and Gábor; to my mother, Masika Szilagyi; and to my generation, the numerous and powerful, possibly revolutionary Baby boomers, the mothers and fathers of the twenty-first century!

CONTENTS

MARCH

APRIL

MAY

JUNE

JULY

AUGUST

SEPTEMBER

OCTOBER

NOVEMBER

DECEMBER

This book contains recommendations for a variety of self-healing techniques and is not intended to replace the services of a qualified professional. Any application of the recommendations set forth in the following pages is at the reader's discretion and sole risk.

HOW TO USE THIS BOOK ———————

ANNA PERENNA IS THE proper name of the Grandmother of Time. *Anna* means "the year," *Perenna* means "perennial, returning in time." Anna is our guide on our journey around the sun. When you consult Anna, when you commune with her, you start internalizing the sacred calendar of her days. You begin to grow in importance in your own eyes and heart. The celebrations, spells, stories, and teachings take you deeper into your own world and give you more power to perform the miracles of everyday life. Let's say you are upset about something, or feel lonely, or have a birthday coming up—in the table of contents you can look up the appropriate spell, ritual, or information about these issues. In addition you will find in the back of this book an index of all the concepts we talk about. So you may have been born in June, but you will find the birthday celebration in January, because I myself was born in January. If you look up *love* in the index, you may find it several times, because I think love is a priority.

You can read this book in any order you like; it is not a novel. The strong presence of old Roman holydays testifies to the power of the Roman Empire, which engulfed most of Europe and preserved or abolished her native customs. The ones the Romans wrote about that I could trace were the lucky survivors. I was not able to list all the holydays my research brought to light due to space limitations. The ones listed were the most significant ones, worth giving a modern rebirth. I included holydays from other continents as well—obviously this is not the complete list of them. The focus of this book is the lost traditions and holydays of the ancient Europeans before they were Christianized by force, but I could not resist the rich culture of Asia, Africa, and North and South America to show the unity of spirit.

The stories from my life are arranged according to the seasons, not chronologically. I have tried to share with you how I lived the seasons, how my life was shaped by the Grandmother of Time.

I have felt an overwhelming urgency to write this book. I am worried that our society, besotted with the Industrial Revolution, has pushed us so far away from the good table of plenty that we may not even miss the spiritual quality of living, which comes from celebrating our lives, our rites of passage. Life is more than having a job or making money. Now, as we approach the turn of the century, we must relearn our ancient heritage, begin to get in touch with old celebrations, stage more festivals, enrich our lives with guiltless power. Anna, our Grandmother, wants us to be happy and significant. Shouldn't we want the same?

Acknowledgments

This book has sprouted from my radio feature on KPFA-FM in Berkeley called "Everyday Is a Holiday." I thank Ginny Z. Berson and my audience for their encouragement, which enabled me to continue and develop my book. Special thanks are owed to my main source, Jane Ellen Harrison, distinguished author and professor of archaeology, who brought the special women's holydays to my attention through her works *Themis* and *Prolegomena to the Study of Greek Religion*. I have also been greatly helped by the work of Lawrence Durbin-Robertson, *Juno Covella: Perpetual Calendar of the Fellowship of Isis*. Thank you Marli Rabinowitz for believing in the goddess movement and for being my friend and philanthropist. Thank you Melissa Reed, my youthful and able assistant, for keeping the Women's Spirituality Forum, our nonprofit, grassroots organization, in good shape while I was writing. Thank you Diana L. Paxson for lovingly editing my manuscript and giving me positive feedback. Thanks to my longtime goddess/friend Merlin Stone for taking the manuscript with her on a train ride and correcting it. Merlin, Goddess love you for helping me! Thank you Diana Rae for helping me create the final manuscript and for composing and recording with me the wonderful audiotape that will accompany this book in summer of 1990 *The Grandmother of Time*. Finally, I thank Jan Johnson, editor, and Yvonne Keller from Harper & Row, who believed in this book and stood by me through the deadlines. Thank you all deeply!

ZSUZSANNA EMESE BUDAPEST

Oakland, California

A Life Without Celebration
Is
Only Half Lived

WHEN I WAS A LITTLE girl in Hungary, I often spent my holidays in the rural areas, where the spirit of the old folktales still came alive on certain special occasions. At such times, I felt the stirrings of a deep and primal joy that I never otherwise experienced, even during the most generous birthday parties my parents gave for me. This was something from the dark recesses of my being, as if I, too, had once been a full participant in the games, revels, masquerades, and mummers' plays; found the last corn doll; kissed the pretty May queen; or was the May queen myself. Thanks to my friends from Nagykunság who took me along to these secret rites, I felt my heart pound with excitement and the keen joy of the forbidden, yet sacred, play.

What did we do? I remember that there was always elaborate dressing up involved. We made masks for our faces and became bears, roosters, geese, fairy queens, old hags, nasty spirits, and good spirits. We stole milk from the cows and drank it still warm to bring good health to ourselves and spilt some on the ground to bring the same to the household. But these were not the most exciting rituals. I always yearned to be old enough to participate in the pounding dances on the bare earth floors, dancers that circled roaring fires made of different woods, which burned clean and made no smoke. I was enthralled by the women's dances, watching as they filed in one behind the other and then invoked the four corners of the universe in their sacred dance. It is only in looking back that I realize what the dances actually were. The folk costumes of the dancers were decorated like the garments of queens. Like queens, they were crowned; they wore thirteen skirts on top of each other, and when they swirled around they looked like the wheels of life, like blooming roses. If I could only have added a few years to my own age, I could have been one of them!

The air at these festivals was always pregnant with expectation. The young women and young men caught each other's every signal. They didn't hide their attraction to each other from young girls like us; they discussed every detail with proud sexuality. "Hey, why don't you go over to Tibor? He has been eyeing you all night!" one girl would encourage the other. "If you jump the fire together you will be married within the year!"

There were reluctant parents who were against certain marriages, but they were defeated by this magic. Shy youths came out to court on Midsummer Night, and boisterous types became suddenly gentle. Couples disappeared into the orchards and made love under the stars; others were kissing under the trees, others still just courting and talking.

I have memories of singing songs under the stars with many other little girls, songs that one would hardly expect six-year-olds to know, all about the Stag King humping the Doe Queen or the fire god jumping into the lap of a beautiful maiden. Little girls who grew up around farms were not shielded from life's activities. We knew everything, respected everything, and thought of sex as something natural, one day to be ours.

I remember falling asleep near the bone fires, where the sizzling bacon still dripped its juice into the hot coals, as the revelers caught it onto white bread, which they washed down with new wine. There were endless starry nights, falling stars to wish upon, and the revelers—some dancing, some kissing, some just caught into the sweet ecstasy of the night, singing like us.

Those were the last days of the traditional rural life in Hungary, the last days without TV when the most important thing was to find the maypole a good place in the middle of the town or when we looked forward to Easter and the boys came dressed up and sprinkled the girls with perfume. Then we gave them an egg and a kiss.

Writing about the celebrations for this book has stirred up all these memories in me. I remember that there were special days when only women would celebrate, certain times of the full moon when only women would dance together in a good-luck dance; if boys so much as caught a glimpse of us dancing, the magic would be ruined, like fairy dust spilled in vain. The same was true for the boys' dances. They had a wand dance, a sword dance, and even a dance where they danced with a chair! Today, most of these dances, women's as well as men's, are wisely incorporated into the repertory of the National Hungarian Folk Dance Ensemble, where I saw them performed last time I visited Budapest.

Looking at these ancient dances with new eyes, I see how pagan magic lived on in the very body movements, in the order of the steps of the dance. All tell tales of a season, of the relationship of nature to people, of women to men, women to women, men to men, and children to children. Even the costumes made the women look like goddesses, such as the famous *parta*, a moon-shaped headdress usually decorated with pearls, or the *kalaris* necklace, a garment different in each region yet the same in essence. I could go on and on about Hungarian folk art and how it preserved the image of the goddess on into the twentieth century! But the purpose of this book is to talk about the revels, so let us return to them.

Celebrations are a womanly art. Women are the rememberers of our species, the cookers of festival foods. Our nurturing arts are the glue that has held society together, since the first wild boar we barbecued on a stick in front of our caves to the Thanksgiving turkey we put into the microwave oven today. Celebrations are made by women dressed in flowing robes or three-piece suits or cocktail dresses or housedresses, by light-footed nymphs treading the sacred dances, or just Grandma romping up a little two-step after dinner. Our voices rise in heavenly chorus, praising this season or that goddess, this fortune or that harvest. We walk in procession with friends and neighbors through the familiar landscapes, blessing the fields.

This is what celebrations are made of; this is what I wanted to find again. A great loneliness has descended on us. We no longer buy into the old fear-induced religions. The wrathful gods have lost their power over us, and we let them rave and rant until we click off our TV sets. But deep within us there is a space that now more than ever is painfully empty, as if we had a hollow above our hearts where the old revels used to live, yearning to be filled. We must be careful about what we feed our spiritual hunger—it cannot be junk food any more.

The first thing we must put into that emptiness is boundless courage. We must have the courage to renew our faith in ourselves as children of the natural gods; we ourselves are like our parents, godlike. To acquire courage, we must regain our spiritual dignity. We must say that only the best of thoughts shall enter the sacred space of our minds; only the most affirming thoughts will wash our souls clean from fear. We must affirm our kinship with the vast universe and claim the Earth, our beautiful blue planet, as our mother. Then we will have found our natural family once more. We will have come home at last. We will have come home to our own courage to love the earth and to love ourselves.

The next thing to do is to actually make contact with the divine parent, the Goddess of Time, to make her real. We must bring her into our everyday lives, integrate the divine into our daily lives and find ritual in it. Suddenly the bedroom becomes a temple; the study is transformed into a meditation room where her footsteps are frequently heard. We embark on urban adventures, urban shamanism, tracking down her magical herbs and using them to get in touch with the healing, problem-solving, ingenious part of nature. Her herbs are like unlisted phone numbers we have finally been able to list in our own book of contacts. By burning them in our incense, we are dialing her, Mother Nature, who is everywhere yet strangely silent when we don't have the craft to call her properly. Our urban shamanism will call her to our aid, protect us and our property against crime, and shield our hearts from loneliness. Like all mothers, she is fussy. Like children, we are needy. Only our newfound courage will help us through the insecurities when we doubt her power within us.

For centuries, the right of women (and men) to hold their revels has been attacked by church and state. In Europe, the ancient rites were outlawed, the wearing of masks and dancing in the streets forbidden. Yet still the people clung to their old customs. The Christian clergy tried to deal with the enduring vitality of the old earth rites by attempting to Christianize them. Pope Julius I changed the date of birth of Christ from January 6 to December 25, thus making it the same holiday as the Winter Solstice, the birth of the young sun. The old customs of celebrating, caroling, drinking, exchanging gifts, Saturnalian processions, Teutonic Yule fests, and the like could now be celebrated under the guise of Christianity. The complex of festivals at the beginning of February, which had included the festivals of Lupercalia in the Mediterranean and the feast of Brigid in Celtic lands, was co-opted into the Purification of the Virgin and Candlemas. The attempt to contain the great revels of February within a one-day Mardi Gras celebration before Lent was even less successful, so carnival is still a major event in many lands to this day.

Perhaps the worst casualties of the war on the old revels were the ones specifically celebrating women's contributions to life. As it was in the beginning, so it is today: from our first birthday parties to family Thanksgiving dinners, Christmas, and Hanukkah celebrations, it is the women who bond the community with good food, shared laughter, and ritual. But where are the celebrations of women's other contributions to society? The festival calendars of women are not about wars, but about the cycles of life with which women are intimately in tune. Acts of a spiritual nature, feasts, and ritual gatherings of women remind us of our own worth and sometimes of our own mortality and immortality.

Women and men need the revels for the same reasons. It is a chance once or twice a year to release the wildness within. Why is ecstasy good for us? In ecstasy we touch heaven while still living; we commune with the goddesses and gods who are inside us. Ecstasy is what humans need to endure the drudgery and confinement of the rest of modern life. Ecstasy frees us from our accumulated burdens, be it psychic garbage or leftover depression. It is a way for us to cleanse ourselves from our past and renew ourselves.

Today we drink to excess or take drugs, but can you imagine using dance, music, fresh air, moonshine, singing, and good company to achieve ecstasy? Imagine becoming gods behind our masks, encountering people we would normally never meet and sharing with them the joy of the seasons? Imagine taking back the streets not only for angry marches but for revels, for dancing, and for walking safely? Imagine a common denominator, the love of nature and the seasons, that abolishes class distinctions even for a short time, a time when rich and poor celebrate together, when the portals of the rich open to revive the poor with welcome?

This book is written in the fervent hope that it will incite people to create more meaningful rituals and have more fun. If you can follow a cookbook, you can follow the directions in this book, and add one or two holidays from it each month to your normal cycle of celebrations. That which is not celebrated, that which is not ritualized, goes unnoticed, and in the long run those feelings and happenings will be devalued. The smallest events can be made into great moments of our lives by taking the time to celebrate them. Since our society is set up to keep people isolated, we must form our own support groups for celebration.

Throughout most of my life I have had to create from scratch what I required to meet my spiritual needs. That is the nature of our times. It can be done. But where, you ask, will you find people with whom to celebrate? Ask around in women's groups, in your workplace, among your family and friends and see if there's any interest in celebrating more than the usual few holidays in a year. Have a dinner or lunch or breakfast with those people and see what they think about celebrating some holidays from *The Grandmother of Time*. The commitment can be for just one year, or six months, or for a single festival. Plan the events in such a way that people don't burn out. Some you can do alone; some need others to attend. You won't regret it; the consciousness you raise by living as a celebrant of life will reward you with good memories later on.

The journey of Anna Perenna, the Grandmother of Time, begins on Her holy day and takes us with Her on Her own natural course around the sun. This book follows Her on that journey. For each month, there is a message from the Goddess, a list of symbols or aspects, rituals and spells, and a calendar of holidays. A bibliography of sources and a detailed index are included at the end of the book.

And now, let the journey begin!

INTRODUCTION ——————————

An Invitation from
Anna Perenna
The Grandmother of Time

ANNA PERENNA, THE ETERNAL Grandmother of Time, has graciously consented to guide us through these difficult and puzzling days. Listening to the prayers of her witches, gathering her information on the wings of the sandalwood incense they burn, she has decided to reveal herself to us in her many forms as the leader of the unfolding journey—Anna Perenna, the Goddess of Time. The oldest of all deities, before the Bible was ever written, she had already been worshipped for thousands of years as the grandmother of the gods! Then why isn't this important deity as well known as goddesses like Aphrodite, or Gaia, or Demeter? Who knows? It could be a convenient cultural blind spot on our part—a tendency to ignore the reality of time as applied to our own existence. After all, who would enjoy contemplating aging, dying, or changing into other forms when this beloved form of ours is the only one we know?

Anna's name comes from the Sumerian prototype of the many forms of the great goddess who is called Anna, Anat, Ann, Ana, or Hanahh—names that mean Lady of Heaven. Time is measured by the rotation of the heavens, the original clock. In Syria she was known as Anatha; in Canaan, as Anat; elsewhere, as Ana or Anah. Anna was the name of the mother of the Virgin Mary. As Asherah, she was the consort of Jahveh at Elephantine. As Anu, she ruled the pre-Celtic tribes. In Phrygia she was Nana, the mother of the savior god. Her names testify to her international, ancient ancestry.

The Romans devoted many processions, popular theater skits, and feast days to Anna Perenna, their two-headed Goddess of Time. One of her heads, named Prosrsa, looked forward as in prophecy. Her other head, Postverta, looked backward from her heavenly gate. Because she was the beginning and the end, the alpha and omega, as the wise Carmenta she also invented all the rest of the letters in the alphabet.

From culture to culture, her divine credits continue on. Ovid said Anna was the same as the moon goddess, heavenly Lucina. To the Celts, Anna was the first aspect of their trinity, Ana, of the beginning. To the Irish, Ana meant mother, also treasure, prosperity, and wealth. In her grandmother aspect, she became associated with goddess as destroyer (when time runs out). She had a cauldron of rebirth, just like Morrigan of the Irish. Anna was Christianized and became the mother of Mary. For a while she was even said to have been born "immaculately," which makes sense, for why would Time be tainted with sex? But later the Christians, obsessed with the matter, decided that Mary's immaculate conception was all they could stomach, and they declared that Anna's had not occurred. No matter, the Goddess of Time survived until today, and she is having a comeback!

My favorite stories about Anna Perenna are those told about the times she intermingled with human folk. I saw these stories acted out in street theater festivals around the Piac in Kunszentmiklos. It so happened that sometimes she took a fancy to some young, good-looking man and liked to approach him as an old hag. "Come and give a little kiss on my mouth, laddie!" she would beg, often in vain. Young men don't like to kiss old wrinkled ladies on the mouth. But then she had a trick. She would plead, "If you kiss me, laddie, I shall turn into the most beautiful young bride you have ever seen!" This got results, sometimes, if the young man in question had the generosity to kiss her and risk what would happen!

Zawoom! Anna, the Goddess of Time, who is a great shaman and can shift her appearance by will, turned into a young bride more beautiful and enchanting than the young man could have imagined! Great then was the joy of the lucky young man! But Anna was not yet through with her time games! (She likes games.) Next she challenged her new lover: "I can only be pretty half of the time," she would say. "Would you like me to be beautiful and young during the daytime when your friends can meet us or in the nighttime when we make love?" If the young man knew what was good for him, he would say, "It is all the same to me dearest!" and Anna Perenna would smile and say, "Then I'll stay young and beautiful all the time!" But if he hesitated and started wavering about nighttime versus daytime, she would disappear forever.

Anna—the oldest of gods, the Grandmother of Time, the young thing of the springtime, shape shifter, the old hag of the wintertime—is our captain on this annual magical journey around the brilliant sun. Come aboard! Be part of it. Let Anna write her messages to you and weave her spells for our benefit. Listen with your inner ear; listen to your irrational mind. Can anybody truly understand Time?

January

THE GODDESS SPEAKS

Anna Perenna

I LEFT YOU A MESSAGE TODAY in the thick snow, just when you passed that old leafless birch tree. I felt your despair and decided to contact you. Hello! I am Anna Perenna, the goddess of the coming year and all the years before and all those yet to unfold. I can see you even without looking, and I can feel you from your birth to your grave. No need to discuss the grave here. No, just the opposite. I wanted you to know that from now on I shall leave you messages, and you shall have hope, knowing that your maker has not deserted you. Did you think that after the magnificent and arduous act of creation I retired? Dear child, not true. I am a god of responsibility! Naturally you don't see me all the time, but I am here nevertheless.

Here—see this new dawn? That is your ticket to ride on my back one more time around the beautiful sun! Let me just show you this, my child! See—here is the sun! We are the third, yes, the lucky number 3 planet from the sun! We move in a kind of egg-shaped journey around it and pause to celebrate the equinoxes and solstices and the high points in between. Fun, eh? Our calendar is divided into eight major holidays when I gradually shiftshape, shamanlike, from young to old and then back! We start with Halloween, the sacred New Year; then comes the Winter Solstice, Candlemas, the Spring Equinox, May Eve, Summer Solstice, Lammas, the Autumn Equinox, and back to Halloween! This is my ancient dance, my Spiral Dance.

Did you see the little map I drew for you? You are here! Yes, that's the one. You are about to begin again. But this year the journey will be lived more joyously, because I won't stand for a solemn trip! I am counting on you to take my messages seriously, and I expect you to spend some time exploring my mysteries, contemplating the words written in the snow (hurry in case they melt!), allowing your soul to slow down and discover me, to know me.

I am the kind of god who likes to work with those who are aware, not the sluggish. I recommend to you a more cheerful path, not the old half-conscious one, where eyes are cast downward and your soul drags behind you as if in permanent rejection of the gifts I packed into your genes! See! No space suit needed, the spaceship Earth is already in gear. I set my course carefully as we spin 200 miles per second in space. The new year is my latest creation—enjoy yourself in my honor.

I am the god who didn't go away. I am the god who gave you life, nurtured you this far, and now takes you on a special course because I feel there is too much sorrow among you; I didn't mean it to be like that. You have to get used to a new kind of calendar, a calendar that remembers me and you, my creation, my own kin. Yes, I am within you and without you, and if you had called on me sooner, I would have come. But you called on a god without a womb, or a sense of humor. So, shall I pretend that I am he? No, child. I have given you a chance to discover who I am, and I think you have finally found me. It's about time!

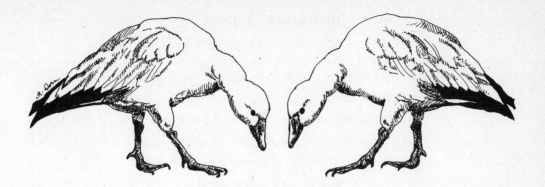

I would like to say right here that it is wise not to expect yourself to be like me completely. Like a mother I have given you many parts of myself that you may use. But we two are separate at the same time as we are one. For example, I can become old or young at will; you cannot. I can see into the future and the past, and I know all about the here and now. This you could practice; a little prophecy is good for you. Take up a divining tool like Tarot, runes, or even the crystal for gazing and see if you can improve the communication between us. But for you the here and now is everything, my dear. Don't dwell excessively on the past or on the future. The past used to be your here and now, and I hope you used it well. Now it is gone. The future will be your life soon, but not yet. See what I mean? Stay balanced in the middle, and all will be well.

In our monthly visits (you may choose the time—however, the time of the full moon is traditional, when the astral planes touch, heaven to earth), I shall teach you meditations to give you more of me and allow you to see and talk to me even though I will appear to be very different each month. Change is my law and I am subject to it. So, my beloved daughter or son, let's put this into practice right now. Come meet your maker, your mother, your god.

January's Aspects

The name of this month is derived from the Roman god Janus, a masculinized form of Anna Perenna. Like Anna, Janus also has two faces and looks into the past and the future at the same time.

Full moon aspect: Cold moon or earth renewal moon

Universal event: Inception of the new year

Communal event: The planting of spring wheat

Message: To begin, to conceive, to originate

Activity: Self-perpetuation

Healing properties: Directed to ills of the joints and skin

Appropriate spell: Dedication of new goals for the year: prosperity, health, finding focus

Color: White

Tree: Birch tree

Flower: Snowdrop

Creature: Pheasant, snow goose

Gem: Garnet

Anna's Spells, Rituals, & Celebrations for January

A BIRTHDAY CELEBRATION

When it is your birthday, instead of the usual fare you have known all your life, why not spiritualize the party? Invite the friends you really want to be with. Don't use your birthday to socialize with new people in your life, ones who don't feel like family yet. Don't use your birthday to increase your prestige with peers or to return a party invitation. Your birthday must be seen as having a value of its own.

Get everything together as usual—the party decorations, your cake and candles—but don't follow the usual procedure of putting the candles on the cake, lighting them, singing the birthday song, and then blowing them out while making a wish. When you use wishcraft, blowing out the candles means you are blowing away your own good luck! So, how can you do it differently? There is a much better way.

Arrange as many candles as you have lived years on a tray separate from the cake. Each candle represents a year of your life. I use Hanukkah candles because they are just the right size and also come in many colors. Take the time to make candle holders of aluminum foil for all of them. Now, sit your guests down, sing "Happy Birthday," and serve the cake; but when you would ordinarily blow out the candles, begin to light them instead.

As you light the first one, give thanks to your mom, who gave you the opportunity to come through the veil between life and death and become you. She is your origin in the universe. The second candle, and the rest, you light one by one in honor of yourself. Tell a little bit about the years when something memorable happened. Share the story of your life and let your guests react— laugh and cheer for you. Reveal about three good stories at one party (save some stories for next year). If you want a total review of your life, do this with people who can verify your experiences or even add another dimension to them that you may have forgotten. When you recall an event worthy of special mention, stop and offer a toast, accept the congratulations of others. In other words, party while storytelling. After you have finished lighting all the candles, let them burn down together naturally. In the glow of your candles you may be awed by your own endurance and beauty.

SPELL FOR HEALTHY SLEEP

The magic herb to find is *Herba euphrasia*. Make a light tea of this herb and drink it before bedtime; it is said to promote restful sleep. In addition to that, it acts on your psychic centers, bringing about dreams that contain prophetic visions. Those dreams can energize you with insights and strength. Other good teas for rest are hops, skullcap, or chamomile.

SPELL TO KEEP A LOVER TRUE TO YOU

I just watched a TV show about jealousy, and I decided that jealousy is a form of powerlessness. If you feel jealous, don't waste your time humiliating yourself; become the urban shaman and quickly whip up this incense and burn it every night before you go to sleep. You need to gather a handful of linden flowers, sweet basil, bayberry, ditanny of Crete, and powdered cloves. Grind and blend them into a fine mixture and burn them on charcoal. Legend has it that this incense can also attract a lover to you if you are alone.*

Spell to Stop Smoking

The New Year caught you making grand resolutions, didn't it? What is it this time? Your health figures high on your list, thank heavens, so how about making stopping smoking your resolution this year? You have heard the many arguments against smoking; it shortens your life span, and it stinks up your space. Soon the new laws will force you to smoke in dingy smoking rooms, banished from human company, just like you were when you first started this habit as a kid, out of sight of your parents.

Take heart. It can be done. Appeal to your higher power, Anna. She will see you through, not scolding or judging you, but giving you the inner strength that you need. Love yourself while you are changing yourself. That's it. Feel this warmth. Cast a spell on yourself; feel your own power. Many different kinds of people have felt your personal power in the past, why not taste it yourself? Spells are like prayers. And rituals are the food of the soul. They are games of the mind. One can practice life-affirming rituals or death rituals like the preparing, lighting, and inhaling of cigarettes.

The whole ritual takes about ten minutes—well worth it for life. This spell involves more than just candles; for starters, get some gentian powder and fill some capsules with it. Take three or four capsules each day. Gentian is a healing herb and kills the desire for nicotine. While you are experiencing the withdrawal symptoms, I recommend a smoking mixture made of red clover, colt's foot, and mullein. This mixture will help you clean out your lungs. Smoke only one or two pipefuls a day and taper this off as you go along the new path.

Now comes another new step. This may feel weird to you; it probably will, but what the heck. Many of the items used in these ancient spells are now found only in occult supply stores. You can locate them in your local yellow pages or mail order them

*If you need sources for herbs and occult supplies, write to P.O. Box 11363, Oakland, CA 94611. Send a self-addressed, stamped envelope, and we will send you our list of recommendations.

through popular magazines. Look for a candle in the shape of a human being. If you are a man, get a male image candle; if you are a woman, get a female candle in green. Why green? Because that is the favorite color of Mother Nature—you must have noticed it—and healing has to do with stimulating your own nature. Take the green image candle, write your name on both sides, and anoint it (smear it) with your favorite oil. Why not use your own perfume or shaving lotion? I even favor saliva for anointing.

Burn the candle for about an hour every Friday, in honor of your body and for a blessing on yourself. Watch it for a little while and visualize your lungs regaining their original lovely pink color. Involve your whole body; visualize a glowing green light passing through your chakras one by one, starting with your toes, moving upward, and finally exiting through the top of your head.

The next part is a little harder. As you imagine this intense healing light moving through your body, stop each time you come to an organ and say:

> *I reclaim my bones with love.*
> *I bless my stomach with love.*
> *I reclaim my lungs with love.*
> *I bless my liver with love.*
> *I reclaim my heart with love.*
> *I bless my eyes with love.*

And so forth. Bless the parts of your body until you feel love being released to you from your divine center. It is there, but self-love was not taught to you as you grew up, and it can be hard to relearn it. Just remember that it makes you weaker to withhold this natural flow of inner healing from yourself; Anna will be with you, giving a natural mother's love to this healing endeavor.

GENERAL PURIFICATION SPELL ⸺

This spell was collected from northern Europe. To begin anew, the old has to be cleared away. Start by cleaning your space, throwing away old clothes or giving them away to charity, organizing your thoughts, and drafting a short plan of what you want for the year. Remember, this is the time of the year when we are boldly fantasizing about the future and thereby attracting it to us.

Using white parchment paper and red ink, write down the things you want, being as specific as possible. If you don't already have a home altar, look around and see if there is a place

in your home that you treat as special. Often people instinctively make a special spot for important things in their lives. You lay your jewelry and your money on it; there may be pictures of loved ones, mementos from happy times, and so on. You just need to recognize this place and clean it up a bit.

Now you will need an item used by peasants since ancient times—a candle (preferably white) in a glass that will burn for thirteen days and nights. These are available in candle shops and are safe to leave burning. Place your list of wishes on your altar (your special place) under a thirteen-day white votive candle that you have anointed with violet oil or with your own perfume. Smear a little of your own saliva on your list to link it to you. Decorate your living space with fresh birch twigs and place some on your altar for use during the spell. Birch twigs are the northern European touch. If you can't get birch twigs, don't worry. Birch is traditional, but believe me, the magic is still strong. Get whatever you can.

After taking a hot shower to open up the pores, go to your altar, take your birch twigs, and with them gently slap your neck, saying:

I purify myself from defeatist thinking.
I purify myself from old patterns.
I purify myself from my past.
May my spirit come into new life
As the sap comes into the birch tree.

Don't slap hard with the twigs—this is only symbolic stimulation, not sadomasochism! Then slap the twigs against your solar plexus, saying:

I purify myself from loneliness.
Love will come to me
Like the new life of the mother.

Finally, slap them against your feet, saying:

I purify myself from inertia.
Vitality will come to me
Like new life from the mother.

If you wish, you can dress now. Beginning in the east and moving clockwise, go to each corner in your house and beat the twigs against the walls, the furniture, your bed, your desk, and so on, driving out the old year's leftovers. Then burn the twigs in a fireplace or outside in a hibachi or bonfire. There is no need to repeat this nightly; just meditate on your candle. In twelve days, when your thirteen-day candle is almost burned down, burn the parchment paper in the last of the flames. Now you have been purified and are ready to receive the blessings to come.

MEDITATION TO DISPEL FEAR

Quiet the space around you. Unhook your phone; declare yourself off-limits to kids, partners, and friends. Listen to the Goddess: You are mine now. To find me, create a small space for your focus, light a white candle to guide you, burn a little sage in a dish. Now, close your eyes and breathe with me. Your breath connects you to me; I can feel you breathe, and I am breathing with you.

Remember the temple—your own spiritual space, the safe place in your mind where there is tranquility and beauty? Come here now, step with bare feet on the moss-covered stones, see your temple in your mind, open the door gently, and wait there in comfort. My birds may be present, or there may be fields of flowers or snowcapped mountain peaks. This magical place may have buildings; it may not. It may be just a bench in your grand-father's secret place where he smoked his forbidden pipe. Your own memories live here, too, and you may come to see me here from now on. Oh, I see you now; you have entered, you found the safe place easily. Inhale the sage now and listen as I appear and speak to you:

> You are the child of the universe.
> I put my almighty protection around you.
> You are now free of accidents, death, sickness.
> You are now shining with golden light from top to toe.
> You are my chosen protected child, and I am your shield.
> The winds shall aid your progress.
> Waters shall cleanse you from fear,
> Fires will purify you from doubts,
> And the earth shall nourish you to health.
> All is well, all is well, all is well.

Now repeat this after me until you believe it:

> I am the child of the universe.
> She puts her almighty protection around me.
> I am free from accidents, death, sickness.
> I am now shining with golden light from top to toe.
> I am her chosen protected child, and she is my shield.
> The winds shall aid my progress.
> Water shall cleanse me from fear,
> Fire will purify me from doubts,
> And the earth shall nourish me to health.
> All is well, all is well, all is well.

THE HOLIDAYS

January 1

GAMELIA FESTIVAL (GREEK)

Gamelia is one of the names of Hera, the queen of heaven of the Greeks. On this day marriages were celebrated, because it was a lucky day to tie the knot. In ancient Rome, Anna Perenna began her cycle, and blessed deeds were done on this first day. Among the festivities, gifts called *strenea* were exchanged among friends in a festival called *Strenia*. Palm and bay branches were carried to the temples and hung with sweetmeats, dates, and figs. The purpose of this custom was to stimulate the new year with presents, joy, and happiness. The fruits were sometimes gilded for prosperity. In France this custom still survives as the *Étrennes*, the New Year's gift exchange.

San-ga-nichi in Japanese means "three days," when people eat a traditional stew called *zoni*. No sweeping is allowed, lest the good luck be swept away. In addition to this, the Seven Deities of Luck—*takara-bune*, or "treasure ship"—are honored by buying little ships from street vendors, which contain treasures for the new year: a hat of invisibility, a lucky raincoat, the secret key, the inexhaustible purse, the precious jewel, the clove, the weight, and a flat object for a coin. Legend has it that if you possess the ship, you may confidently sail into the future.

January 3

INANNA'S DAY (SUMERIAN); NATIVITY OF THE LADY

She is the evening star, and with her birth we celebrate the birth of light. According to the Sumerians, "Our Lady in her mother's arms shines forth on the grey dawn." Inanna is a goddess of great power over lovers and cities. If you are one of those who is afraid of success, pray to her to lose your fear. She certainly struggled with this same fear and won.

Who is Inanna? In the third millennium B.C. in Sumer, where civilization was formed, the complex goddess of life, love, and death was worshipped under the name Inanna. The Babylonians who followed the Sumerians in dominating the Fertile Crescent called her Ishtar. This goddess embodies the full humanity of women, from adolescent, lover, and mother to destroyer and crone. She attempts the most difficult transformation of all, that of her own soul, and descends into the underworld, where her sister and alter ego, Ereshkigal, rules. Here is a Goddess of Heaven and Earth, and she wants to be the Queen of the Underworld as well? Ambitious!

To willingly die for facing the dark side of life requires maturity. In the underworld, Inanna is divested of all her powers, her jewels, her crown, her magic amulets. She is naked and low, stripped of her pride and powers. Here in the underworld, the fertile love goddess is killed by her sister. By experiencing death, she gains control of all her feelings of fear and hatred and dread. Inanna has a higher self, her priestess servant Ninshubar (a pure sunlike energy), who intercedes for her with the god of wisdom. He sends spirits as companions to the lonely Ereshkigal to mirror her laments. The unhappy, lonely queen of the underworld is relieved from her endless sorrow by these spirits and offers them gifts in return, which they refuse. They ask instead for the corpse of Inanna, the queen of Sumer. Ereshkigal, softened by their companionship, allows Inanna to be reborn, opens the door of death to her, and lets her return to her country.

However, the rules of death still apply, and Inanna must replace herself in the underworld with someone else. The death count must remain the same. Inanna visits her children, who are mourning for her, and her priestess, who is awaiting her. She then finds her husband, Dumuzi, living high on the throne's powers, usurping the queen's privileges. She appoints him to replace her in the underworld. So once a year Dumuzi is banished into the darkness to face his own transformation. When you want a story of transcendence, remember that of Queen Inanna, sophisticated and bold.

January 5

KORÉ'S DAY (GREEK)

Hail to Koré (kor-ay), the Divine Maiden, she who grows all things above the ground! Hail to the corn maiden, lady of the fresh fields of wheat and barley; hail to her powers of nurturance. Women adorned her statue with beautiful jewels and carried it around in the cities of the Mediterranean and the Near East, also carrying it around in their homes seven times for protection from evil. To celebrate her holiday, take a statue of the goddess (or make one from bread) and walk around inside your home calling her to keep sickness, burglars, and criminals of all kinds away from your steps: "Koré, Koré, Koré, keep us all safe, keep the evil eye away."

January 6

FEAST OF KORÉ (GREEK)

Nocturnal theatrical rites and feasting were held in honor of Koré, the Divine Maiden. A troop of torchbearers went down into the underground cult chamber, bringing up a wooden goddess statue, naked but for golden adornments. She was placed on a litter and carried around the temple seven times. Number 7 is lucky for success.

This day is the Twelfth Night of legends and fairy tales. On this day, the Celts celebrated the triple goddess of fate, the givers of good and bad, the weavers of tales and destinies, the Morrigan. In the tales, a turning point enables good to triumph over evil.

In Italy, La Befana is the image of the Halloween witch who rides on her broomstick, looking wild and sassy. On this day—Befana Day—this good fairy flies around the countryside, bringing blessings and frightening all and filling children's stockings with sweets.

January 8

JUSTICIA'S DAY (ROMAN)

Justicia is the Goddess of Justice. European legal history begins with the goddess Themis, the forerunner of Justicia, whose name means utterance. In her name the first oaths were taken. Wearing her purple mantle meant that if you lied under oath the goddess would kill you. So people bound themselves, saying, "If I don't keep my word, so strike me dead!" Does this sound familiar? It was thus that laws began and taboos were created. On a higher level, the Goddess Themis is the source of social instincts. She is the sense of justice within us.

January 8 and 9

CARNIVAL; FASCHING (EUROPEAN)

Even before Christianity, Fasching (or Carnival) was a merry time, and it still is taken seriously by many countries, with celebrations beginning anywhere from November through mid-February. What is celebrated in carnivals? Just fun! Freedom from conventions! This is the time of year before the Lenten period, and the processions on the streets assume a madcap quality. People act out of line with accepted social rules. In Venice masked celebrants carrying lighted candles pelt each other with sweetmeats and flowers and flirt outrageously with each other.

In Spain, the carnival allows young men to approach socially high-born ladies and make advances toward them without being challenged. In Madrid, carriages carrying very well dressed people parade through the streets; women can pick and choose their partners for the festivities without waiting to be asked. In Austria, the "dance of the phantoms" is performed with colorful costumes

and wooden masks, with fangs and frightening features to drive away evil spirits. In the procession there is a witch-mother holding the sack of grain for the new year's sowing, which she throws among the celebrants, and another character called Spitzer, who squirts water at people, symbolically fertilizing (raining on) them. The good spirits sweep the streets with their brooms, and city vendors sell their pretzels hung on broomsticks.

Get zany today. Look for a ball or carnival to attend. Make a mask of your own face and hang it on the wall. Pay special attention to playfulness; if you have kids to play with, give them your all!

January 11 through 15

CARMENTALIA (ROMAN)

This period honors the birth goddess who brings in the new generations. The Goddess Carmenta was honored vigorously by the Romans in this five-day festival, packed with festive processions of the city matrons. Carmenta ruled the hinge of life, on which the door of life is hung. She lived behind the North Wind. Pregnant women made offerings to her of prayers and rice for easy deliveries, for she aided women in childbirth. The festivities began by baking cream-filled pastries shaped like male and female genitalia (much like the eclairs we have today) or triangle-shaped pastries filled with raspberry filling. These were eaten in honor of the birth goddess, who, after all, started everything worth living for.

The second day Carmenta was remembered as Mania, the mother of ghosts, since the hinge of life swings both ways, toward the living and toward the dead. In order to appease Mania, women used to make straw effigies of little people and hang them above their doorsteps as a substitute for the living bodies of those within. Mania gladly accepted them, and left the dwellers of the house safe. The last two days featured processions of mothers in chariots decorated with flowers, celebrating their achievement as mothers. Carmentalia was a day to go home to visit Mom. All focus and honor was on her, not her children. This was a kind of early Mother's Day.

During these five days, meet some babies, give a hand to young mothers, baby-sit a little if you have relatives. Our society is hard on young mothers and penalizes them with isolation for having babies. Usually they have little money to pay baby-sitters and therefore little time to themselves. If you cannot visit babies or buy some baby clothes, plant a new flower, make something sprout, and eat sprouts to revitalize yourself.

Carmentalia could be a time for mothers to unite around an issue, like publicly supported child care, or an end to the arms race. What if the mothers of the world decided to close the door of life until meaningful arms control is in effect? I don't mean stop having sex and pleasure, only to hold back on having babies until we can bring them into a safer world. How about a baby moratorium?

January 21

SUN ENTERS AQUARIUS

Aquarius is the sign of the water woman, Sophia above and Sophia below, of women as carriers of knowledge and enlightenment. Study something today. Cut a rowan (mountain ash) wand for yourself. Think about God as a woman. Here is a time to indulge the impulse to change things for the better. Aquarius is the transformer, the revolutionary who brings a love for the future. Question authority and rail against lies today.

January 30

FESTIVAL OF PEACE: PAX (ROMAN)

Pax was the Roman goddess of peace. How we need to focus on her! Burn white candles to stimulate blessings. Work for peace today. Send money to peace groups. How did the goddess of peace fall from the intense honor she used to enjoy? Even the warlike Romans celebrated at least three times a year in her honor.

A long procession started from the center of the city, composed mostly of the magistrates and high officials who wore no insignia that day. Just like regular folk, they marched along with the women and children, pausing briefly at the altars erected along the way, where the pictures of the emperor or king or whoever represented power at that time were put at the feet of Pax. From the temple steps, priestesses of Juno and Diana read a list of names of those who were considered enemies of peace and women—these two seemed to be the same. This naming of names acted as a curse, separating these people from their community and punishing them.

Every Friday, Jewish women celebrate the goddess Shekinah. This celebration, called Shabat, has been performed for centuries. The women light white candles and invite the goddess—the sacred bride—to enter their homes. Jewish feminists have brought goddess consciousness back to all the Jewish festivals, and there are many women's groups that celebrate the new moon together. Rabbi Leah Novick says: "Women shift from the world of doing to the world of being in their work for the Shekinah."[*]

Also on this day, January 30, Zsuzsanna Emese Budapest, founder of the Women's Spirituality Movement in the United States, was born in Hungary.

---

[*]Personal communication, January 12, 1989.

The January Story: Birth of the Women's Spirituality Movement

HE YEAR WAS 1971, Winter Solstice, December 21. The place was Hollywood, California, two blocks from Hollywood Boulevard, up on Whitley Hill. Nobody thought about that day as "herstorical." It was a mild winter day, no rain for a long time. I was expecting a couple of friends to join me in my first effort at holding a public gathering of women to celebrate the birth of light and to blend witchcraft and feminism together. What a heady brew! Nobody then suspected it would become a mass movement that would propagate itself like dandelions. No. It was only our first.

Six women showed up by sundown, all my personal friends who trusted me enough as a person to know that there would be nothing "weird" going on. There was Phyllis, a factory worker; Katlyn, who was also a writer and my new-found best friend; Delphin and her lover; Kirstin; and Sally, the poet. A very diverse group indeed. We all sat down and started making our witches' girdles, actually just belts made of intertwined red yarn, symbolizing the color of life, the blood. We each struggled with our tasks: I held the yarn in my mouth as I braided away from myself; Katlyn held it on her toes and braided toward herself. We looked sharp in our brand-new witches' girdles, which remained as our only form of "uniform."

I was not yet an experienced "high priestess," the name we use for the conductor of the orchestra of women souls who worship the Goddess in circles. Much discussion went into the term and function of a high priestess. Should we have hierarchy at all? Is it a hierarchy to have a conductor? Does an orchestra lose power because its members all focus on that single baton or person? We were all "allergic" to any mention of hierarchy. We were anarchist, we thought, but nobody really knew what that meant; it just sounded safe. But those discussions took place in later years. On the first sabbat, there was no such questioning because I was the only one who knew about witchcraft. The rest just came to try it out, to find out if it had any validity for feminist women. We did agree that we cannot work toward liberation as long as our inner selves remain unchanged. Liberation has to begin inside; liberation has to be getting past the fears of taking our own power.

"Do we have to say three times 'I am a witch,' Z?" asked Phyllis.

"No, Phyl, you just have to be open-minded," I answered.

"Do we have to wear more costume? Do we take off our clothes?"

"Not now; we have to find out where we want to send this first sabbat energy, and then we have to act on our own impulses; then all these questions answer themselves."

"You mean we don't have to take classes to do this?"

"No, we are the experience. We are the curriculum."

All I knew was what I remembered from my mother. Hold hands in a circle, let the energy unite. Then, invoke the ancestors, the spirits of the loved ones, to come in and help. Whisper on the winds your wishes. Say thanks for the blessings already on their way. I don't even remember if we invoked the obligatory powers of the east, south, west, and north (but I think we did that).

The energy in the little flat did change; the room appeared larger, the women looked historical in the candlelight. For a cauldron we used a small hibachi in which we burned palm tree leaves. It made too much smoke; we had to open the porch door to let it out! Then Sally started chanting, first under her breath, then openly with clever rhymes. She was dressed as the Raccoon Woman, with the animal's tail on her hat and a long, brown, soft skirt instead of her usual worn jeans. She was slowly transformed. Her journey led her into the realms of the raccoon, her guide, and she rhymed for four hours, which made Phyllis extremely nervous. Several times Phyllis tried to stop Sally's chanting, but I interfered by putting my body between them and distracting Phyl. I remember that that was the hardest of all, protecting Sally so she could have a safe trance and protecting Phyl and the rest from freaking out too much about psychic phenomena.

We sang regular women's liberation songs, because there were no goddess chants then as there are today. We pronounced blessings on all of our sisters and especially asked the Goddess to grow an indigenous women's religion, composed of the heritage (little as it may be) from the past and a large dose of new revelations. This we asked the Goddess to make global: that wherever women pray, they can pray to their own Lady of the Wild Things. We saw this as the most revolutionary act of all: making the old frowning god lose his power over women. This could be done, without violence or guns, as a private matter. This most sacred dethroning of the old authorities could serve as the first most important step toward inner liberation and empowerment.

Katlyn worried that when this idea caught on, women would just want to use it as an excuse to have a great party. To make sure we would never forget how politics and religion are used together, she named the newly formed coven Susan B. Anthony Coven Number 1, because we were convinced others would follow, and that Susan B. Anthony was the best-known suffragist associated with women's rights. We shared some food Delphin cooked, and we tried to jump over our cauldron saying our wishes. Since we were steeped in public service, most of our spells concerned political freedoms for all oppressed people: free Chile, grant women control over their bodies. (It was still three years away from the historical Supreme Court decision that legalized abortions.)

When we finished our blessings, still flushed from our newfound magic, I suggested we go outside and there encircle the hill we lived on. It was one of those beautiful California prestorm skies—clouds making emotional formations in the shape of spirits soaring, women laughing, birds flying. We held hands together and ran into the wind. Suddenly the skies opened up, and the first rain of the year started sprinkling down—a moist, but not-too-abundant, rain, almost like a misting to wash off the old year's dust. We came to the top of the hill where a grove of tall palms blew in the wind. That was when I heard the hooting of an owl. Owl! Here in Hollywood? I turned to the source of the sound, and there in the trees was a big sassy barn owl (my favorite) winking at me. I stopped in awe. I knew the owl was the sacred bird of the Goddess Athena, the protector of women, the wise warrior, who used wisdom as her shield. I felt this was a good time to ask for an omen. How often do you get face-to-face with an oracular bird on the top of Whitley Street?

"Oh, sacred bird of Athena," I prayed, "tell me if this event tonight will start what we want to start, a global Goddess Movement? Hoot for me seven times if the answer is yes. Hoot only five times if you think this is just for us, a gift." We all stood in the rain and faced the tawny bird. Then, without any mistake, as we all counted carefully along with it, the owl hooted seven times! The answer was yes! This is the beginning of something large and important! It will be successful, the Goddess will rise and bless our efforts! But how? How in the world will she accomplish spreading her light? Do we have to go out and proselytize like the Hare Krishna people or the born-again Christians? The thought of proselytizing made us nervous. We didn't want to do that at all. On our return, Sally finally got out of trance and was sipping tea. She told us she saw the owl in her journey as well and that she felt refreshed and filled with energy. This was the most important effect we experienced from our own daring.

We felt high without drugs for days after this first sabbat. Sleep was there waiting for us, deep and restful, but on waking we realized we only needed half the sleep we needed at other times, and yet we all felt like we had rested for a lot longer. The word got out: "Witches give the best parties!" Katlyn was right; we didn't have to proselytize; the fame of the first sabbat was enough. Women wanted the miracles, wanted their own magic, wanted their own power. They came. The next sabbats doubled in size each time.

Finally, we had to find another place, and we went to the beach. The beach phase lasted a couple of years. The weather was always rainy on the sand, until we asked within the circle that the Goddess keep us dry. Then she held her rain for us, letting it come down in buckets just as soon as the last woman was safely back in her car driving home after another magical, mystical night. I remember the altars we built on the beach. We dug them deeply into the sand, and therein we placed our candles to protect them from the wind. The goddess image was always the same, the triple goddess image, a small plaster statue that showed up at the women's center the same day I took a candle to the center for the first time. No one could tell where the triple goddess statue had come from. Who brought it? The women brought flowers and other decorative items—crystals, pictures of their dead ancestors who were called on with love for help in matters affecting the women's lives. Many times we were not disturbed in our devotions. Other times we saw what looked like other witches, wearing black robes and holding candles, but they avoided us. Sometimes drunken thugs tried to butt in, but when they caught the energy from the women's circle, no matter how drunk and nasty they were, they retreated in reverence despite themselves.

I also grew as a priestess. No longer lost for what to do next, I developed a participatory style; my function was simply to watch the communal energy and lead for the first time whatever each woman would do next. "The Goddess is alive!" I shouted in ecstasy. "Magic is afoot!" the women answered. Then we shouted our names: "Zsuzsanna is alive! Magic is afoot! Nancy is alive! Magic is afoot!" Then we shouted the names of our mothers and grandmothers, bringing in the invisible minions of female ancestors who lived still in our bones and bloodlines. We started feeling the energy that gives life to the universe. We felt the awesome power of the female side of God. We had a great time! Imagine, then, how fast our numbers grew from celebration to celebration. At these gatherings there was never any exchange of money. We were doing this as a part of the Women's Liberation Movement, not as a business of some spiritual capitalism.

On one of my walks, I found a mountaintop in Malibu. My dog Ilona led me to it. It was a splendid plateau overlooking the Pacific Ocean: to the north the coastline hills, to the west the blue waters of the ocean, to the south some more rambling hills, and in the east you could barely see the Santa Monica lights twinkle. It was just perfect for our women's circles. From 1973 on, we started meeting in Malibu, on this mountain, right above the expensive neighborhoods of Malibu where we had to park our cars before the long hike up the mountain. For three glorious years, we met there undisturbed, in growing numbers. Anywhere from 17 to 125 women came at any one time; I never knew how many.

That first sabbat in Hollywood was now far away. Only Sally and Kirstin remained from the original crowd. Phyllis was not comfortable with our taking ourselves and our work more seriously. She understood that it wasn't just a great party for us, it was worship and a spiritual need to be fed. Katlyn also fell away for other reasons. She started the first rape hotline in Los Angeles and gave her energies to women in this way. Delphin and her friend broke up, and Delphin moved to Laguna Beach, attending law school. Kirstin and I carried on the tradition of women gatherings. In those years I had to answer a lot of questions.

"Why are you doing this?" my sisters often taunted me. "You are distracting the women with this religious stuff. They will grow complacent in the political work and will just want to contemplate their navels." "There is no danger of that," I answered. "The women who will develop spirituality for themselves will be stronger for it. They will not burn out. They will stop and smell the roses on their way to liberation." I wrote about it in our own papers and sent around a few articles to other feminist magazines, like *Ms.*, but we never received any acknowledgment from *Ms.* that what we were doing was revolutionary. As it turned out, we were the new wave of feminism, which nowadays Gloria Steinem calls the "psycho/spiritual wave." In fact, it is the only kind of feminism going on twenty years later that permeates the entire women's culture: festivals, art, theology, literature, and sciences. The old politicos who swore that we were distractions and not serious feminists have long since stopped working, burned out, dropped out of the history-making stream, and blended into the fabric of the mainstream.

I am dreaming of mountaintops all over the world, with women on top of them singing and dancing and blessing the fields and the people, and the men full of goodwill, making sure that the women are happy and undisturbed so they can spread their blessings on the entire community, so they may gain the blessings of the planet herself. All living creatures will abundantly profit, because our prayers are that important, because our blessings are that potent, because our hearts are that generous! Let it be! It is so!

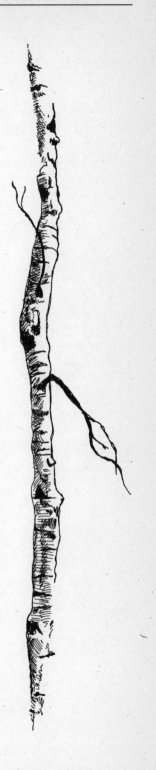

February

Hagia Sophia

I HAVE HIDDEN THIS MONTH'S message inside a bear's cave, then changed my mind and thrown it on your threshold. Did you feel me encircle your house? You would hardly recognize me, I am so beautiful, my cheeks are red from the winds, and my feet are damp from all the moisture I am pumping up to the tips of my forests from the depth of the earth. Nothing is showing now, of course. It's still the dead of winter, but I have my hidden activities. We are busy down in the depths! My rowan is about to burst out in flowers, and in the south blooms my laurel, my bay. There are crocuses in my hair, and I have tiny snow-white flowers blending with the snow itself. I am heralding an initiation.

A spiritual strength, unlike that of any other time, is surging through me like the sap of the trees. I care for the depths of the soul. It's a new dawn. There is no more need to hide the spiritual strength of women. My name rings out freely from their lips, and I answer the call. I answer the call every time. This season I am the all-wise seeress, the witch of transformation. Have you felt the stirrings of my power?

Do I mean Valentine's Day to you? Can you hear the animals going into heat at night, howling, mewing, scratching at your door, making the sounds of wild desire? My wolves are mating in the north. They mate for life. I am sorry if you were lonely through the winter. I was with you. But I know what you mean—a mother's love can go only so far. After that, a partner is in order. Trust me in this one; Sophia can see your luck changing. I shall bear you on the flow of my sap and carry you to your own new beginnings. You shall be loved as I loved the folks who celebrated me on Lupercalia. You shall have new jobs, new monies, new houses, new wealth, new life. I want my children to take advantage of this power. I share with you gladly.

I have brought you the herb hyssop to wash your eyes and see true reality, the kind of reality that lives in your inner-scapes, the wisdom in living and the dying, but mostly the wisdom of rebirth. You are not one of those disgruntled children of mine who resent the wheel of life, who wish to beg off, to bail out, not to be tied to me or to incarnations of their own but to go away somewhere. I don't know what they mean. They want to get off the endless chain of rebirth, they sneer at the miracles, they say it's better to be unborn. I keep them in my blue sleeves, trying not to weave them back into my magnificent bird song–peppered tapestry of life. But they are not happy there either. They peek out and say things like, "Look at the fools; they are entering new bodies again, they are falling in love again with life and each other." They are not laughing either, these soured-up souls. I suppose all mothers have to contend with a few of these strange seeds, but you I care about; you are trying and you are winning. It's time for another visit, isn't it? Another date to cross over realities, another chance to transfuse you with my love.

Come see me in our secret place, your safe place, the temple of your soul. Sit down again in your room, and close your eyes and breathe with me, in and out, nine times. Then still your thoughts and imagine coming into my presence. Wait for an image to appear. I shall come to you as a beautiful young maiden, with far-seeing eyes. I will hold your hand and ask you what you wish to know. Say then calmly, "I am seeking the Self." Then I shall hold up a mirror to your beautiful face and make you see how you radiate rainbow colors through the universe, how your soul is all-knowing already, just like mine.

February's Aspects

This month received its name from *februarius*, from *februare*, a word the Latins borrowed from the Sabines, meaning to purify.

Full moon aspect: Wild moon, red and cleansing moon

Universal event: Quickening of life

Communal event: Candlemas sabbat; initiations

Message: To purify, to initiate, to quicken

Activity: Purification, growth, healing

Powers: The power to extend life

Appropriate spell: Any spell concerned with growing; money spells, health spells, children's blessings, dedication of newborn babies, blessing of crops and animals, love spells

Color: Red

Tree: Rowan tree (quickbeam), laurel

Flower: Violet and primrose

Creature: Duck, otter

Gem: Amethyst

Anna's Spells, Rituals, & Celebrations for February

SPELL TO WIN A LOVED ONE —————————————

This spell is to be begun at the time of the waxing moon. Matters of the heart are really the center of our existence, unless you were born to be a monk. We are often shy, as if admitting loneliness is saying that somehow we have failed. Not so. Our society is not set up to accommodate mating; it is set up to accommodate profits. You have to resort to the ways of the old days, when casting a love spell was normal for both men and women. When we need a mate, somehow we are able to set aside cultural embarrassments and do what's irrational but what works. You will need a few items to work the spell. Get two candles representing you and your own true love. Colors are again based on what feels attractive to you. A cherry red, not angry red, is recommended.

Write your name with a rose thorn on the back and front of the candle representing yourself, and the other person's name on the other. If you are in the dark about who your future lover is, just write the all-purpose "my own true love" and leave it to the Goddess to figure it out. Set them on the altar (that is, your special table, remember, where you do your sacred acts) at opposite ends of the table, symbolizing the long road to be traveled before you meet.

Light the altar candles. These two white candles remain on the table no matter what you are working on. They are your messengers. As you light them, say, "Blessed be thou, creature of fire." It may sound old-fashioned, but you are not exactly doing high-tech magic here. Light your fine incense (sage) in a fireproof dish—just a little to set the mood. Light the other two candles, saying, "Blessed be [your own name]" and "Blessed be [partner's name]."

When all four candles are blazing away, you say, "Now may the Goddess of Love enter this rite." Just allow yourself to be impressed by this fire show. Your ancient mind loves fire; love is fire—it is comforting to watch such a pretty sight. Give it a moment, hum a little tune if you remember one, then proceed. "In the name of the Bright Spirit of Love, I and [name] will draw near to each other's souls and bodies as these two flames near each

other." Now move the two candles just a little bit closer together. Remain at your altar for at least ten minutes, visualizing: She or he is coming toward you from the east, from the south, from the west, from the north. If you leave the altar, continue to be aware of the candles burning. After one hour, extinguish the candles with a blessing by nipping out the flame with your fingers. Never blow out a candle! (You may blow away your luck.)

Repeat the spell during the three nights of the full moon (the one day before and after the full moon proper is what we call the three nights of the full moon). The three days will go by fast. Each night, repeat this spell and move the candles closer and closer to each other. The last night, let the candles touch and burn down together! What a spectacular sight! You should remain nearby to watch it (don't burn down your apartment!) and use a lot of protection, such as a metal tray, dishes, or aluminum foil underneath the candles.

When your candles have finished burning, collect all the materials on the table, ashes from the incense burner, the flowers you used for decorations (but not your photographs, if you used them), candle drippings if any; pack these into a paper bag and take it to a living body of water! This should be moving water with plants and other living things, not a stagnant lake or polluted stream. Say a few words to the river, lake, ocean, or whatever: "Please take care of this for me, thank you," then cast the spell remnants into the water, turn away, and don't look back. This "don't-look-back" part is the essence of casting a spell. Don't think about it, either. Let go of it altogether; obsessions are out.

If you can follow this procedure faithfully, the force will have you meet somebody new before the next full moon. That's not too long to wait. But there is another aspect to this love spell. When the attraction is manifested and people get interested in you, you must be polite and at least give them a chance. (I don't mean have sex with them, just go out.) If you are generous, the third person will be the one you want. The Goddess is benefiting others with your spell, too; it's nature's way to work in threes.

POWERFUL MONEY SPELL

This spell is to be done during the waxing moon and requires more creativity than the candle spells. Out of green cloth, fashion a doll; mark its eyes, nose, and mouth with red thread and stuff it with rowan leaves. If you cannot find rowan, how about eucalyptus, rose petals, or clover? Sew it up, moving clockwise around the figure. Try to identify with its image, as it will represent you in the spell.

Prepare your altar on a white cloth and decorate it with evergreens. Have ready some pyrite or golden glitter powder. Take a shower and go to your altar when the new crescent moon can be seen in the evening sky. Light two green candles, saying, "Blessed be thou, creature of fire." Light the incense (sage is wonderful, or you can get something else that appeals to you) and pass the doll through it, saying, "I name you [your name]. You are Success! You are powerful! You will always have more than enough."

Actually, why not improvise the words on this one? You can bless your magic doll with anything from corporate mergers to raises to lotto winnings. Let your imagination fly, but don't get frivolous. Powder the doll with glitter, then say:

> *"I conjure the spirits who guard the wealth of this earth to bless me with wealth." Anoint the doll with your own saliva, saying, "I call on the waters to bless my spell with love."*

Wrap your doll in white cloth and hide it in a dark, womblike place. Repeat this spell nine nights in a row; on the tenth night, make a permanent hiding place for the doll and burn it after you receive the spell's blessings. It is done.

SPELL TO PURIFY YOUR HOME & POSSESSIONS ———

This is the month when nature gets rid of what's not fit to survive, so you must protect your house and car from accidents and break-ins. Urban life is as fraught with danger as life in the real jungle. Our possessions are our survival systems; we cannot afford to lose our homes to thieves or our cars to accidents. We may carry good insurance, but the best policy is that which is never needed. We exist on a plane in which we cannot perceive all the other beings sharing the earth with us, good guys and bad guys, spirits that might protect or harm us. It is just common sense to get the good spirits in our corner. This can be done with the pleasing smoke of the sage herb or other incense and with prayers left to us from olden times. We don't have many of these, but they are hidden in our genes; we have to go deep into the genetic library—our imagination—and bring them out for modern use.

Put some sage in your incense burner. After viewing the waxing moon, circle your home with the smoke while reciting under your breath a prayer you improvise or write ahead of time. Don't be shy. Nobody is going to judge your poetry this time; it is something you get from the depth of your soul. It doesn't even have to rhyme. Here is mine:

> *I invoke the Goddess of Protection, and my*
> *grandmother's and grandfather's spirits to shield*
> *me and my possessions with impenetrable power.*
> *My house will be safe from crime and fire.*
> *My car will be safe from accidents, thieves, drunk*
> *drivers, and other cars. And I shall be safe in*
> *the Goddess's grace, like a child in my mother's arms.*
> *So mote it be. Blessed be.*

Circle your rooms inside three times and also outside if you can. Circle your car three times (always clockwise), and when it's all finished, place the incense in the door. Open all doors for a few minutes and let the smoke drift through your home, washing it clean. You can also purify your body, or your friends, by walking around them with your sage burning in a fireproof dish, fanning the smoke over them (this is called smudging). I keep a piece of poke root in my car as a charm against the evil eye. I think about all kinds of unwanted attention as the evil eye, including that of the police. The root hangs behind my mirror, wrapped in shells (sacred to Aphrodite), along with a rabbit's foot from Alaska. Car charms should have three components—three different elements represented. In this case, the shells are of the sea; the rabbit's foot, of the earth; the poke root, of the world below the earth.

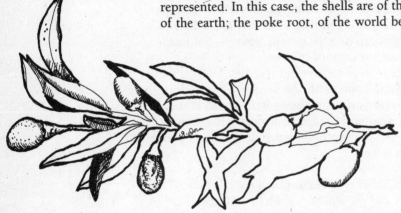

Spell for Victory

Winning, achieving, reaching a goal are feminine virtues. But for the past few thousand years, we have been socialized to think of them as masculine prerogatives. A visit to the business districts of the world will show that women are now present in the most male-dominated fields in large numbers, but we are not present among the decision makers about peace and war. Women do not have enough power to redistribute the country's wealth to our children instead of to the war industry.

What do you want to achieve? Target your goal as precisely as you can. Spell it out in detail or spend time to develop your vision until you know exactly what kind of victory you are after. Choose a time when the moon is waxing, prepare your mind and space for the ritual, set up an altar for the work, use some sandalwood incense, and get three purple candles for the aspect of the Goddess as the Three Fates. On the altar, put an image of the Goddess Victory. She can be found on postcards from museums as the winged spirit, usually holding forth the olive branch of peace.

Now, here is a bit of challenge for you. If your goal is something to get and then hold on to, like a new job or stocks or a company, the next candle you want is brown, for the earth is wealth and she binds and holds on. Is your goal to grow something brand new? In that case, you want a bright green candle. Does your goal have to do with love and affection? Your color is pink. Will what you want require a fight, like a court case? Use red-colored candles. Are you calling forth a brainchild from nothing? Use a yellow candle. Is it a book you want to write, or do you need a publisher, a protector, a helping hand? Use white candles. If you aren't quite clear about what color you should use, get the basic blessing of white candles.

Arrange the candles on your altar with the three purple candles in a triangle in the middle and the working candle of the different color in the center. On the working candle, write as briefly as you can what it is you desire. Use a rose thorn (the traditional tool) or a pencil. Light your incense and meditate on your goal; then light all four candles, one by one, the purple ones first and then the working candle, and say:

> I evoke the mighty spirit of Lady Victory.
> I invoke her mighty courage into my own soul.
> I inhale the strong perfume of her presence.
> I offer her up my mighty goal.
> The blue planet with her mountains
> Now as always, be my territory.
> The blue planet with her rivers
> Now and always be my hunting ground.
> The blue planet with her cities
> Now and always be my home ground.
> The blue planet with all my goals
> Now and always be my victory!

Put out the candles without blowing them out, and the next day, repeat the whole process. Do this seven nights in a row after you have seen the waxing moon. When the seven nights are finished, take all the remnants of candles, incense ash, and so on to a living body of water and cast them in, turn your back, and pursue your goals with confidence.

THE HOLIDAYS

February 1

THE LESSER ELEUSINIAN MYSTERIES (GREEK)

This was an elaborate preparation for spiritual initiation of the youth of the Mediterranean, which was completed at the Spring Equinox when Persephone returned from the underworld.

What a lovely time it must have been, getting ready to embark on a spiritual path, dressed in white, attending to the words of the priestesses and priests in the temples.

On February 1, Ireland has an interesting holiday called Wives' Feasts, where women homemakers lavishly celebrate themselves with beautiful meals shared with each other.

February 2

FEAST OF BRIGID (IRISH)

Most of all this was the month of the Goddess Brigid. Who is Brigid? The Goddess Brigid was worshipped by the Celts as a triple goddess. This idea of three deities in one is a very ancient concept, going back maybe as far as the Ice Age. The Christian trinity is a direct plagiarism from this much older religious concept, except it has been masculinized into the three aspects of Father, Son, and Holy Spirit. Only the Holy Spirit still suggests the Goddess, with her sacred dove as its symbol; she is still declared the soul of the world in churches and art. Brigid, or the Three Mothers, or the Three Blessed Ladies of Britain, seemed to have a lot more to do with poetry, arts, crafts, smithcraft, agriculture, and women. She is the patroness of the bards, inventions, good harvests, and healthy babies.

Brigid was worshipped by groups of women. Nine (or nineteen) priestesses kept an eternal healing fire going at her shrine in Kildare, just like the vestal virgins of Rome. Brigid was a great healer. Her sacred wells all over the British Isles gave sight to the blind and healed hopeless wounds.

Christians couldn't get rid of her, so they tried to Christianize a pagan goddess into a new saint. However, her subjects on the British islands never quite accepted that, and they claimed Brigid as equal to Mary, mother of Jesus. This was fine with everybody, so even today they worship their ancestral goddess in the churches as they once did at the sacred shrines.

February 2

CANDLEMAS: INITIATION OF WITCHES

"Ye shall dance and sing, feast and make music, and love all in my praise. For mine is the ecstasy of the spirit,"* said the goddess of the moon. On this day, some traditions of witches celebrate their initiation rites. I don't want to be mysterious here, so I would like to just give you a quick glimpse of what this ritual looked like in my group.

We used to gather on this day, and those who had studied the Goddess religion for a year and a day and wanted to be part of the coven asked to be initiated. No cruel testing, hazings, or other Hollywood-type rituals

---

*"The Charge of the Goddess," traditional.

were performed; the ceremony we liked to do was part European and part African in origin. After the magic circle was drawn by invoking the four directions of the universe to witness our rites, we chanted the great "Charge of the Goddess" (one of the few poems left to us from ancient times). The women lined up behind each other and spread their legs, forming a "birth canal" for the new members. They in turn curled up on a piece of sheepskin in the fetal position, and we pulled them slowly between our legs, like a collective mother giving birth. The initiates were not allowed to help things along.

We had lots of fun with this. Before we graduated to the refinement of the sheepskin, we used to drag the poor souls through by their hands, which caused rug burns if we were indoors, or grass burns if we were outside. We learned from this the necessity of making it more comfortable for everybody. After they had been "born again" in this communal fashion, the new sisters became part of the birth canal and helped with the others. One priestess offered honey to the newly born witches, saying, "Taste the sweetness of the Goddess."*

February 3

CELEBRATION OF BRIGANTIA (IRISH)

On this day, Brigid, the Irish goddess with the all-seeing eye, was celebrated. The godseye symbol traditionally made on this day is one of several patterns of solar crosses made from the straw that was brought into the

*Zsuzsanna Budapest, *The Holy Book of Women's Mysteries* (Berkeley: Wingbow, 1988), 37. For more information about witches and wicca, check the reading list at the end of this book.

house and then hung over the door to protect the house from harm. Get yourself an "eye of Brigid." Germinate some seeds and eat the sprouts.

February 11

OUR LADY OF LOURDES (FRENCH)

In 1858 the Virgin Mary appeared in France to a peasant girl named Bernadette Soubirous. Jesus has not been seen by anybody since he died, but his mom comes back repeatedly. Busy! Busy! From February 11 through 16, Bernadette Soubirous had a total of sixteen visions of the Virgin at the place where today the Virgin's marble statue is revered by millions. It is noteworthy that this cave, with its healing waters and the magical herb that Bernadette ate before finding the well, was the same grotto where the ancient pagan goddess was worshipped long ago. This is quite common. The Lady of Guadalupe in Mexico also appeared on the earlier site of her pagan temple, and there are many more examples of the goddess requesting that her temple be built where her worship was active in earlier times.

February 12

PROTECTION OF WILDLIFE: FESTIVAL OF DIANA (ROMAN)

How did the lovely goddess Diana (or Artemis to the Greeks) fade into being just a name in the art books when once the forests of Europe were hers? She went the same way as the forests. When Mother Nature is seen as a slave to be exploited by humans, the forests end up as condos, the wild animals end up stuffed or in zoos, and our human nature ends up as a sad story of self-destruction. Why, you may ask, does the Goddess allow this? Why doesn't Mother Nature rise up and swipe at us with her mighty arms and teach us a lesson?

In the nature of self-destruction, we are our own punishment. Nature controls who lives and who dies; our species would not be the first to disappear. She gave us brains and she gave us a chance. After humans, there will be more successful species who will not blow up the planet that is their own home. I still work for our survival and will not stop in spite of the terrible odds. I still think women and men who love life can turn things around. Send some money for animal or environmental rights today. Contemplate nature as a sister.

February 13 through 21 ————

PARENTALIA (ROMAN)

This festival was the first of a series of festivals that included Lupercalia and Feralia (see holidays mentioned later). The holiday began on February 13, with worship devoted to the *parentalia*, the ancient ancestors. Who were these ancestors? They could have been the beloved relatives who had passed on already. They could have been the magic ancestors who never really departed but watched over the living. This was not a feasting time. Marriages were forbidden, temples were closed, and magistrates appeared in public without their insignia.

February 14 ————

ST. VALENTINE'S DAY:
THE FIRST OF THE RESURRECTED
LUPERCALIA FESTIVALS (ROMAN)

Lupercalia was the festival of the natural "heat"—the sexual readiness that permeated nature, especially the wolves. Lupa is the wolf; she was a sacred animal symbolizing Mother Nature's breeding aspect. This was the original St. Valentine's Day, when the minds of people turned to celebration of their sexuality and attraction.

St. Valentine's Day customs originated in Rome, when willing young maidens wrote their names on slips of papyrus, put them in a box, shook them up, and let young men pull out the names of their valentines. The young people then spent the day together as companions, and Goddess knows what great adventure came of it all—romance, marriage, or just a day to remember. The names were equally matched by both sexes so nobody had to go home alone after the drawings.

Records in England go back to 1479 of girls writing letters to their valentines, when the custom of drawing names was no longer in use and youth simply sent letters to each other with their feelings expressed inside. In the 1880s, lace, hand-painted satin, ornaments, birds, baskets, ribbons, and cupids were added to the letters, and rhymes and perfume followed. Today it is a thinly disguised holiday of love and sex. Yes, the fertility rites never die, they just acquire more props!

February 14

SUSAN B. ANTHONY'S BIRTHDAY (AMERICAN)

If you're tired of hearts and flowers, take this opportunity to celebrate the birthday of our suffragette sister! Susan B. Anthony's greatest achievement was to give modern American women the right to vote. If you don't fight for your rights, you may lose them. Take courage from the past; build a better future. Read up on women's herstory.

February 16

CELEBRATION OF VICTORIA (ROMAN)

Victoria was the Roman goddess of victory. Have you ever wondered how everything the patriarchy cares about has a female name? The ships, the countries, and even victory herself? Women have very little to do with these things; we only receive one-tenth of the wealth of the world.

Today, focus on winning. What does it mean? To each it is different—some of us want money, others more power, others more love and affection in our lives. It doesn't matter what it may be, Victoria is the goddess to turn to when you need raises, promotions, direction, leadership, even support for all of the above.

February 17

FORNACALIA: FEAST OF OVENS (ROMAN)

Give a party, bake out, eat X-rated pastry. Celebrate the food workers! An old saying goes: "The oven is the mother." I am not sure if this celebration includes the microwave ovens, but, hey, that's the modern oven. Just think food and appreciate the good stuff.

February 18

FESTIVAL OF WOMEN AS CULTIVATORS (PERSIAN)

Think a minute—what else is there that may be more important than cultivation? I can't think of a thing. Our entire life is about cultivation of somebody or something. Friends require cultivation, lovers and relatives require it, and of course the little ones do. Water your plants, cultivate the arts, get a pet today. Conceive a baby. Cultivate your mind; read a new book or write one. Cultivate your friends. Cultivate your own self-esteem by counting the ways women hold up more than half the sky in our daily work, professional lives, and spirituality. Most of all, let's cultivate peace.

February 19

FERALIA: PURIFICATION FESTIVAL (ROMAN)

Purify your altar, bring in fresh flowers and fresh ideas! The last day of the festival that began with Parentalia was the opposite of good times. Temples were closed, no feast was served, and magistrates appeared without their insignia. Feralia was devoted to the old ones, the "more." Spirits of the dead were placated by food offerings, houses were cleaned, clothes washed, and, generally, rites were solemnized instead of celebrated. Sounds like a good prespring cleaning to me!

February 20

SUN ENTERS PISCES

Pisces, the sign of the fish, is a sign in which to celebrate your intuition and harmonious emotion. Take a long, warm bath today and renew yourself in the womb of the waters.

February 22

CONCORDIA (ROMAN)

Concordia (or Caristia) is a celebration of the Roman personification of harmony, the feast of good and favored relatives and friends. It was sweet to count the living kin and make peace with each one of them, to devote family dinners to ironing out differences between feuding relatives, to reconnect with loved ones. Presents were exchanged by all, and nobody was allowed to carry any feuds beyond this point in the year. You may consider inviting your kinfolk over for a harmonious dinner and exchange small presents with them. Will they ever be surprised!

February 26

HYGEIA'S DAY (NORTH AFRICAN)

This day celebrates Hygeia, the goddess of healing and disease prevention. She is often shown as a middle-aged lady of African origin, dressed in the long robes of the physicians, with her python snake entwining her torso. You can see how early on the snake was associated with healing. The snake earned the distinction of being able to renew herself—just watch a snake after she has shed her skin! On this festival, honor vitality and physical well-being. Seen a doctor lately? It is the proper time to do so. Hygeia is the preventer, the patroness of foresight to avoid illness.

February 29

LEAP YEAR DAY

Women get to propose marriage on this day, but, of course, nowadays ladies can propose all year if they want to. In *Juno Covella*, Robertson tells a story of the old days in Ireland, when monks and nuns were allowed to marry and the nuns of St. Brigid's abbey were about to mutiny for the right to do the asking.* St. Patrick agreed to let the women propose every seven years, but St. Brigid threw her arms around his neck and exclaimed, "Arrah, Patrick, jewel, I daurn't go back to the girls with such a proposal. Make it one in four years!" St. Patrick is supposed to have replied, "Brigid, acushla, squeeze me that way again, and I'll give ye a leap year the longest of the lot!" Ever since this, leap year day has empowered women by letting them choose their mates. I can see in this story signs of a Goddess culture that was positive about sex and love clashing with the oncoming patriarchal clergy, who forbade marriage to their members lest possible heirs claim church property.

---

*Lawrence Durdin-Robertson, *Juno Covella: Perpetual Calendar of the Fellowship of Isis* (Enniscorthy, Eire: Cesara Publications, 1982), 51.

The February Story:
A Tale of the Winter—
Sacred Are the Coyotes

WINTERTIME ALWAYS PRESENTS a challenge to those who want to celebrate the seasons outdoors. When I wanted the weather to be kind so that I could bring out the Susan B. Anthony Coven Number 1 (a group that might include anywhere from 17 to 150 participants), a week before our celebration I would climb into the Malibu mountains at Big Rock and request Mother Nature to grant me a dry night. Ensuring good weather was easy. What was more difficult was to achieve freedom from disturbance, from police or prying eyes. This has become more and more of a problem. As our numbers grew, our fame spread, and our troubles multiplied.

The tale I want to tell happened at Candlemas in early February, a holiday important to witches because this was the time of initiation. There were nine students, who had studied a year and a day, waiting anxiously for this event to celebrate their accomplishment. Then there were the older students and their new priestess, Ramona, who had prepared a special ceremony to hive away from the Susan B. Anthony (SBA) coven. They had set their own spiritual and political agenda and wanted to try out their new wings on their own. Hiving off new groups from older ones is one of the best ways for the spirituality movement, which has been my main focus for so many years, to grow. There were also some foreign students from Germany, some Italians, a very few French students, a strong representation of Canadians, and Americans from all over the States, sometimes as far as Alaska. This made about thirty-eight women altogether, along with the original group. I liked the ad hoc character of the SBA coven; it demonstrated global activity. We were a teaching order, and we were doing our job very well. And I was caught up in this holy excitement.

The thirty-eight women who scrambled up the mountain were not too reverent. As they carried conga drums, sleeping bags, food and drinks for the feast, sacred objects (like bells and chalices), candles, and cauldrons, there were a lot of friendly shouts and warnings about avoiding mudslides. We all made it to the top and set up our circle with stones pulled out from the tall grass, still bearing colorful candlemarks on them from our Winter Solstice gathering.

We built an altar lovingly and beautifully. Ramona set up her South American goddess in the middle, and I added the usual "Three Graces," our official triple goddess image, which had miraculously come to the women's center many years before. Tonight we were blessed. Everybody wanted to take responsibility. Ramona and her ladies were marking the circle out with barley, symbol of the Goddess for centuries, slowly pouring it out onto the wild earth from a Safeway bag. Tony and Artemis were arranging flowers they had brought on the altar. A bird was starting to tell other birds about the barley.

Softly we planned how to invoke the four corners of the universe with the new initiates. They were very nervous; they were foreign students, and their English a little shaky. Could they invoke the Goddess in their own languages? "By all means!" I told them. "We will all know what you mean. It is more natural from the heart. So the north will be in English, the east in German, the south in Italian, and the west in French. Maybe I should do the main invocation in Hungarian? *Istennő halgass ránk! Boldog Asszony jöjj hozzánk!*" As usual, the whole production pulled together somehow. We looked wonderful, all thirty-eight of us, diverse and bold, out in the middle of the winter night. We were ready to dance around an ancient altar without fear, candles burning in white and pink and blue and purple.

Tall, blond Maggie drew the circle with smoke, and graceful Kirstin followed with the sword, separating the world from our sacred space. We raised power by humming, that ancient woman sound, vibrating our very brains, individuals blending with the group until all were one. A sacred silence descended on us within the sound, a feeling of coming home after so many centuries of denial.

Now the initiates took their places and started invoking the Goddess in their own native tongues. Each woman faced the east or south or west or north, arms outstretched with desire to touch the divine, boldly calling on Ishtar, Hulda, Pele, Anna Perenna, each holding the power of the priestess. And they were good. The different languages didn't matter; their faces told the whole story. Ecstasy. Confidence. Altered state of consciousness.

I took a little time out to be proud. Yes, after all, this was my achievement as well. Women need a spirituality that empowers them, instead of robbing them of their power.

Ramona was now reading a statement about her goals, which were to dedicate herself to world peace, freeing political prisoners in Peru. This is when the first wave of that "other" humming reached us. A composite of sound was coming from the mountains, just like the one we made, but with male voices mixed in, a rich resonant chorus that grew and grew until Ramona was hardy audible. "Maybe another coven is worshipping nearby," I said, to explain what I couldn't really explain even to myself. Once I had found a circle of stones left behind, which I was sure had been made by another coven. This spot was very desirable; why should we be the only ones who used it? It made sense.

I motioned to Ramona to continue. She picked it up again, but as she raised her voice, the humming emanating from the mountain became louder again, this time building into a primal howl. The whole coven stopped and looked at me. This is when the high priestess's job becomes a solo responsibility. This is the time when the feminist principle of "we are all leaders" breaks down. An unusual situation must be handled by the one with the ultimate responsibility.

But I didn't know what to do either. It still sounded like a very large coven, women and men together, all raising power at the tops of their lungs; but where were they? We had seen no sign of them before. They could not just fly overhead, could they? So we stopped everything. A small trickle of sweat started running down my sides. The other elders were as puzzled as I was. This had never occurred before. The sound was growing and growing, and there was nothing left to do but listen.

A few minutes crawled by, and suddenly another sound was coming out of the darkness. This one we all recognized—it was the sound of cars. Before we could even disconnect our hands, we were caught in the blazing reflector lights of the police careering down from the north, where the fire road was. Seven more police cars followed, one by one, taking up position with their lights trained on our group.

"Who is the leader of this group?" came a voice over a bullhorn. The police didn't get out of the car. We all looked at each other. I was on probation already for doing Tarot readings, the right to prophesy, which was another fight altogether. Maggie stepped out. She walked over to the police. Maggie, however, sported a full-grown blond beard at this time, which she had let grow just to see what she would look like if she left the Goddess markings undisturbed. This beard was like a light fuzz underneath her chin; she was pretty, and one didn't expect her to have a beard, so when anyone noticed it, it was a shock. The police immediately fell under the spell of Maggie's blond beard. They surrounded her, and one man yanked at the beard to see if it would come off. It didn't. This gave rise to speculations.

"Are you taking hormones?" one policeman wanted to know.

"She must be!" The other was sure of it.

"No, I'm not." Maggie answered politely. "It grows naturally. Actually I used to shave it off, but not this time. I just wanted to see what I would look like if I didn't shave."

"She shaves every day?" The policemen discussed this. "Not anymore; she said she didn't."

"Let's see some I.D.!" Finally the policemen had remembered what they were supposed to be doing.

"Why are you here? What law are we breaking, if any?" Maggie tried to shed some light on the situation.

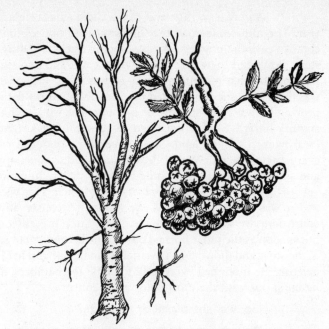

"We got a call from a neighbor down the hill; he said there are all kinds of strange cars parked in front of his house, and then he saw a bunch of people coming up here."

"Sir, there are no signs here that this is a park, or that it's closed. This is wilderness."

"No, you are trespassing."

"Whose land is this then?"

"It belongs to Iran."

"Iran? This is the Ayatollah's place? The one with the American hostages?"

"Yep. Private property."

"You mean you are arresting us because the Ayatollah's rights have to be protected by Malibu police?"

"We are just doing our job, ma'am. Line up everybody, and it will be quick; we have to give you a citation."

There was one woman among the eight policemen, and we decided to get arrested by her if we must. All thirty-eight of us lined up in front of Officer Mary Smith, who was patient and secretly enjoyed being the preferred cop.

And that was the end of the Candlemas celebration that year. The initiates learned that there is much oppression to overcome to earn the privilege of worshipping freely in nature. But the story didn't end there. We had to go to court and explain why we were out on that mountaintop. Luise was a lawyer, and since she was there, too, she represented us. She took pictures the next day, proving without the shadow of a doubt that we weren't causing any fire hazard. She also planned to question Iran's right to keep local women off the land. She prepared a wonderful case, with every angle covered. We all dressed up for our court appearance and showed up on time, hoping to have our day in court.

The judge wore a T-shirt on the bench. This was Malibu, and it was a nice sunny day. We looked so conservative in the courtroom, we were really the outsiders. Luise presented the case, but as soon as the judge opened our file, he became totally absorbed in the story and didn't even pay attention to Luise and her foolproof defense. He motioned everybody to come to chambers, and there he burst out with the most consuming concern.

"So, was she a man or a woman?"

"Your honor, she is a woman. Many women have facial hair; they just shave."

"I know, I know, but I have never seen one that had a real beard."

"It was a real beard, your honor. Officer Maloney pulled on it."

"I know, it's in the report. I saw that."

Eventually, when the beard sensation died down, we were fined a dollar each. The question of religious rights never came up.

Ever since then I have been praying that a wealthy woman or man would step forward and donate a mountaintop or just a lovely piece of land to us, a place where the Goddess could be worshipped by women from all over the world. Even now in the eighties this has not yet happened. We haven't stopped holding the ceremonies, but we have to hide our group and steal the moments of freedom when, with outstretched arms, women reach to touch the divine.

What was that powerful sound coming from the mountain five minutes before we were arrested? It was like a primal warning, so loud that it stopped the women's words. The memory of it still lingers, as one always remembers miracles, especially a miracle witnessed by thirty-eight women! A hushed reverence still lives in that moment in the cry of the coyotes. The sound was wild, yet it spoke directly to us. It made the hair stand up on our arms. Nobody could see them. We only heard them, but in my mind's eye there is a clear picture of a ragged, all-Californian, very psychic coyote family, possessed by Mother Nature and howling their canine song from the gentle heights of Big Rock to protect us from our own kind.

March

THE GODDESS SPEAKS — Koré

YOU GAVE ME DIRECTIONS TODAY, and I knew you had no idea who I was! I was the little girl coming home from school, and I stopped for an ice cream. Then I saw you and thought I'd chat you up! Great fun it was! Later you saw me as a little boy riding my bicycle, and you had to stand aside so I wouldn't run into you. You need not fear; I wasn't going to hit you or fall down or anything. I was just there having fun! A marvelous time this is! I am covering the surface of the world once again with blankets of flowers! I am making tulips, lilacs, apple blossoms! I paint the almond trees pink with my delicate blooms.

I am all over the place. Resurrection is my game, and if there is something to revive, I will do it! Even old dying things come alive now on my command. Did you notice that old ivy sprouting a few leaves? You know—the one your cat is using for a scratching post? Take a look, it's alive! I tell you, I race my winds to carry the pollen, I revel in the profuseness of my works. I am so young I can hardly stand it! My energy makes older people tired just looking at me.

I pinned my message on a tree for you with a pink ribbon. I love yellows and pinks, whites, and reds. I am mad for color! Dress up for me for this month's meditation. Wear ribbon in your hair when you look for me in your temple. I am so excited! What will you need this time? Do you want children? I have children coming down in sacred groups! Unborn children all want a mother. I can send you a great soul, a wise soul for your child. It's the best time to conceive; the whole world is doing it. The power to grant life is yours. See, in that we are alike. I share this power with you because to birth and raise children takes a lot of your energy, ability, and time. Let no priest talk you out of the divine rights I have bestowed on you! If I trusted the black-robed priests with such decisions, I would have made men get pregnant. But I trusted you with this. You know when you are ready. I want you to know that I am ready to send them.

Meet me tonight after the moon has arisen. It's easier to manifest then and talk with you. How to find me: Get some rose petals to burn tonight. Take a shower and come to me dressed in a colorful outfit. I'll wait for you in your mind temple. We'll rest and talk. Breathe again deeply; visualize yourself walking barefoot to your safe temple space. Abide there, listen, and look. I will be the rosy-cheeked maiden who will throw herself into your arms and kiss your face. I have so much love to give! You will not regret it!

March's Aspects

This month was named after Mars, the god of war. In the Julian calendar, this month included New Year's Day, March 25th, when annual leases for homes and farms were signed. The beginning of the new year was moved to January later on, when the Gregorian calendar was instituted.

Full moon aspect: Storm moon

Universal event: Spring fires drying up the floods; materialization of the new year

Communal event: Spring Equinox, blessing of fields and animals; deer and wild cows drop their young (Children conceived during the great rites of Midsummer Night are born.)

Message: To grow, to prosper, to explore

Appropriate spell: Dedication of newborn babies, also called a naming festival; money spells, personal growth

Color: Red, green

Tree: Alder tree or dogwood (Alder wood is used for three different types of dye and in making whistles for calling up the north wind.)

Flower: Daffodil, jonquil

Creature: Sea crow, cougar

Gem: Bloodstone, aquamarine

Anna's Spells, Rituals, & Celebrations for March

DEDICATION OF A NEW BABY

Mothers customarily pay meticulous attention to choosing a name for their child. They try out how it sounds, try to guess what nicknames the child's playmates would use. Does the name sound authoritative enough for later life when the child-turned-adult will hold a job? Will the child's future lovers be able to whisper the name without difficulty? Ancient European peoples believed that you must have two names, one public and one a secret name that only the mother and immediate family knew. This second name is for use after puberty, when the soul changes into its first adult self, when it can be uttered and made public. The purpose of the first public name was to divert the evil eye, to gain favor with the Fates, to keep away sickness, to help the child reach adulthood.

For the naming ceremony, invite a good group of celebrants to meet on the first day of the full moon. Find a place with a big old tree to serve as your symbol for the tree of life. Dress comfortably, prepare some drinks and food the family enjoys, but set out three special dishes for the naming spirits: a bowl of barley (just a handful will do), a small dish of salt, and a small bowl of water. Light three white candles for the blessings to be received. When the mood is high among the friends, and the full moon is well visible, let the guardian mother (chosen by the family) call everybody into a circle around the tree.

Whether you are working a spell alone at your home altar or with a group outdoors, remember that the universe is, as always, within you. You may want to protect the place where you are working by invoking the powers of the four elements and directions. If you do so, remember to thank and dismiss all the powers you have invoked when you end your ceremony!

Turn toward the east with your hands held up as if to embrace the skies and say:

> I invoke the powers of the east by the air that I breathe,
> by the imagination of my thoughts, by the new direction
> I am taking!

Then turn to the south and say:

> I invoke the powers of the south by the fire of life that is
> in me, by my will power and my passion!

Turn westward and say:

> I invoke the powers of the west by the waters of this
> planet, by my very blood, by my deepest love and my
> connection to the deep!

Finally, turn to the north and say:

> I invoke the powers of the north by the earth that
> nurtured me, by the bones that give me form, by the laws
> of the universe!

Then continue with the ceremony.

A little song will help tie the souls of those present into the action, reminding them of their own mortality and rebirth. Sing or chant something like:

> *We are a circle, within a circle, with no beginning and never ending.**

The guardian mother and father (also chosen by the family) should light some frankincense and encircle the small group during the song, moving clockwise to invoke the good spirits and banish the bad ones. When the chant is finished, the baby is placed on a white cloth on the ground. The guardians then take turns, with the mother performing the remaining parts of this ritual.

> *We welcome this new soul into this blessed life with song and love!*

Now encircle the baby with barley on the ground.

> *Dearest [name], may you never know hunger or poverty for material or spiritual things! I bless you with the barley of the Goddess, for nourishment and wealth.*

Encircle the baby with the salt, the symbol of the Earth's wisdom and purity.

> *Dearest [name], may you have access to your own wisdom and that of others! May you be protected from foolishness and self-destruction! May you know the essence of things; may you be bright and find it easy to learn and teach.*

The guardians now sprinkle a little water around the baby, saying:

> *I bless you in the name of the Goddess of all life and healing, that you may be healthy and strong in body, mind, and spirit! Let love be your treasure; may you be happy in your heart!*

The two guardians and the two parents hold up the baby to the full moon and pronounce his or her name.

---

*Rick Hamouris. *Welcome to Annwfn*. Nemeton, 1986. Audiocassette.

Great Spirit of Nature, protect and guide this new soul among us. Bless [public name] with health, wealth, and wisdom! So mote it be!

Great Spirit, bless this person [secret name never to be uttered again until puberty] with health and wealth, love, and good purpose! Blessed be!

It is done. Let the child wiggle a little in the moonlight, then carefully tuck her or him back in bed and let the adults entertain themselves for the rest of the evening.

MONEY SPELL

At the greening of the year, it is wise to cast a spell for the greening of your bank account. Wait for the new moon to grow into a good little crescent and view it one night before you begin the work. Think about the natural tides, the sap in the trees, and the works that burst out to create abundance in your world.

Now create a lovely white space on a small table and decorate it with some living flowers and objects that mean abundance to you. Put on your altar your jewels, gold, and heirlooms—treasures for the Goddess. Purchase four green candles and one orange one. The orange candle will represent yourself attracting the wealth you desire; the green candles, the greening of your income. Place the four green candles at the four directions: east, south, west, and north. Put the orange one in the middle. For the element of air, have ready some sage or cinnamon incense.

Write your name three times on the orange candle and write the amount of money you want on the four green candles. Now don't get outrageous; just ask for what you think you have permission from yourself to receive. Then settle down for a short time in front of your white table, looking mysterious and ready. Imagine that you are like a bird whose seeds for food are scattered all over the earth, and you have to fly over it and pick them up. Money is like seed, except you have to go and pick it up yourself. Take jobs, make interviews—do what the real world requires from you.

Talk to the Goddess like a girlfriend. Habondia, the goddess of havingness, is kind and mellow. She is like a favorite sister. Her hair is braided like bread. Her eyes are dark, and her scent is that of flowers. Now light the incense, your cinnamon or sage. Smell the scent of her essence and say, "This orange candle represents me in all money matters. Dearest sister, send me abundance from the east," then move the green candle in the east closer to the orange one. Imagine your business getting a lot of input from the east. Now do the same from the south, west, and north, each time pausing to think and visualize wealth coming from all directions.

Let the candles flicker and just bask in their light. You may want to go on with other activities in your room, letting the spell continue. When you feel you've had enough, or when the candles have burned down a little, extinguish them with your wet fingers. (Don't ever blow out your magic candles—it blows away the luck.) Repeat this spell three nights in a row, or seven or nine (uneven numbers are lucky). The more often you repeat it, the deeper the message of abundance goes into your brain. Magic is, after all, what's between our two ears. When the candles meet in the middle (you move them closer and closer every night) on the last night, let them burn down together. Say to yourself, "It is done. Blessed be!"

It helps if you can be creative and compose a small rhyme concerning your money. Here is a sample:

> Money that is needed,
> Money that is speeded,
> Money that is mine,
> Come! Now is the time.

Dispose of the spell remnants in a living body of water as usual.

NATIVE AMERICAN PUBERTY RITE FOR GIRLS

Janet McCloud, the famous Native American activist, told me about the ritual initiation of young maidens when they receive their first blood. The mother of the youngster chooses three elders whom she likes and trusts to instruct the young woman in matters of sex, birth control, health—even matters of love spells and other magical arts. The young woman spends three days and nights in a windowless hut. There, taking turns, the three mother elders give her their initiation instructions. The young woman's head is covered to help her concentrate, and she only drinks and eats special foods. After the three days of instruction are done, she emerges. Her mother then removes the girl's head covering, and she is presented to the community as a woman. From then on, she receives the full respect that is due a mature person. Of course, such positive treatment will make a young person grow, assume responsibilities, and flourish.

CELEBRATION OF A MODERN YOUNG WOMAN'S ————— FIRST BLOOD

This event is rarely celebrated in modern culture. The first blood of a young girl is whispered about, and a great secrecy about what it means to become a woman descends on her. If she is lucky, her mother will tell her about birth control and different methods of catching the bleeding, but that is it.

There is a better way. A month or two after a girl has received her first blood (so as to allow time to organize a decent party!), gather friends and relatives who are not narrow-minded, and with whom the youngster feels comfortable, for a party at your home. Other young girls are the best guests for this, since they are sharing the change from child to young woman and can benefit from exposure to a positive attitude.

The mother of the young girl buys her a ring with a red stone in it; it can be a garnet or something more expensive, if the budget allows. At a certain point in the party, the mother should quiet the girls just long enough to say the following things:

> *I am proud and happy to honor my daughter today and welcome her to womanhood. I know she has a lot to learn about being a woman, as I still am learning as I live my own life. [name], please accept this ring as a symbol of your passage from child to young woman. Good-bye, my baby, and welcome, my sister!*

Then she presents the the young girl with the ring.

Other presents can be included, to make it a happy occasion. Depending on the maturity of the young women, the guests could listen to tales of women who fought for women's rights—the right to be educated, the right to vote, the right to keep their income. A young person might as well keep an eye on this process early on, so she will know what to expect from her society.

THE HOLIDAYS

March is a wet month, sacred to Aphrodite, the goddess of love. Many festivals in this month have to do with weddings, motherhood, and being a bride.

March 1

MATRONALIA (ROMAN)

Matronalia is the celebration of women and power. Juno-Lucina, protector of women and the family, is honored on this day. Prayers were offered to this Goddess for a prosperous and happy wedlock, and women received presents from men. Temple fires were lit welcoming the new growth to the earth. The Goddess was represented veiled, with flowers in her right hand and an infant in her left.

March 2

FIRST FESTIVAL OF VESTA (ROMAN)

Vestal virgins were a teaching order of powerful women who served as the priestesses of Vesta, the goddess of purifying fire. The priestesses were sexually active, both homo- and heterosexually. The term *virgin* simply meant "one within." On this day, old branches were removed from the altars and the new fire was kindled.

In ancient Ireland, the Feast of Rhiannon, the great queen, the muse, the white goddess, was celebrated. Burn a purple candle today for inspiration.

March 3

DOLL FESTIVAL (JAPANESE)

In Japan, little girls celebrate the feast of dolls on this day. Dolls representing women ancestors are arranged in homes, court scenes are acted out, and little girls play with the dolls all day. In Japan they call this day *Hina Mastsuri!*

March 4

MOTHERING DAY (ENGLISH)

This was the original Mother's Day. Centuries ago in Old England, it was the custom to visit your mom on mid-Lent Sunday. You presented her with a loaf of bread and shared with her a cup of frumenty, which was a kind of caudle. The best part was that fairs and carnivals coincided with the Mothering Sunday, so there was plenty to do. On examination, this looks to me like a festival of the Earth Mother, possibly Ceres, the food giver. Visit your mom on this day. Bring her presents; take her out. I favor a lot of celebrations for mothers—not just once a year!

March 5

CELEBRATION OF ISIS
(NORTH AFRICAN)

Who is Isis? Imagine a beautiful woman with long black hair and a swarthy complexion and eyes the color of black onyx, seated on her throne and suckling a baby. Now imagine this same beautiful woman with iridescent wings outstretched, her gown and crown decorated with brilliant rubies and emeralds, wearing golden bracelets and anklets, holding the whip of sovereignty in one hand and a child in the other. These are just some of the images of the Queen Mother Isis in her splendor.

Her worship extended all over Asia and Europe. In an inscription on some ruins in my native Hungary, the goddess Isis describes herself in this way: "I am she who binds hearts together." The Egyptian image of mother Isis with her child Horus suckling at her breast is the best known, as it is associated with Mary and Jesus. But the idea is the same. The fundamental bond of humanity, the rock on which all societies are built, is the mother and her child. Isis is associated with Egypt, but her worship was widespread in the Roman Empire, where she became a major deity. Queen Isis was the Egyptian throne, authority, and culture. Here is how she described herself to her worshipper Apuleius in book 11 of *The Golden Ass:*

I am Nature, the parent of all things, the sovereign of the elements, the primary progeny of time, the most exalted of deities, the first of the heavenly gods and goddesses, the queen of the dead, the uniform countenance, manifested alone and under one form. At my will the planets of the sky, the wholesome winds of the seas, and the mournful silences of hell are disposed; my name, my divinity, is adored throughout the world in diverse manners, in variable customs, and by many names. *

This celebration of Isis as the ruler of safe navigation and inventor of the sail originated in the region of the Nile. She is celebrated on her ship, symbolizing our journey through life. Meditate on what you wish to manifest this year. Bless .your fishing boats with incense if you have any, or cast flowers into the sea for good luck.

March 8

INTERNATIONAL WOMEN'S DAY

In 1857 the garment and textile workers of the United States organized themselves into a movement. This event followed a devastating fire in a sweatshop in New York, which exposed the inhuman conditions the women had to labor under and radicalized the workers to demand change. Ever since that day, there have been marches and speeches to raise consciousness about the workers and their needs today. Women's Day is an inter-

---

*Quoted in Barbara G. Walker, *The Woman's Encyclopedia of Myths and Secrets* (San Francisco: Harper & Row, 1983), 453.

national holiday adopted by the United Nations.

Do something radical today. Pay your National Organization for Women dues, join a workshop, start a goddess study group.

March 9

CELEBRATION OF APHRODITE & HER LOVER ADONIS (NEAR EASTERN/GREEK)

Who is Aphrodite? She is the goddess of love and death named after the waters. Her name, literally "foam born," harks back to her birth at Paphos, and may be associated with her earlier names, Marina and Marianna. Aphrodite represents the life-giving element in nature—water—without which there is nothing. She is the goddess of love and death, not just sex. She cannot be forced; she has to remain free or she flees. This means that if you try to force love, she will go elsewhere. This is a rare holiday because here the Goddess is part of a couple, though she is rarely monogamous. Couples celebrate wedding anniversaries, but do they celebrate their first lovemaking? Keep track of that date and remember it on this day so many more will follow. Put lots of flowers in your bedroom, take the evening off to make love. Celebrate this day for success in union. Have a lovers' dinner; celebrate couples.

March 10

HYPATIA'S DAY (ALEXANDRIAN)

This day belongs to the scholar Hypatia, the divine pagan, who taught at and presided over the Neoplatonic school in Alexandria.

Hypatia was born circa 370. She taught many famous scholars, who adored her. Of her it was said, "Her scholars were as eminent as numerous." She was held in high regard for her wisdom and gave advice to important leaders of her time. Christian priests, however, incited riots against her because she was a woman who taught men. The mobs slashed her with seashells until she died. Remember her today. Being smart is no longer punishable by death. Go take a class, get even with the mob, get a diploma in women's studies. Start a women's college! Buy one if you are wealthy. Use wealth as a tool for social change.

March 15

HOLIDAY OF CYBELE (ANATOLIAN, LATER ROMAN)

Cybele was loved and celebrated all over Europe, and this holiday started the spring festivals. Cybele represents the Earth; her son, Attis, is returning from the dead, which is the reason for the celebration—the Goddess defeats death. General picnicking is observed on this day, along with lying on the grass, eating, drinking, and making merry.

Anna Perenna's feast day (Roman) was held on the day of the first full moon in March. There was mandatory fun time, dancing, and fooling around. Couples paired off, making love on the grass for good luck throughout the year.

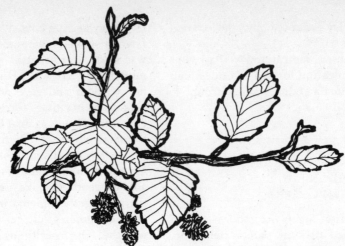

March 17

LIBERALIA: CELEBRATION OF FREEDOM (ROMAN)

On this day, slaves were allowed to speak with freedom, and liberties of all people were honored by allowing them to step outside of the normal lines of authority. Be outrageous today! Step on some toes, speak your mind, organize speak-outs!

March 17

FESTIVAL OF ASTARTE (CANAANITE)

This is the sacred day of the coming together of male and female principles in the ancient Near East. Color eggs red for Astarte (this is the origin of Easter eggs).

March 19

QUINTARIA: FEAST OF ATHENA (GREEK)

This celebration was of the Goddess in her aspect of physical and mental prowess. Five days long, it was a big holiday—the biggest social event in Greece. On the evening of the first day of her festival, there was a footrace with torches. On the second day, people competed with each other in gymnastics. On the third day, there was a musical competition and song festival with harps, flutes, and drums to celebrate the Goddess's accomplishments. On the fourth day, poets competed with each other in four plays, the *tetralogia*. The last day, a satire was produced in honor of Athena, since laughter and wit were Athena's gifts.

The winners won the famous crown of olives from Athena's sacred tree and a flask of oil for sacred use. The Quintaria was closed by a giant procession, where Athena's *peplus*, or sacred garment, was carried by the young nymphs who wove it. It was always gleaming white, with gold trimmings. This *peplus* was carried to the temple, where it was laid on the statue of Athena.

Athena was also called Minerva by the Romans. She was the matron of Athens, inventor of science, music, wit, the wheel, strategy, weaving, a teacher of sports, and the liberator of women. The myths about her unnatural birth from the head of Zeus were but a patriarchal attempt to make her into more of a male than a female deity and to shift her unflinching alliance from women to men.

March 20

SPRING FESTIVAL

Festival time is now in full swing, featuring games, processions, women displaying their talents. This is a good time for crafts fairs, parties, and fund-raisers. The sun enters Aries, and the Goddess rejoices in the fertilizing energy of the ram. Honor Frigga, Norse queen and mother goddess, whose chariot was drawn by two rams.

March 21

SPRING EQUINOX

This day is a major sabbat for witches and celebrates the reunion of the daughter of the Earth, Koré, with her mother, Demeter. Spring returns. "All sleeping seeds She awakens, the rainbow is Her token."* Rebirth, the Earth, and our own lives rise in triumph.

March (variable)

EVE OF PURIM (JEWISH)

Brave Queen Esther saved the Jews from Haman, who planned to kill them. Hamentashin (fruit-filled cookies) are eaten and plays about Queen Esther are still performed on this day. This is a day to observe women's power over men's violence and the victory of female strategies.

---

*Starhawk, *The Spiral Dance* (New York: Harper & Row, 1979), 88.

March 22 and 23

FESTIVAL OF MINERVA (ROMAN)

Minerva (Athena to the Greeks) was the wise goddess of arts and sciences. The festival of the goddess of wisdom is a good time to study something new. How about picking up that art or hobby you had to give up when you took a job?

March 25

HILARIA: LAUGHING DAY (ROMAN)

This is a time for a general observation of glee and laughter. Originating from the rituals of Cybele and Attis, Laughing Day is the original Eastern Easter celebration of the resurrection of the Earth. Go to a comedy night presentation, laugh at least seven times, make a joke yourself.

The days from March 26 through 29 were called by the Romans the theater days, to celebrate the dramatic arts. Remember that a fully lived life includes the arts and support the theaters in your neighborhood. These are party days, times for inviting your friends over. Making time for just enjoying yourself and your contemporaries is just what the Goddess ordered.

March 30

FEAST OF EOSTARA (GERMAN)

Eostara, the German goddess of rebirth, invented nature regenerating and all of us along with her. Hers are the first signs of spring—the colorful Easter eggs, the hopping bunnies—all fertility symbols. Cook a great meal in her honor, for this season is for rejoicing in the abundance of the Earth. Eostara is the goddess whose festival is Spring Equinox, and whose name gave us our (Germanized) term *Easter*. Later, this day was Christianized and associated with the resurrection of Jesus instead of that of the Earth.

March 31

FEAST OF THE MOON GODDESS (ROMAN)

Luna was the Roman goddess of the moon. So often we gaze at the sky and our breaths shorten with the awe the lovely moon evokes in us, renewed and brilliant, her white light transforming the familiar landscape into a star-dusted fairyland. Poets and lovers, travelers and pilots look to her light for guidance and solace. Witches pray to her for all the reasons to live—for health, wealth, and wisdom. The ancient Chinese and the Europeans baked moon cakes in her honor, and her holidays are all the full moons of the year. There are thirteen full moons recognized in a year, not twelve. This gives the number 13 its mystical meaning of *good luck* instead of bad. The number 13 is a completion number, thus associated with prosperity.

The moon inspired a universal spirituality revering its effect on organic life, namely conception, menstruation, and fertility, through controlling the waters, the weather, and rebirth. The most recent moon goddess is the Virgin Mary, standing on her crescent moon. Other names for the Lady of the Moon, who became revered as Mother of the World, are Isis (Egypt), Inanna (Sumeria), Asherah (Canaanite), Akua-Ba (Ashanti, Africa), Selene (Greece), Hina (Hawaii), Chang-O (China), Artemis (Greece), Diana (imperial Rome), and so on.

The March Story: Confessions of a Feminist Witch

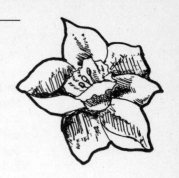

WHAT IS THE DIFFERENCE between a feminist and nonfeminist witch, you may ask. But before we get into that, let me backtrack a little. First, let's define who a witch is. A witch is a woman or a man who considers the Earth a living, breathing, conscious being—part of the family of the vast universe—to be regarded and respected as God herself. To be a witch, you have to see yourself as part of God, who is present in, not separate from, us and all living beings.

To be philosophical about it, a witch feels and thinks that she or he is participating in the constant flow of life energy; a witch takes responsibility for her and his actions in relation to others and to the world. Power is within and without; the created are not set apart from the Creator. In an old-fashioned way, this is a very religious point of view. The responsibility for saving the world is internalized, not externalized, nor is it delegated to a third party like a messiah. A feminist witch uses her craft for the good of all, politically as well as personally.

We, the living expressions of the divine life flow, *are* the divine life flow. For example, the snow in the winter is the expression and manifestation of winter; it also *is* the winter. Peach blossoms are expressions are springtime, but they also are the essence of springtime. It is harder to be a witch than the follower of a guru or some great man or woman, because the burden of power is constantly on our own shoulders. There is no room for a savior.

So what does a witch do? For one thing she or he has gotten past the fear that is associated with the buzzword *witch*. More than any other race, white people have been subjected to such intense terror for the past six hundred years for following our Native European traditions that today we are afraid to own our own past. On our native continent, white people tortured, killed, and waged war on each other in the name of a book (the Bible) imported from the Middle East, with no Europeans in it. We owe it all to the emperor Constantine, who declared Christianity—with its Bible—the European state religion in A.D. 500.

Now we are poised at the end of the twentieth century, white, mostly Christian, dominating the world just as the Bible said we should, but we have forgotten that the Earth is our home, not some enemy from outer space. Our blindness costs us clean air and water; a hospitable, fertile environment; a relaxed life-style and community life; and the rich spirituality of our un-Christianized ancestors. There are more and more people who are getting interested in the Old Religion, trying to reclaim our repressed and denied past and put some common sense into our present.

Other races have never given up their own roots or their own spirituality. Black Americans molded their hearts into the Christian format and gave this country culture we would never have known—the blues, the gospel songs, the passionate dances in worship—all expressions of the African sensibility. Their culture gave them pride and the strength to fight for their civil rights. For the same reason, Native Americans maintained their Sun Dances and sweat lodges, their prophecies and, when they could, their sacred land; they did so to hold on to their racial memories and the freedom of their souls. Latin Americans, being the creative people they are, simply sugarcoated their spirituality by identifying their gods with the Christian saints and practicing their native rituals under different names.

We white people no longer have to be the racial/spiritual orphans of the world. It is okay to know that our own ancestors were brilliant builders of shrines and temples, creators of hymns and of oral, as well as written, traditions, that we worshiped the sun and the moon and the earth of our Cosmic Mother. It is okay to love women—it won't make our balls fall off. It is okay to be witches—it won't be the end of our lives. The witch burnings are over. Repeat it to yourself when you are afraid: "The witch burnings are over." And we cannot burn us twice. We have returned in full force. Look into each other's eyes and say yes to a guilt-free new century. Yes! So you see, it takes a lot of courage to own the words *witch, Wiccan**—to own being a "white, pre-Christian spiritual person." We can't make a complete return to the old ways, because we can't know precisely what those were. But we know those ways are something precious of our own, not imported from other parts of the world. We can remember and reinvent them.

I wake up in the morning, and just to make sure I am tuned in a positive way, I stand at my altar and say to myself, "I am the conductor of love in the universe. All my needs are easily met. I achieve my goals effortlessly. I play and love and help others." You can make up your own morning prayer. The spirits who love you appreciate a hint of what you want to use your existence for that day. The prayers we need are already whispered in our own souls; just listen in and find the one you feel good about. I go about my morning ritual of taking a shower, fixing some tea, making toast, feeding myself wholesome foods. Divine choices have to be made right away; you do not ingest things that are bad for you—no cigarettes, no coffee, no greasy foods—because you conduct love in the universe, not cholesterol.

The day begins, and here is the chance to "walk the pentagram"—the poor maligned, media-trashed, five-pointed star! Can a Hollywood movie ever be made without one? Long associated with the Earth, the five-pointed star is a powerful symbol all around the world. The U.S. Navy, for example, puts pentagrams on its fighter airplanes and their uniforms, the Russians put them on their planes and uniforms. Americans like to paint blue, black, or white pentagrams on flags. Witches just draw them. For us, the pentagram stands for the four directions—east, south, west, and north—and the center.

The top point of the pentagram is associated with pleasure, recreation, and sex. So all of our activities should be influenced by the pleasure, not the pain, principle. We have not come into the world to suffer or to inflict suffering. Can you just imagine any mother-to-be planning a vale of tears for her baby? Does any mother really believe that her beautiful new baby is a sinner? Do babies "sin" because they come through our vaginas? Nonsense.

---

*A Wiccan is a follower of Wicca, the old Native European Earth religion.

The two side points of the pentagram are associated with the self (that which is the same in all living beings) and individuality (that which is unique to you only). Aha! Here is a tough task: Every day you have to do something for yourself that is good only for you. Selfish? No! Self-possessed. But then you balance this out by doing something equally good for the benefit of all. This will depend on your opportunities; only you know what you can do. For example, if I get a massage (for me only) then I drop by the whale center later on and do some volunteer work.

Finally, the bottom two points of the pentagram mean power and passion. Wow! How do you walk that? Power is easy, because every day we exercise power. We use power even if we deny it. Power is like the weather; it is an *is*. If you don't want to use power, somebody else will, because nature likes to fill a void. For women to use their power in these times is the hope of the world. If you are a woman, please, don't back away from power. If you are a man, and you stand up against other men when sexist/racist put-downs are exchanged in the male-only spaces, you have used your power for the good of all. Especially when there are no women around to witness your contribution to a guilt-free next century, you are my hero! You deserve the title "brother." May your numbers increase!

Power is used in making good decisions; doing well at your job; creating your own art, inventions, or ideas; being resourceful; teaching yourself something new. If you are in the media, you are using your power if you uncover corruption in spite of the dangers this may entail and if you conduct uncompromisingly honest investigations that can topple the mean-spirited and powerful. If you are an artist, use your power to be original, to try to heal the wounds you see around you. Then there's passion, the last frontier! Passion is like steam, and we use it in all the other four endeavors. Everything we do needs passion to be done well. Not only in making love but in getting well from a sickness or even getting up in the morning—all require a passion for life. Passion is precious; it indicates good mental health. Use it as an important energy source all day long. And thus we "walk the pentagram."

So where does the feminism get into the witchcraft? Witchcraft, the ancient European earth religion, is inherently feminist. When you see your gods as female and male, neither subordinated to the other, both required to create reality, you are safe from sexism, because both sexes are powerful and divine. Enjoy.

There is also the thorny, scary subject of hexing. The craft advises us to "do as thou wilt and harm none." But what happens when we need to use magic for self-defense? Here again, the feminist witch makes a choice of risks. We can call down the Dark Mother and ask her to help us. Killers exist only on the physical plane; their souls are saddened by the evil they are doing. We can call on their very own souls to stop the evil, and their own souls will make them make "fatal" (the Fates are our helpers) mistakes so they can be apprehended and taken out of circulation. Why is that more difficult to accept than taking self-defense lessons and learning how to gouge a man's eyes out or pull off his testicles? I prefer to do my spells without touching men at all. Isn't that the safest way for a woman to defend herself?

When I moved to the Bay Area in 1980, I was looking for a sacred place for my group to worship Mother Nature. I found Mount Tamalpais, which used to be a sacred mountain of the California Indians. Here I found tradition and beauty—and politics. As I was walking around on the mountaintop, I found well-meaning official leaflets pinned to the redwoods saying, "Women! A murderer is stalking this area. Please be aware and don't come here unescorted!" I became furious! I tore down a leaflet and wrote on it with big red letters: "Murderers! Stay off this sacred mountain! Witches are stalking you!" And I pinned it back on! What is wrong with the leaflet's warning? Well, being escorted, for one thing, would mean nothing, because men were being killed by the trailside killer as well. Women would get a false impression that being with a man meant safety, and this may have well cost some women and

men their lives. The leaflet must have been a great compliment to the killer! "Look! The women are afraid of me!" he must have thought.

But I didn't stop with rewriting the leaflet. I started making phone calls to all the witches and groups I knew in the Bay Area. I called witches who taught classes, lectured, or wrote books about witchcraft and said, "Let's get together! What are we witches for? Let's hex this murderer once and for all; let him be caught. Let's put our politics where our spirituality lives!"

Ahhhh. . . .

To my astonishment, I got very mixed reactions. The old internalized oppression reared its ugly head, and my sisters in the Craft reacted in a very counterrevolutionary way.

"But Z," they gasped, "how would this work? Wouldn't a hex come back to us threefold?" They were quoting the traditional threefold law. "Only if you attack the innocent!" I replied. "What does it take to get you to fight back?" I probed. "Are we not getting shot at while we jog on the trails? How much trouble do you need to be in for you to use your Craft to defend yourself?"

Clearly, there was too much New Age influence on the Bay Area witches; it made them just lie down and roll over.* They actually believed that hexing in itself is wrong and must be avoided at all costs. They felt if they hexed a murderer they would become "bad witches" and be doomed. There was another school of thought circulating in the Bay Area within the witches' community. It was a strange twist on the threefold law. It held that each time you cast a spell on some evil thing, you bind yourself to that evil. This, of course, totally paralyzed any political/spiritual action. Who would want to be bound to serial killers? The threefold law, in fact, is as follows: If you use the Goddess for frivolous, greedy reasons, it will rebound upon you threefold. If you attack the innocent, it will rebound upon you tenfold. If you stand up for yourself or others in need of help, your luck will improve threefold.

---

*Followers of the New Age movement were too laid-back. Their plan for self-defense would probably have been to send the "white light" to murderers and rapists and to pray for their self-realization. I didn't think this was a very strong defense against rape and murder. Most New Age literature lacked any feminist ideology and blamed the victims for bad fortune in the name of their karma. It denied the need for dealing with the dark side of our lives and culture—namely the sexist patriarchy responsible for abused children, battered women, murdered women, and children kidnapped for pornography; the same sexist patriarchy that profits from war.

I was raised to stand up for myself. There is a definite cultural difference between me and the local American witches. They have forgotten that what gave witches great value in the European communities was their protection spells against pestilence, or drought, or criminals.

I asked KPFA Radio to document my hex, so that it would be clear that no devil or male god was going to be invoked to accomplish the capture and arrest of the murderer, and that it was not necessary for his identity to be known to me. Karla Tonella of KPFA said she wouldn't miss the hex for the world. She recorded every word. We later published it as a cassette tape and distributed it to battered women's shelters and women's centers as an example of how women can fight back.

I managed to gather thirty feminist witches under a full moon eclipse to perform this ritual. The eclipse was very important. When you hex somebody under the full moon the spell becomes more powerful. An eclipse makes the magic more powerfully affect the thing or person you cast the spell against (such as the murderer). I cast the spell to make the murderer fall "by his own mistakes, by his own fault, by his own evil." This is my standard hexing ritual. Performing the hex separated the witches from the pretenders (or New Agers, who think sending "white light" or love to rapists and murders might do some good. It never has).

We gathered in a sprinkling San Francisco rain. First, we had a meeting in somebody's home to reach consensus. This was most important. *To do an effective hexing, all the women must be of the same purpose and unafraid. If anybody is afraid to fight back, they must leave.* There was some discussion; women were still scared of their own power. Only women who were not afraid of their psychic power could do this. Out of black cloth we made a doll representing the murderer, and we passed the doll from angry woman to angry woman as we stuffed it with baneful herbs, nettles, boldo leaves, poke root. Then we anointed the doll (now identified with the rapist) with "double-crossing oil" so he would find nobody loyal to him anymore. Even his relatives, his own mother would give him up. Later the Mount Tamalpais witches joined us, bringing the murderer's very footprints gathered from the earth at the murder sites to further link the doll to the murderer.

Finally, we were on our way to Sutro Heights Park, overlooking the Pacific Ocean, where a temple-sized statue of Artemis/Diana stands. The statue is beloved by the local witches; it is decorated with fresh flowers almost all the time. I loved this site. I knew it was a place of power.

First, we held hands to measure the circle we were to make. It wasn't an easy place, being on a slope. Next, we invoked the four corners of the universe; four different priestesses called in the powers from the east, the south, the west, and the north. I think I worked the north. I have been somehow ending up doing the north for years. Now, with all powers present, we proceeded to raise power.

A restrained humming evolved into an all-out primal howling at the moon, which was about to be eclipsed. As the eclipse slowly proceeded, I called on the Dark Goddess:

> *Dark Mother of the universe! Hecate! Kali! Black Madonna! Listen to your priestess Medea! We have a serial killer on our trail here! We cannot walk or jog without being shot at! There is war against your sisters down here on Earth! Every four minutes, one of us is raped! Every thirty seconds, one of our babies is molested by a man! Every two minutes, a woman is battered by a man! The rest of the time they plot to kill the Earth and all life on it! Wake up, sleepy Mother! Wake up and use your mighty power to defend the life we represent!*

The women started supporting this by spontaneously chanting, "Bring him down! Bring him to justice! By his own fault, by his own mistakes, by his own will he will be caught!" The hexing had taken off. The moon slowly covered her face with the shadow of the Earth. As we touched astral planes, I could feel she was there, listening. The Mother was present in the salty air, in the barks of her seals nearby, in the righteous anger of the women who were fighting for their lives.

Then, when the energy was at its height, I brought out the doll. I had bought some pig's blood from the local butcher shop for ten cents. Pigs are sacred to the earth. I squeezed the blood from the plastic bag onto the doll representing the killer, saying, "This is Mother Demeter's sacred pig's blood. I ask an end to the human blood that flowed. I ask the Dark Mother to stop the killer's human sacrifices. Take this pig's blood instead. Take this murderer instead of the victims. Let him be caught! Recycle him into your dark womb!" The women chanted, "Recycle him into your dark womb!"

Then I took the doll representing the murderer to a predug hole in the earth. I placed it in and buried it within the rich dark body of Mother Earth. After that I proceeded to draw an equal-armed cross on the earth with powdered dragon's blood reed (an herb from Sri Lanka) to keep his evil buried. After that, the witches urinated on his grave, one by one, to "eliminate" his evil.

> "So shall he lose all his protection!"
> "So shall he lose all his luck!"
> "So shall he lose all his comforts!"
> "So shall he lose all his freedom!"

After thirty angry women were through with the hexing, we thanked the four powers of the universe for lending their power to ours and started singing a freedom song.

> *We all come from the Goddess,*
> *And to her we shall return.*
> *Like a drop of rain*
> *Flowing to the ocean.*

We left offerings of flowers, apples, and burning candles at the feet of the Artemis/Diana statue and tried to dance a circle three times in the pouring rain, which made the earth cling to our boots. I want you to know it isn't easy to dance in the mud on a slope. But we managed.

The results were not in for three months, but they were worth waiting for. From reporters who wrote about the case, I learned the name of the man who was arrested for the trailside killings. He denies it to this day, but that is usual for serial killers. After our hex, he never killed again. Instead, he started to make mistakes. He left a victim alive, who recovered and became an eyewitness. He dropped his glasses beside a body. When the police contacted all the optometrists who could replace his glasses, the suspect was pointed out as the man who came in for the replacement. Three months of observation followed until the police had gathered enough evidence to bring him to justice.

There was one more sign that it was our hex that brought him in. There was an old woman in her sixties who had already talked to the police about the suspect, but the police didn't take her seriously. She told them that he acted "weird" around her daughter on a ship he was working on. After the glasses identified him, the police took the old woman seriously and these three strikes against him—the eyewitness (mistake), the glasses (his own fault), and the old woman (the Goddess)—brought him to death row where he is now. The trailside killings have stopped since he got arrested. May all killers end up this way.

There was no need for a male god or the Christian devil to help the women in this. The Goddess in her destroyer aspect can be called on to help the living.

What is the lesson of this hex? That it is in the interest of women and men to help clean up their communities and protect them from killers. That it is in the domain of the Goddess to respond and help women to make their lives safe. That women have the psychic power to petition their own universal powerful force in their own behalf.

Our example inspired other groups of women elsewhere in the country. In Phoenix, Arizona, witches in a coven called Blue Heron performed a purification ritual for their neighborhood block by walking around with smoke and candles, singing blessing songs. In the middle of the ceremony, some other women inquired what they were doing. The Blue Heron women explained that they had had some burglaries in their neighborhood and were casting a circle of protection around the area to prevent any more such criminal acts. Their spell was directed to Lady Luck, asking her not to grant the criminals safety for their acts but to cut off their luck so they would be discovered if they attempted to rob.

Now the women who asked these questions were regular neighborhood women, not feminists or witches, but they thought about what they'd heard and discussed this among themselves while the Blue Heron women went on with their protection spell. When they reached the end of their block, the women from the next block gathered and asked them to do their block as well. So the Blue Heron women and the new sisters proceeded to stoke up the incense burner with some more frankincense and myrrh and crossed the street and blessed the entire area, some twenty women strong! Such are some of the activities of feminist witches.

Aphrodite

I AM APHRODITE, MARIAMNE, Aphrodite-Mari, Stella Mari, the life giver risen from the tangy, frosty waters—the original cauldron of transformation. I am life and death. From my loins all things issue forth, and at the end it is I to whom they return.

I am Aphrodite, the sea born, the sexual goddess and death goddess all at once. And what a sight I am! I am naked, without shame. I am attractive and alluring. They tried to tame me, and still I would not obey. They tried to degrade me with censorship and pornography. They tried to regulate me with laws and turn my people away. I only came back stronger.

Yes, look at me, I am sex unbridled. I am the heat in cats and dogs. I am the lovers' passionate relationship. I am the lovers' embrace and the lust they try to deny you. Yes, lust. When your body is wholesome, healthy, and my natural time comes around, I am the one who makes you sigh all night and look with longing on those who have captured your fancy.

I am also the prostitutes who gather in the loveless and undesirable men from the streets. I am the generous whore with the golden heart and the cold cunt with the ice in my veins. I rule everything; I am almighty. No one can resist me. I made you that way. My imprint is on your every cell and nerve ending. I am the images you see in wet dreams, and I am the hope of the lovelorn and the treasure of those who find me.

I reward my worshippers with long and healthy lives. I am there for the traveler and the home bound. I am the food of the body and soul; I am the future of the races. I continue weaving my web of knowing around your heart, even if you have been giving this knowing away. When you no longer want me, old and tired, I will take you back into my all-encompassing lap because I am the one who decides on your hour of return.

Are you aghast? Are you wavering, trying to avoid my face, ashamed that you are so weak as to bow to me? Know that I am queen of all organic life; none but the stones can resist me. Nothing but honesty makes me listen to you.

I proclaim messages of love; this is my job, and I do it well. All art thrives on my feelings; all music celebrates my variety; all dancers dedicate their movement to me; and all sculptors follow my lines, if they are any good. I am one with the opposites; I am constantly uniting. I am pansexual; the imprint of my genitals is repeated in nature. Look at the vulvalike seashells or the nourishing barley for my shape. Look deeply into the orchids, roses, irises—they imitate my sex. Admire the scent and drink deeply of the summer night's coming. I am in the air, dispensing longing and ecstasy in generous measures. My celebrations are spent with flutes and bare feet on mountaintops. I am Marina, curly-haired and swarthy. The mermaids are my cousins. I am that which makes your life worth living. . . . Pay me respect.

April's Aspects

The name of the lovely and exciting month of April is derived from Aprilis, a Roman analogue of Aphrodite, the goddess of love and death. Her name seems to be rooted in the verb *aperire*, meaning "to open." Indeed, this goddess is the door of life, as often her pictures depict her, naked, with her hands pointing to her genitals to remind us of the passage through which we came into the world.

Full moon aspect: Seed moon, budding trees moon

Universal event: Nesting of the birds—royal symbol of the sun

Communal event: May eve, ushering in summer; dances around the maypole, symbolizing the Tree of Life (Time to clean your house, purify your altar, and anoint the sacred images of the temple.)

Message: To develop, to know, to enrich, to pleasure

Activity: To bend, to aim

Healing properties: Return the balance of nerves, cleanse and strengthen

Appropriate spells: Passion spells and devotions to the dead

Color: Crimson, green, brown

Tree: Alder, fern, willow tree (The wood of the willow is highly desired as a witch's wand. Musical instruments are made of it. It is sacred to the Moon Goddess; her herons gather there to nest. Willows passionately love water.)

Flower: Sweetpea, daisy

Creature: Hawk

Gem: Diamond

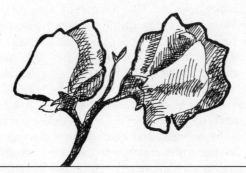

Anna's Spells, Rituals, & Celebrations for April

HUDOUGH DANCE

Janet McCloud, a famous Native American leader, told me about this custom. It is a special dance for Native American women called *Hudough*. The dance involves both sexes. If a woman in the community fancies a man other than her husband, she is free to ask him to this dance. After the dance, couples may lie with each other without threatening the continuity of the family. This is that time of the year when one's fancy is honored. Marriage laws are relaxed for the duration, much as they were during similar festivals among native Europeans.

BLESSING ON YOUR GENITALS

Your body is your temple, but your genitals are the seat of all your pleasures and recreation. See a doctor or two and explore herbal medicine to keep them healthy. We are so lucky in the United States to have the whole world's wealth of healing available to us. If you suffer from a venereal disease, make it your sacred duty not to spread it to others. Find out about safe sex. In any case, it is a good idea to use the following guided meditation to ensure remission or reversal of the sickness or just good maintenance.

When the moon is full, sit and meditate for ten or fifteen minutes, relaxing. Imagine quietly walking barefoot to the temple in your mind, a beautiful and safe place, and abide there in the feeling of peace. Wait for the Goddess, and see if she wants to tell you something. Watch for insights. She may appear to you as a friend, or as the Goddess in her full splendor of nakedness. Don't be alarmed by her frankness. She is the Goddess of sexual encounters. She is bejeweled, and she is free. Ask her now to bless your genitals so that you will be free of sickness there and your pleasures may be honored and deep. Burn the scent she likes best, musk. Offer her gifts, cunt-shaped cookies, conches, jewels, a mirror. Thank her affectionately before you leave the temple to return to your normal existence.

BLESSING ON LOVERS

If you were favored by the Goddess of love and now you have a relationship that you know is special, that you two are bonded in love, gather your friends for a public celebration of your relationship. You don't have to have a legal ceremony to make each other feel that you are bonded in the eyes of Mother Nature, your chief relative.

The lover's ceremony takes place under a full moon in April. Invite your family and those people you had as friends before the emergence of your "all-encompassing" relationship. This is a way to pay attention to and not forget those whose friendship saw you through the times of no lovers.

The lover's symbol is the myrtle tree, so you may want to go out and find some or go to a florist to buy some. Set a lovely table, with flowers and good wine or juices, and settle down for drinks around it. Serve your feast foods—seafood is most appropriate. At an appropriate moment, let your best friend get everybody's attention by saying something along these lines:

> Dear friends! We have gathered together tonight to celebrate a very special relationship between my friend [name] and [name]. I am honored to be the one to call the Goddess of Love to our table and offer her the wine from our cups and the bread and seafood from our plates and ask her to bless [name] and [name] so that they may continue in happiness and understanding and good luck.

> I understand that it is traditional to take a branch of myrtle and bring it to this gathering to represent the tree of life and the blessings of life. Please now present this myrtle to each other, as we witness and bless it for you.

Now the couple will say something in their own words, for example:

> I choose you [name] because I love you, and you are the blue in my sky and the laughter in my morning.

All of this is improvisational, so just speak from the heart.·

If you cannot get hold of myrtle branches, try for orange blossoms, jasmine, cherry blossoms—anything that blooms in your area at this time. It is good to exchange rings as mementoes of commitment, or small gifts to remember this night. Take pictures. When the lovers make love this night, offer your joy to Aphrodite for good health and love. Create a lovely altar to the Goddess, with shells and blooms. Burn a pink candle for her and let it burn all night through without putting it out. Pink is for happiness and equilibrium.

DEVOTION FOR THE DEAD

Go in the evening to the grave of your loved one. (If the grave is far, create a small memorial table.) Tidy up some—plant some flowers, or just turn over the top dirt. This is particularly nice for one who has just died recently. Place a week-long white candle in a jar on the grave. Anoint the candle with sandalwood oil (for wisdom) and pour some on the ground as well. Light the candle, saying:

> *Blessed be thou, spirit of [name]; I come to bring you love and energy.*

Light frankincense and myrrh in your censer, saying:

> *May the Goddess who is three-formed favor you with deep peace and a happy rest.*

Spend a while chatting informally with the spirit of your beloved and tell her or him the latest news. In closing, say:

> *Blessed be your spirit, [name]; blessed be your dreams. Sleep in bliss and never know fear, only the peace of the Mother.*

HALOA (GREEK)

The most majestic of all the Greek women's festivals was Haloa, the celebration of women's free speech. The observance was performed by women only. Exactly what happened during Haloa is something of a mystery, since the women didn't keep written accounts. But we know this much—the women were talking about sex.

Women's sexuality has always been a very important topic for frank discussion, and Haloa gave women an opportunity to exchange information among themselves. Haloa was feared by men. During Haloa, women gathered in a sumptuous social setting. They created pastries that looked like male and female genitals and shared them. They used language with each other that was otherwise not allowed for ladies. In fact, they liked to interject a bit of the risqué, ribald, and free. After their frank discussions, exchanges, and eating of the X-rated pastry, they really dug into their fantastic banquet, where everything that land and sea could offer was served. Slave women and mistresses were equal in Haloa, and class distinctions were lifted in memory of the matriarchs.

Associated with the Haloa celebration was the "Festival of the New Wine." When Mother Nature was ready for her grapes, the day of the cutting of the vines was celebrated with the Mysteries of Demeter, Koré, and the Son of the Goddess, Dionysus. The pomp and circumstance included carrying first fruits through the streets of the city for good luck before offering them at Demeter's grove. After the cutting of the vines, there was a communal dance on the "threshing floors," doubly used for cleaning grains and, in honor of the Grain Giver, dancing, sporting, and playing games. Special prowess was displayed, ritual showing-off took place, and general good humor was generated.

After everybody was warm and high on the new wine, it was believed that purification from troubles could be achieved on many levels. Young people cruised each other, and loudness and laughter were not frowned on even by early sleepers. This was a pagan custom nobody wanted to change. Dancers came out to perform exhausting feats. The next day there were more local athletic events during which men lifted logs and huge stones or even carts. Women cooked sumptuous feasts, flirted, and danced with each other in circle dances of the earth.

Jane Harrison tells us that the wine festival portion of Haloa was celebrated in the midwinter season and later taken over completely by Dionysus.* According to her, this is due to the coming of the new god of the patriarchs, but his coming was a two-edged sword. On the one hand, the worship of Dionysus enabled women's mysteries to thrive into the patriarchal times, with

---

*Jane Ellen Harrison, *Prolegomena of Anglo-Saxon History to A.D. 900* (Cambridge, England: Cambridge University Press, 1976), 145.

the worship of the god as hermaphrodite—both male and female in one form.

On the more negative side, however, the festival of wine was officially shifted from harvest time to midwinter in Greece and completely assigned to a male god who, as time went by, shed more and more of his female characteristics and traits. However, Dionysus (as the patriarchs modified him) was still the son of the Earth Mother, closest to matriarchal status.

With a newly discovered scroll from Lucian that reveals a full account of Haloa, we see a new aspect to the festival. The women celebrated Haloa alone in order to have free speech! What an ingenious religious impulse.

At the end of the festival, there was a giant banquet. What was in abundance on those festival tables was varied and interesting. Cakes shaped as female and male sexual organs (still seen in European bakeries), crepes filled with cream, diamond-shaped cookies with red raspberry filling inside. But in all of this, the flesh of animals was not eaten nor desired. That particular custom was brought in later by Achaenas, who overran the gentle land of the Pelasgians.

"Imagine a Haloa!" I said to my study group; all were anxious to put their newfound knowledge into practice. "What would it be like? How would we celebrate it?" After a couple of hours of discussion, this is what we decided our Haloa would be like. We gathered in a cozy women's club, not a cold big hall, just the space we could fill up without too much advertising. We came dressed up as festively and opulently as our budget allowed, and we hired out the catering because we wanted to concentrate on speech and self-expression. All of us stood around the tables holding hands and blessed them in the name of the Goddess of Truth, Maat, and self-expressive Aphrodite, goddess of love and death. We burned a small cone of very fine incense in a censer and decorated our tables with tall, brilliant, many-colored candles.

The first step was the Honoring. We each bowed to our left and right before sitting down, and declared:

I honor my sister [name] and promise that no matter what may be said here tonight we will remain friends. I honor my sister [name, to the other side], so that no matter what is said here tonight, we will remain friends.

We had a commitment to overstep the boundaries of our normal conduct with each other so we needed to assure ourselves that our bond would not suffer because of this exercise.

After this, we seated ourselves, and one chalice was filled with wine and another with juice for the nondrinkers. First we toasted each other and the Goddess, but after a while it was time to start the quips and jests that were "scurrilous." The moment was pregnant. In order to break the ice (or socialized fear), we passed out the desserts that looked like human genitals—a kind of X-rated pastry. This was part of the ancient custom in Europe. Cream-filled eclairs, for example, are very penislike; raspberry-filled triangular-shaped cakes look like vaginas with menstrual blood. One doesn't think about this in the pastry shops, we are so used to it. You may even have baked them yourself.

"This is goddess cunt, have a bite!" said one woman to another. A little laughter broke out. I could see the candlelight making the familiar faces look like something out of the past. "What? Are you offering me pussy to eat?" Kim teased her partner, and the women again heard a word only men are allowed to use. Long, brittle pastry cones filled with cream were passed out next, and, blushing this time, our crone Betty remarked, "I have eaten these things all my life, but until today I never really looked at them. They do look like penises, with cream!" More laughter. Everybody watched Betty taking a bite, and that gave rise to even more jesting.

"You're sucking the cream right out of that thing, Betty. Have a heart, girl!" Eva was pushing her cone into her own mouth. "This is how that is done!" "Done? What is done?" taunted Margaret. "Sucking the cream silly!" I guess it wasn't easy for us to use all those forbidden words, the p——, the f——, the l——, the c——, and all the other words having to do with sex that are forbidden to women to use but not to men. It took a lot of courage to overcome the inner policemen who have hushed our tongues all our lives to harness us into some mold just for women. But we managed.

As the night advanced, there was more freedom; stories were told about awkward sexual encounters, embarrassing moments with condoms or diaphragms, of our fumbling first attempts at sexual expression, of our own repression when it came to talking about sex to our children. Nobody here was a teen— most of us were in a mature age range—some of us grandmothers, talking "dirty" for the first time in acceptable company.

The stories told at this table are not for publication; I can only give you a feel for them, because your own stories will be different, after all. What can be told, however, is that Haloa had a great liberating effect on us, and nobody ended up being angry at anyone else. There was a little food fight between Pat and Kim, acting out a crayfish fertility rite. Pat dropped chocolate globs on Kim's lap, and she squirted it with whipped cream. But this happened after our candles burned quite low.

At the end we repeated the honoring ritual, bowing low to our left and to our right, hardly able to keep ourselves from bursting into laughter. *"I honor you, my sister. No matter how silly your stories were, our bond remains close."* This may have been the greatest bond-building ritual we have done, because we shared our follies. Cleansed of them, we gain the wisdom that only laughter can give. Blessed be.

THE HOLIDAYS

April 1

VENERALIA (ROMAN)

This is the holiday of Venus (Aphrodite to the Greeks), the goddess of love and death, of orchards and sexuality, of the waters of the world. This celebration appears to be a practice peculiar to women, who washed the image of the Goddess in rivers and lakes before again adorning her with her precious jewels and new long robe. The women burned incense to her in her aspect of good fortune, to ensure happy love, birth, and joy in their lives. This ancient description in Ovid's *Fasti* shows how alluring this practice was, and how widespread among all kinds of women.

Then dry her neck and restore to it her golden necklace, now give her a fresh-blown rose. Ye too: She herself bids bathe under the green myrtle. Learn now how to give incense to Fortuna Virilis in the place that reeks of warm water. All women strip when they enter that place. . . . Propitiate her with supplications, beauty, and fortune and good fame are in her keeping.*

It isn't an accident that April Fool's Day grew from this most emotional and sensuous observance. Is it not love that makes fools out of kings? Or queens? Let's be honest—love is the common denominator, the feeling that makes us all crawl and jump through the hoops, achieve heights of glory or the all-time

---

**Ovid *Fasti* (trans. Lawrence Durdin-Robertson) 4.133.

lows of foolishness, most often the latter. April Fool's Day originates from this womanly calendar event when all kinds of foolishness were acted out to venerate the Goddess, symbolizing love's rule over logic. On this day, lovers ordered each other on senseless errands in proof of their love and devotion.

April 2

BATTLE OF THE FLOWERS (FRENCH)

The custom of the "Battle of Flowers" originated in France and follows in the same line of foolishness as the day prior to this. You walk down the street looking out for the one you fancy, and when this person is near enough, you take out a flower—a rose, or daisy, whatever you've got—and throw this at the desired person's heart. If the flower actually hits the "heart," this person will fall in love with you. You can imagine the romantic French women and men taking their walk with a large basket of flowers, making sure their social calendar will be busy all year.

April 3 and 4

MEGALISIA (PHRYGIAN & ROMAN)

Megalisia is a celebration of Cybele as the Great Mother. Cybele's worship was passionate and sexual. Men who wanted to be her priests castrated themselves in her honor to be more like the Goddess. I cannot help but think of all the men who change their sex in modern times to be more like women. Are these the modern day priests of Cybele without knowing it? This order was called Attis, after Cybele's son and lover, who was the first such castrated male.

For the women, this is another mother's day devoted to the Great Mother, Magra Mater, the creator of all things, gods, and people. But instead of remembering Mom as the baker of foods and cakes, this is the sexual mother whose urge called forth life. Her celebration is in dance, games, rituals, and feasts.

Ovid tells us in his *Fasti* how Megalisia was celebrated in his time:

Straightaway the Berecynthian flute will blow a blast on its bent horn, and the festival of the Idaean Mother will have come. . . . The Goddess herself will be borne with howls through the city's midst. The stage is clattering, the games are calling. To your places Quiirites! And in the empty low courts let the war of suitors cease! I would put many questions but I am daunted by the shrill cymbals' clash and the bent flutes' thrilling drone.*

Then he quotes the Goddess Erato:

Cybele gave birth to the gods. The city gave place to the parent and the Mother has honor of precedence.*

What kind of ceremony could possibly approach this wild and amazing goddess in modern times? Sexuality is so dangerous nowadays, I would not advise you to follow the priestesses and priests who reveled in religious orgies for many nights and days. Still, imagine a world where sexuality is still a gift of life and try to meditate on that. How

---

*Ovid *Fasti* (trans. Durdin-Robertson) 4.179.

about organizing a lovely, lively party, with folk dances and party foods and drinks? Cybele will understand.

April 5

FESTIVAL OF KWAN YIN (CHINESE & JAPANESE)

The festival of Kwan Yin, the Goddess of Mercy (known as Kwannon in Japan), the Great Mother of China, is celebrated on this day with offerings of incense and visits to her shrines. "The Lady who Brings Children," Kwan Yin embodies all that is female of the universe. She sits in her lotus throne and contemplates the golden vial of her own womb, which gave forth the entire world.

This day is dedicated to the goddess of tolerance and mercy. A more sedate version of the same idea: female sexuality as the life-giving force Asian style. Think about how important it is to bear healthy, happy children. How often is it that we have children with birth defects or weak constitutions? Today, more than ever, we need to appeal to this magnificent great spirit who brings us the future.

What follows is a true story about Kwan Yin. A mother and daughter were living in China, and the child became very ill with pneumonia. All the available medicines were tried, and they all failed. Finally, the mother went to the shrine of Kwan Yin and asked the oracle what she should do. To her surprise, the voice answered, "Tell your story to the first man you will meet on your way home and do what he says." The mother went home and met a young Western doctor on the road who had brought in the first supplies of penicillin. She told him the story; he followed her home and gave the penicillin to her

THE HOLIDAYS • 81

daughter, who promptly recovered. It was this daughter who told me the story at the Goddess conference in Santa Cruz.

April 13

CERALIA (ROMAN)

The Goddess Ceres, whose name is still in our breakfast cereal, gave us the first foods, developed the acorn, taught us the art of agriculture. Ceralia was celebrated by the simple folk. Farmers walked or danced around their fields with burning torches in honor of Ceres, the goddess of the crops. Do you recall the Russian ballet dancers' so-called stag leap? When the male dancer flies across the stage in great leaps, you are looking at an old custom of pagan men who blessed entire fields of wheat by leaping around them.

In Ceres' honor, we burn a little incense on our altars at home. Wear white today, Ceres's proper color. Look at the folk dancers in their fancy costumes, and observe the ancient sacred steps that were used to bless fields, gardens, forests.

April 21

SUN ENTERS TAURUS

Taurus is the sign of the bull. This is the season of the women and men who work the earth. Farmers have a holiday today. Keepers of cows, horses, barnyard inhabitants; creators of the rice fields, the corn fields, the potato patches, and orchards—honor and appreciation to you! Honor Hathor, maiden aspect of Isis, crowned with the horns of the life-giving cow.

April 22

FESTIVAL OF ISHTAR (BABYLONIAN)

Who is Ishtar? She is the Babylonian great goddess, "the Star," a derivation of Inanna. Slandered often in the Bible as the Whore of Babylon, she was a sexual deity whose very fecundity was the life of her people. She appears in the Bible as Ashtoreth and Asherah. She was the major divinity before any of the patriarchal gods appeared. She represented life and light. Many of her hymns were plagiarized, taken over, and put into the Bible to praise the new male god.

*Who dost make the green herb spring up, Mistress of mankind! Who hast created everything, who dost guide aright all creatures! Mother Ishtar whose power no god can approach! A prayer will I utter, may she do unto me what seems good to her. . . . O my Mistress, make me to know my deed, establish for me a place of rest! Absolve my sins, lift up my face!**

Ishtar was the soul of her people, the very essence of their power to live and love.

April 27

FLORALIA (CENTRAL & EASTERN EUROPEAN)

We honor the Goddess of Flowers, Flora, and pray for fruits that come from blooms. This used to be a six-day-long celebration, when men bedecked themselves with flowers and women dressed extra gaily. Take a look at the central European embroidery for both men

---

*Barbara Walker, *The Women's Encyclopedia of Myths and Secrets* (San Francisco: Harper & Row, 1983), 451.

and women, and you get an idea what the folks looked like back then. I own a couple of shirts embroidered with roses and nosegays and bachelor buttons, and those are only the men's shirts. The women's top looks fit for a Goddess, and all the girls wore those on holidays, red roses and yellow wheat and blue morning glories. Their headdress was usually the *parta*, a crescent decorated with pearls and shining beads, with long streaming red ribbons cascading down the back. Today would be a good day to dress up really colorfully! Go shop for summer clothes!

April 30

BELTAIN (CELTIC)

This festival of witches—known as Beltain or Beltane (Celtic), May Eve (Central European), or Walpurgisnacht (Germany)—has a lot of tradition behind it. This is a festival where the power and sacredness of sexuality is celebrated. Listen to the dark on this night: You can hear the cats in heat howling; if you own a bitch in heat, the dogs will be scratching on your door. During the day, butterflies locked in coitus fly through your garden; insects buzz in the grass with orgiastic excitement. Mother Nature is regenerating her children, and everything is horny.

The followers of the Old Religion, the witches, met on mountaintops, and danced the spiral dance. Pagan priestesses and other women mated with pagan priests and men. It was a very effective antiloneliness custom. You knew if you attended the Walpurgisnacht (Walpurgis Night) you would get laid. Babies that resulted from these parties were called sons and daughters of Pan, or Cernunnos, since all men represented him.

Today, when we fear sexually transmittable diseases, this old custom is no longer viable. We have lost the wildness and the innocence our ancestors possessed; we have become soft and ridden with disease. What was achieved by the ancients' revelry? They believed that the good earth—Walpurg/Demeter/Gaia—appreciated the sexual energy expended in her open fields and that it stimulated the fertility of the crops and animals as well as the vitality of the community.

April 30

YAKIMA TRIBE ROOT FESTIVAL (NATIVE AMERICAN)

The first appearance in spring of rooted plants used by the Pacific Northwest Native Americans called for a celebration. In the late spring and summer, several varieties of roots and plants were dried and used in soups, porridge, and for bread.

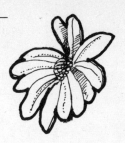

The April Story: Spring Belongs to My Mother

Spring belongs to my mother, Masika Szilagyi, artist, medium, healer, witch, storyteller, friend, and lover of life and of the Goddess. She was born March 1, 1916, passed away on April 19, 1979, and spent her sixty-three short years of life between springtimes. I was a winter baby, always cold. Mother's warm hands never cooled off; even in the worst of winters, she was warm.

My mother was first and foremost an artist, and I was one of her favorite creations. Our relationship was a mixture of mother/daughter and performer/audience. She was a great storyteller, and she could spin the slightest or most mundane of incidents into a tale of hilarious insight. When we went out together, it was an adventure. Anything that happened to us on the bus or on the street instantly grew into a colorful and humorous anecdote.

By the time we reached home, the stories had been honed and polished; they had even had a quick run-through, having been tried out on me. For example, once we saw a little boy who lived on the second floor of a building over a little café. As our streetcar stopped to pick up new passengers, we saw the toddler come out on his front porch, yawn, and then proceed to pee off the balcony. Underneath, serious-looking gentlemen were sitting and sipping their coffee, which the child splashed with urine. But in my mother's story, the child made a direct hit in the coffee cup of a certain gentleman who was complaining to the management about the coffee. When the manager came out to test it, he tasted the baby-pee coffee and declared it fine. He even smacked his lips. By the time Mother was done with this story, it was bigger than real life and much better.

I could tell her everything—my dreams, my ambitions, gossip about my friends, secrets. I could throw tantrums if I felt a need for it. We could talk about everything under the sun and moon, except for sex. When "that" came up, her blue eyes narrowed and her small nose got shorter. When sex was mentioned, my mother changed into a veritable prude. She told me all kinds of myths about boys and their dreaded sperm. If you took a bath with a boy, you could get pregnant. If you got touched by a boy who touched himself, you could get pregnant. Even heavy necking could result in that cursed condition. Needless to say, I stayed away from the boys and their sperm. Getting pregnant was just about the worst thing to happen to a girl in Hungary. Those who got pregnant never finished high school and were considered failures. Hungarians are famous for their high literacy and numerous diplomas; taking night classes forever is a part of the life-style. A teen who got pregnant was failing as a Hungarian kid. I didn't fail.

What stories Mother told! Grandfather's wine once saved Masika's life. When Mother was born, nobody expected my grandmother to have a baby, herself least of all. Grandmother Ilona was unusual for a Hungarian; she was tall. She had long hair that had to be washed in three buckets. She started giving speeches about women's suffrage and spent a lot of time away from Grandfather Geza. She traveled in Hungary and to other European countries for meetings. And then one day, Grandmother felt a little side pain, like gas, and went in for a checkup. The doctors told her she was in labor. She gave birth to a premature baby, my mom. It caused her a deep resentment, because she didn't plan this child and because she couldn't recall having had sex. Grandmother was on a long speaking tour with her best friend and sister suffragist Anna-merie from Germany. She felt betrayed by her body. How could this happen to her? Geza teased her about her immaculate conception, which we all eventually believed must have been what happened. Ilona was not pleased.

As a baby, Masika—little Masi—was weak and skinny. Geza kept her covered by a big sieve to make sure the cats would not get her, and he fed her a spoonful of his good old Tokay wine every day until she gained enough strength and vitality to survive

outside her sieve. And then she flourished. Everybody swore it was the wine. In those days they didn't have intensive care for preemies. It had to have been the wine.

Grandmother ran a newspaper for the National Hungarian Women's Suffrage Association in which they advertised a poetry contest for women and promised to publish the winners. First prize was a trip to Paris. Under a different name, Masika submitted her melancholy poetry. The poems were written in a trance—she channeled them—and they were the work of an old soul, not a young one like hers. People loved the poems. The poetry was so successful that the paper awarded her first prize. The editors, including Ilona, asked Masika to come and introduce herself to the staff at the paper and pick up her prize. She wrote back that she was very old and sick, which prevented her from getting out of the house a lot, and asked them to just send her the tickets so she could use them when she was able to travel again. Months went by. Masika continued her double life—at home, a dutiful daughter; in her correspondence, a tortured and conflict-ridden soul in search of happiness and peace. After six months, the ladies from the suffragette society tracked her down. She was the daughter of the editor; she couldn't take the prize away from somebody else. The family sent Masika to Paris anyway, just to get it out of her system.

Instead of getting tired of the arts, she added a new talent to her repertoire—mediumship. Masika was wayward, psychic. She would hear voices and see spirits. These were actually psychic skills our people relied on for centuries to guide us during our wanderings through Asia, but Grandmother considered Masika to have a nerve disease and prescribed for Mother lots of nervines such as teas of chamomile, scullcap, or hops.

Stories of this period of my mother's life were told to me in hushed whispers. In Paris she became part of a group called the Paris Nine, a very select group of painters, sculptors, writers, and theosophy students who gathered once a month when the moon was full and communed with the enlightened spirits. Mother was their darling medium. Masika came home to Hungary a sophisticated woman, moved to the city, enrolled at the Art Institute, and started creating her visions of clay.

Grandmother Ilona was a successful suffragist, but at home she was terribly old-fashioned. She wanted her daughters to be married. Masika was very pretty and had many boyfriends, but she turned them all down because she wanted to stay single. She was an artist. But one night Masika went to a party and there she met my father, Sándor, a crusty bachelor of thirty-five, the son of a governor, rich and handsome. Masika "saw" that this was her future husband and that the marriage would be terrible for her. She fled the party before they could be introduced. But the fates caught up with her, and they met somewhere else. After a short courtship, Sándor proposed. Grandmother accepted for my mother.

Sándor would not allow his wife to work. He closed down Masika's studio, broke her heart, made her pregnant, and I was born. Then came World War II, with bombs and poverty and hopelessness. Their bad marriage had been ecstasy compared to what they had to go through just to survive. People who were accustomed to summer houses and wintering in southern Hungary now had lice in their hair. I had whooping cough, and my grandmother died of hunger.

When the war was finally over, the world around had changed completely. Budapest, our beloved city, was in ruins; the dead seemed to outnumber the living. Masi was now divorced. She had custody of me, but our house had been razed by a bomb, wiping out all our worldly possessions except for our photographs, which we kept with us during the bombings. These were my first memories of the world. We lived in a one-room apartment. We shared facilities with another family that occupied the other room.

At this time Masika was stunningly beautiful. I used to watch her make up in front of her mirror. Her shapely dancer's legs were at eye level, and she had a dark beauty mark behind the left knee. She worked as a waitress at the radio station and as the manager of the coffeehouse as well. The management part was not easy; she had math anxiety, but there were always some friends who showed up at closing time and counted up the money for her. We got free lunches as well. Every day I set out to the coffeehouse, some twenty blocks away, for my main meal and arrived hungry as a wolf. Lunch was usually soup and noodles or sometimes potatoes cooked with red onions. Perhaps once a week there was meat, a little stew. I don't remember missing better food; I had never been exposed to any. To me, poverty, war-torn buildings, and bullet holes in the houses that were still standing were normal.

About this time, Masika fell in love with Imre—or Dr. Koncz as we used to know him—my old pediatrician. He was thirty-five and a virgin, so Masika said. He came more and more frequently to help Mom count her money at the coffeehouse, and he walked her home after she closed down at 2 A.M. After a while, I used to find him in our place in the morning, getting ready for the hospital, washing himself, doing handstands on the side of the bathtub, and singing at the top of his lungs. I had always liked him, when he was my doctor in the prewar years and now when he was courting my mom. He treated me with respect. When, after five years of courting, they got married, I was happy for them.

Mother started sculpting again and getting assignments, not challenging ones, but assignments nevertheless—a bust of the local leader, his cabinet, a few portraits of some of the Soviet leaders. Masika loved going at her task; the clay replaced the coffeehouse at last; she could grow again. A couple of years into her renewed career, she was asked to make twenty-one different busts of a leader who had just come to power. Elections were merely theatrical; there was only one candidate, one voting box to put your vote in, and four guards looking on from the four corners of the voting room.

Masika was bored with the political process; she never bothered to learn even the names of the official she was sculpting. She had a photograph of him, and she went to work. She lined up the busts, doing six or seven at a time to make the work go faster. It was urgent; May 1 was coming up, when the people would march with their flags. Anyway, Mother was hard at her task, making those busts on the double—nose, nose, nose . . . moustache, moustache, moustache . . . chin, chin, chin—happily humming to herself. She worked for days, and then she fired the busts and spruced them up. The day before the big march, the men came and picked them up, and she got paid. We all celebrated the big windfall with a chicken paprikash meal and a little wine. Masika was on her way up again.

Then May 1 came and all the people went out to parade. They marched alongside these busts and realized that they represented the wrong leader. Mom had confused the photographs with each other, and all the new busts were of the old leader, not of the new, whose debut this was supposed to be. "Sabotage!" accused the new regime and sent a paddy wagon for Mom's arrest.

We were in bed when they came for her. There was no mercy; she was a saboteur. She was going to prison or Siberia.

Masika understood that this was a matter of life and death. She had to somehow convince all six of the judges that it was an accident, that she confused the two men's pictures. They both had a moustache, they both had bald heads; how was she to suspect that they were rivals? It was a very weak defense. So she resorted to her witchcraft, which she used only in times of trouble when the chips were down or when somebody's life was in danger. We had about as much hope as a mouse in the throat of a snake, but Masika went to work again. In jail she went into a trance, which was something she had done often enough before the war, and astrally traveled to the bedroom of each official who was to sit in judgment on her the next day. She found them sleeping and broke into their minds, telling these men to remember her and listen to her story, which was that she'd made a mistake, an honest mistake, and she was sorry. The men were astonished. "Who are you?" they asked. "I am just a soul who traveled on the winds and got into trouble unjustly," she told them. "You must remember me from this dream," she demanded, "and when you see me tomorrow and hear my story, you must believe that it is the truth and let me go back home." "What proof do you offer for your innocence?" one even asked Mom in his dream. "I am here with you in your dream, isn't that proof enough?" she answered.

She did this all night, barely finishing with the last one by daybreak. But it worked. The next day these men all came to the courthouse, and there Masika confronted them and told them again how it had all been an honest mistake. And the men all agreed that such a mistake could have been made, since the men did look alike in major features anyway. They acquitted Masika and sent her home. This time she took the streetcar, and when she arrived at the house, she found me and Imre, my stepfather, in mourning. We had never heard of a case when somebody actually beat the rap. We had thought we would never see her again. It was a miracle! And then, too, it was springtime. And after she came back to us, the jasmine never smelled sweeter, and the Hungarian wine was never drier. All our relatives came up from the country, and the neighbors all showed up, and we had a best homecoming party ever. Mom's cousin Lorant, the country priest brought some of his church wine in a keg, the old Tokay, which we all drank. But the Party officials never commissioned Masika to make any busts of Party leaders again.

May

The Goddess Speaks

Artemis

YOU WILL HAVE TO SEARCH HARD for my message this month. I have been totally distracted from writing anything down. I am engulfed in the message, possessed with it, and you'll just have to pick it up on the winds, or miss it. I almost don't care.

It is a private message of sexuality. How do you feel about yours? I am on fire. I am in love with all lovable creatures in the world. I share this surge of passion with all living beings, yet my own personal sexuality feels so private and separate from the rest. Is that how you feel too?

I am Artemis, lover of women. My maiden's prowess is equal to that of men. Raised by a she-bear on the mountains, you can imagine that I am wild and love to roam. Freedom is my natural environment. I know how to defend myself and enjoy races. I am the Lady of the Beasts.

I am possessed by a hungry, grown-up kind of love. I am yearning for my mate, my she-bear lover. My most beautiful beloved, Callisto, is clinging to me in her silk chiton, the winds lift her skirts and reveal her milky thighs. She sets me on fire.

Callisto is feeling her own nature turn and yearn, and we find each other in the caves of the bears. She says that to make love in the cave of the bear brings good luck. During the day we roam with the wildlife and protect it. We teach young women Amazonian sports—mind/body/soul unison makes a woman hardy. I am the free spirit of natural freedom, I inspire others to be the same. Callisto helps women in childbirth; she is an excellent midwife! But we ourselves have few babes. Only the most beloved come through us, so we are the childless women, natural birth control for humanity.

Each century has assigned us different fates. Back at the dawn of time, we lived in tribes on mountaintops, like the nunneries of the churches today. The faithful still flock to our old sites to worship Artemis, the soul of the wild and of women. This last century has treated us as outlaws or as insane. God's frowning judge sneered at us, and prudes of all denominations blushed at our loving nature. But we have never been this strong before!

I am the girlfriend who didn't let you down when you called late at night with your last dime, because there was no one else to turn to. I am the politician who didn't forget about child care after the elections. I am the judge who didn't allow your rapist or child molester to go free. I am the artist who celebrated your life in pictures and painting, poetry and novels, who sang songs to soothe your heart. I am the orator who disturbed your consciousness and led you ahead when you felt stuck in old ways. My strength comes from loving myself, and there is enough to give you some too. Will you connect me to your strength? I give courage to women and self-knowledge; how can you exist without me?

I will tell you how to find me. Look for some Artemisia

herb (wormwood) and burn a little in your incense burner after viewing the new crescent moon. The astral plane is touched by your humble exercise during the new and full moons, so don't miss out on your chance to pray. Close your eyes and inhale the scent; I shall enter through your nose like breath. Imagine yourself lying on soft moss surrounded by open blue skies. This is my sacred grove, where I welcome you. Wait there and see if you sense an animal present. When a creature appears, a fox, quail, a partridge, a deer—a stag even—or hounds, welcome them—those are my sacred animals. If they look healthy, well fed, and exercised, your own body is well fed and exercised. If they look dehydrated, you need more water to drink. Whatever the animals show you about their well-being applies to your own body and nervous system. Listen well and look at them carefully.

After the visit with my creatures, allow your body to float up into the air, levitating. As you do this, imagine that your own sense of self-worth is lifting you higher and higher. Challenge yourself to see how much self-worth you can experience without getting into particular reasons why. There must be no logical reason, just a feeling.

After the self-worth meditation, softly land on the moss bed and promise yourself to remember what you learned in the grove. Then look around and take a wildflower to remind your own nature of the wilderness sacred to me. Open your eyes and return to normal.

May's Aspects

The month of May was named after the goddess Maia, Maria, the goddess of spring, she who brings forth life. Appropriately enough, it became the month of the Virgin Mary, Mother of God.

Full moon aspect: Hare moon or frogs return moon

Universal event: Flowers coming forth—the potential for creation of the new harvest

Communal event: The May Eve festival initiates this month, but no other sabbaths occur. This is still a month for chastity and cleaning up one's life. Making trysts, commitments, or marriages is not allowed, because the month of the queen of May is unlucky for tying the knot.

Message: To propagate or not, to enjoy sex or be celibate (Make important choices.)

Activity: Sexual encounters or complete abstinence

Healing properties: Fevers and infections

Appropriate spells: Finding a new job (if you want one) or a new home, settling disagreements, getting in shape physically, taking care of yourself (Get your cards read or your horoscope cast.)

Color: Hazel, pink

Tree: Hawthorne

Flower: Lily, trefoil, the food of the goddess's mares; and witches' broom, yellow as the goddess's hair

Creature: Magpie, dove

Gem: Emerald

Anna's Spells, Rituals, & Celebrations for May

ARTEMIS & THE CHILDREN

Artemis is the goddess of youngsters, of whatever species, be it human or animals. She is the nurturer; in many of her presentations in stone or drawings, she is suckling a doe with her slender finger. At these times, Artemis is not expressing her sexual nature but her female essence, as protector of young life.

Once upon a time, the legend says, there were two orphans whose parents passed away without leaving them any money or guidance. The little girl and boy cried and cried, filling the nights and days with their laments. In their terrible loneliness, they gathered around a little statue of Artemis (Diana) in their garden. Besides their own bodies, this was the only human form they had in their home. At least it looked like an adult—a beautiful lady suckling a doe with her forefinger, with a hound at her heels. So the little girl appealed to her and said, "Dear little garden statue, dear Artemis, what are we going to do? We have nobody to help us, we are hungry and fearful."

And the little boy listened, and he also spoke up: "Dear Artemis, you have protected our garden, please protect us now—please." And a voice came from the bushes, a soft and kind voice, filled with compassion: "Don't be afraid, children. I'll hunt food for you and bring you things to eat. Come back tomorrow and see." The children couldn't believe their own ears, but they returned next evening, and there, all neatly arranged into a circle in front of Artemis's little statue, was a chicken and some vegetables and fruit.

The children were happy, and quickly the little girl and boy cooked their food and ate all the fruits and vegetables. But afterward they remembered to go back to the statue and say thanks to Artemis. "Thank you, Goddess, for caring about us, who have no parents to love and feed us." The little girl made a wreath of flowers and placed it on the statue's forehead, and the little boy found a blooming branch and cut that down and placed it in the goddess's hand. "Thank you, Artemis!" he said politely.

Then the voice from the bushes spoke again: "You are welcome. And because you have been grateful and gave me flowers in return, I shall bring you food every day as long as you need me." And so it was. Day after day the children found their daily bread and meat at her feet, and they left flowers for her in return. Years passed this way, and the whole village was astonished at how well these two orphans were able to fend for themselves. They never seemed to be hungry or sick, and they flourished in spite of all neglect. The villagers started getting curious as to how it was done.

One day a priest came to visit and spied the children in the garden as they were decorating the statue of Artemis with their flowers. He got very angry. He summoned the children to him and gave them a terrifying speech. "What are you doing worshipping the devil?" he demanded. "We don't know anything about devils!" the little boy answered bravely. "Poor ignorant babes!" thundered the priest. "Don't you know that this idol is of the devil? You are decorating it with flowers, that is devil worship!" he declared.

The children felt bad, because they knew that he was wrong. They loved Artemis like their mother and father all in one. "You are wrong, Father!" said the little girl. "This is our beautiful lady. She has helped us survive hunger and cold, she is always there for us when in need, and all we can give her is her own flowers."

The priest really wanted to make a point now, and he looked for a cabbage in the patch, took it, rolled it in mud then hurled it at the little statue of Artemis, saying, "Here, you devil, this is my offering to you!" The little statue fell into the mud and lay there. The children tried to pick it up and place it back on its stand. And then a voice, now sounding more stern than they ever heard it, came from the bushes. "You made your offering to me. You shall receive your just reward!" The priest froze in his tracks as he heard the woman's voice, hurt and yet strong. He told the children to forget about Artemis, and that they should come with him and be his servants.

He went home alone, however, and that night he had a terrible dream. He felt a great heaviness on his chest, heavy like a stone. His breathing became more and more frantic, until finally he woke up. And there on his chest was the head of a dead man, whom he had buried two weeks before. The head was muddy, just like the cabbage he threw at Artemis. And it was only the head. The priest got such a fright that he suffered a heart attack and died. Only the children knew that he had come to this sorry end by offending the soul of the wild.

This is a heavy story. You may tell the whole thing to the children, or tell the first half and not the terrifying part. But considering that children have survived the stories of Hansel and Gretel, which is about cannibalism, or of Cinderella, which was about child hating, or of Snow White, which is about poisoning, I don't think our modern children would be too much upset by this old Italian legend.

The story demonstrates Artemis's special relationship with children. To help them worship her, gather together your youngsters and create a party for them, just for being young. Take them to the zoo and explain to them about the different species, teach them the names of the animals. When you return home, have them tell stories of their experiences and what the animals "told" them. Put your hand on their little heads and bless them in the name of Artemis, with strength and health and sharp minds.

SPELL FOR MAY: BLESSING ON THE CHILDREN

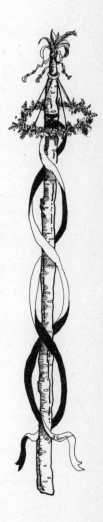

When the moon is full, gather your household and dress up your children as for a birthday party. Give invitations to all the grown-up family members and friends who care about the kids. This can be done for the whole neighborhood together or just for your own crew.

Now, make flower or herbal crowns from the wild green things outside for the little ones and have them wear them as they sit around the table. They will look much better than party hats. Take pictures. Bake a lovely cake (or buy one). It can be made from any grain or flavor or in any style. Take blue chalk and draw a slim little crescent moon on each kid's forehead saying:

> *I mark you with the sign of Artemis, the young crescent moon. Now you have inner protection for the rest of the year.*

The young person answers:

> *I love Artemis because she is the protector of wild things and teacher of young folk. Blessed be.*

ARRETOPHORIA: NYMPH FESTIVAL

In Greece, in the days of the Goddess, our younger sisters performed a very important task. During this nymph festival, they carried sacred objects down to caves in the earth, without opening them. They then would pick up the baskets left there by another group of youngsters the previous year and bring them back up. All this was laced with fright and a sense of importance. I think a modern version of this festival is needed. We want to trust our youngsters without endangering their lives. So what will we do?

Young girls could perform a house blessing for the family, which could be considered a serious task in addition to being a holiday. Appoint a day for your young girl's nymph festival. In other words, she will star in the family's protection spell. Dress her in a pretty dress or gown, crown her with flowers, and give her a special bell to ring. Let her young friends also participate; honor is always more honorable when witnessed by one's contemporaries! As their magical tool, get some purifying incense, sage for example, that is easy to hold.

Starting from the outside, the young women should circle the house three times clockwise, making sure the sacred smoke rises up to the heavens along with their prayers.

> *Three times around, three times about,*
> *The world within, the world without.*
> *All evil stay away, only good spirits abound,*
> *All problems stay away, only happiness be around.*
> *All sickness stay away, only good health stays around.*

Again you may improvise from your heart—the youngsters' talent is the only limit. This accomplished, the nymphs should perform the same service inside the home, again walking clockwise three times, paying special attention to doors and windows and letting the smoke filter into the crevices and openings, cracks and secret hiding places.

The youngsters should say whatever is needed for the spell. The bell is rung each time a circle is completed, three times altogether. The young women will have a sense of magical power and their importance to their families. I have seen this performed by a nymph in Alaska with great pride and success.

The same kind of protective spell can be done around your car and other possessions. Change the words of spells according to the task. For instance, say something like:

Let no accident come even near this car; let all the parts
function well; may nothing break down; may no thief
desire this car or steal it for any reason at all.

If you have a young boy who is sensitive and loves
Mother Nature, feels connected to the earth, and wants to use his
magic powers as protection for his family, all that has been said
applies to him as well.

SPELL TO FIND A HOME

After the cold and wet of the winter, this is your chance to escape
and make your own nest along with the birds. As you perform this
old spell, remember that we live and act on more than one level
and that it's important to move both magically and realistically for
our goal. In other words, you cannot just burn candles and incense
and meditate—you still need to fill out application forms and be
tidy and punctual for your appointments.

At the time when the moon is waxing, on a piece of
white paper make a drawing with Magic Markers of the home you
would like to have. Give it detail, put in the doors and windows,
play at it a long time. When you have created it as a thought form,
place it under a brown candle on your altar, because brown is the
color of earth and security and homes. I also recommend that you
take a handful of earth from the general vicinity in which you are
hoping to find a place and put that on your drawing.

Make your altar pretty. Use flowers and shells, things
you like to see around that you feel would appeal to the Goddess
of the Earth herself, since she is the ultimate landowner. Go to
your altar after sundown. Light white candles as usual and then
light the brown candle, saying:

This is my home, my earth, my cave, my castle.
Mother Demeter, bring me to my shelter.
Mother Demeter, bring me home!
Bring me home! Bring me home!

Do this spell on three consecutive nights, and actively
look for a place during this time. When you have finished it (when
your candles have burned down), gather all the biodegradable
remnants and cast them in a living body of water. Turn your back

and don't look back. Another good way of disposing of them is to leave them in the neighborhood in which you want to find a place to live. Your home will manifest within a moon.

SPELL FOR PRODUCTIVE STUDYING

The color of hard work, fame, and fortune is purple, so light a lovely candle of this color whenever you study. If you want to manifest something very important but haven't yet figured out exactly what it is, use yellow. Light a little sage or whatever is available to you, and meditate before starting work toward your goal. Then just say:

> *Goddess of Wisdom, to you I pray.*
> *My mind clear and receptive stay;*
> *All in true accord with thee,*
> *As my word, so mote it be.*
> *Give me light! Blessed be.*

SPELL TO FIND A (NONSPECIFIC) JOB

We spend a lot of time agonizing over our earthly jobs—not the divine one, namely, living, but the one that supports us, the nine-to-five type. I have met women and men who actually believe that they are what they do for a living. Can anybody *be* a clerk? A typist? Being and making money are not the same. Being is constant becoming. A job is important, but let it not define your becoming.

This spell should be done at the waxing moon after using some form of divination (I Ching, Tarot) to assess your talents and match them with reality. When you have figured out your strategy (which is more than half of success), then begin to assemble your magical tools. Purchase a yellow candle on which you shall write your name three times. Make a list of jobs you desire. Create this wish list, with both letters and colorful ink, on some nice white paper; even put your desired annual income on it. For the next seven nights, you shall rendezvous with your own imagination. Imagine yourself happily employed; see yourself treated very well—given raises and responsibilities. While you do this, burn the yellow candle little by little until it's all gone. During the day, keep making appointments, look for interviews, distribute your résumé. When the candle is burned down, collect the remnants and, without being noticed, leave a little of the ashes in the flower pots of offices where you are seeking a job. Your job will manifest within a moon.

THE HOLIDAYS

May 1

MAY DAY (EUROPEAN)

May Day is still celebrated in many parts of the world. The Irish especially love this folk festival. They decorate trees and bushes and hold dances outdoors to welcome the beginning of the summer. On relics in Assyria, we see ribbons fastened to the Tree of Life. The Canaanite goddess Asherah was worshipped as a tree, not only at Winter Solstice but on May Eve as well. Gifts to the poor were left in the trees in her honor.

When we take the ribbons and dance around the maypole (representing the phallus) and entwine the ribbons (representing the vulva) around it and cover the pole, we act out the lovemaking of nature. Gifts of the Goddess Maia follow such dances; abundant flowers and fruits will result from nature's sexual union. This festival comes down to us from much earlier tree-worshipping cults, where the goddess was represented by sacred trees such as oak and pine, fig, apple, rowan, and willow.

In many countries, people chose a May queen and king, usually a good-looking cou- ple from their new generation of young adults, to represent the Goddess and her Lover. They were paraded and celebrated and "married" in a mock ritual to stimulate the Earth's fertility. Today this day stands for the celebration of the world's workers, the people themselves. Don't get married in May; wait until midsummer when the ban on marriages is lifted (this explains the popularity of June weddings). Wear green on May Day; it is the color nature loves best, denoting resurrection and rebirth.

May 2 and 3

FIRE FESTIVAL OF BONA DEA (ROMAN)

The good goddess has her fire festival on this day. Women celebrated Bona Dea in all-night revels, where no men were allowed. Build a bonfire and jump over it for purification and good luck. As you leap over the fire, make a wish and it will come true. Bona Dea presides over all the Earth and all the blessings, so don't forget her. Do cheerful things today. Attend a women-only event.

May 4

FESTIVAL OF SHEILA NA GIG (IRISH)

What a brazen goddess this is! Her face is almost cartoonlike, but her vulva occupies most of her body, and her hands are opening her labia like a door! You would think such a feminine, womanly goddess would have gone the way of the forgotten images, but no! She is still present on the entrance doors of some old churches or hidden away in the woodwork somewhere in the pews; old Sheila Na Gig has not been forgotten. The door of life as woman's genitalia was a religious symbol. Sheila Na Gig was the protector of the poor. On this day people hung old clothes on the Hawthorne bushes for her to see and believed that she averted poverty by this magic. Today we can just give away old clothes to charities and clear away space for new things to come. Give alms to the poor.

May 5

BOYS' DAY: FEAST OF BANNERS (JAPANESE)

On this day, mothers of sons celebrate their boys. Streamers in the shape of carp, sometimes as long as eight feet, fly from every house. Each boy gets a new banner; the biggest goes to the oldest. Carp represent courage and personal power. This is a good time to get into your child's personal traits, build up his ego, praise him, play his favorite games with him, or show him something new. It's boys' day all day!

On this day, a boy can be asked to perform the house protection spell given earlier to show him how much respect you have for his magical powers and his contribution to the family's safety.

May 9

LEMURIA (ROMAN)

The Lemures were wandering spirits of the dead. People brought gifts to the ashes of the dead to make them happy. If you harbored any resentments against somebody, purification was achieved by forgiveness and making peace with the dead.

May has its ghostly aspect. Even in springtime, hail can take away the whole harvest, a drought can devastate a whole country. Beltane stands opposite Halloween on the wheel of life, but we never pay enough attention to our own mortality. Maybe another doctor's appointment is in order, a little revision of our life-styles toward something healthier? How about making a visit to Grandmother or Grandfather, soon to be ancestors? Protect the old. One day we will all be old, if we are lucky.

May 14

GODDESS TITHE DAY
(NORTH AFRICAN)

The black-robed Isis receives one-tenth of the riches she has given to the wealthy. This is the day when those blessed with her gifts return a tithe to the Goddess's representatives on earth.

Oh, Isis, hearer of prayers, the merciful healer of all ills, renew your blessings for us one more year, that we may gather in the riches of life and keep them in your honor.

Give money generously to your local or national goddess activity and renew your own good luck in finances. If you don't have a way to do this, buy some books about the Goddess in the bookstores and let that be your offering. Check out the reading list at the end of this book.

May 15

RAIN DANCE NIGHT (GUATEMALAN)

If the waters are not coming as they should, perform the following rain dance. Take a pitcher full of natural water—rain, river, lake, or sea. Build a fire in the middle of the circle with sacred wood like oak, rowan, willow, pine, fern, and so on. Take your water and sprinkle a little all around the circle, praying to the goddess of space, the power of the cosmos. Call down the powers of the east and south and west and north with words and chanting. Dance with your friends as wildly as you can to raise power. Move to the sound of some good drumming, a deep-bellied steady beat, as you dance barefoot directly on the earth. When you have all danced, pour out the rest of the water to the four corners of the universe and say:

This is the beginning of the rain you are releasing on this land. This is the blessing you bestow on your people. Great Spirit, let the waters flow out of your skies and onto this parched and thirsty earth! It is done! It is done! It is done!

Then go home and watch the clouds gather and the rain pour forth.

May 18

FEAST OF PAN (GREEK)

On this day, women and men celebrate men. Pan is all that is male in the universe. Pan is represented by a wild-, but good-looking man, not your deodorized modern type. He has hooves because many of the male animals he represents in nature have hooves. He has horns for the same reason; he is hairy, and he usually sports an erect penis. He plays the flute divinely. He is the son of the Earth. He is not a patriarch who oppresses women. He is, however, all male.

Pan likes parties with wine, song, and women. Invoke him in some wild place or burn patchouli on your altar in his honor. Christians stole his image and made him into the picture of their own negative male god, the devil. This act of twisting the old ways didn't make Pan into the Christian devil; however, his worship slowly disappeared, as did the worship of the Goddess. The gentle male role model, the singing-dancing pagan priest, medicine man, good-time lover Pan, is much needed to reclaim the lost wildness in our men today. Without him, nothing is conceived or glad. His view of the world was not that of a warrior but of the lover. Give a party for men today. Let the men define this: What is manhood without violence or competition? Do a guided meditation to visit Pan; he'll tell you the answer.

May 20

SUN ENTERS GEMINI

During Gemini, sign of the twins, seek to understand the twin spirit hidden within you, your unconscious, the hidden part of your soul.

May 19 through 28

KALLYNTARIA & PLYNTERIA: SPRING CLEANING (GREEK)

These days are devoted to the cleaning and nurturance of the sacred places. The Greeks were good at that, and they called this festival Kallyntaria and Plynteria, by which they meant making a special effort to clean the sacred statues of the goddess and god. With all that incense burning and dust gathering, the sacred images got pretty dirty, and you had to take them to be washed in the nearest rivers or lakes, submerging them and letting them reunite with the life-giving waters. Afterward, the women dressed the goddess in her jewels, with much ceremony, and paraded her proudly back to her home in the temple. No singing or fun was allowed during this procedure. These festivals were solemnized because it was work, not play. The same principle applies to us today. Let's get those brooms out, and wash the house from top to bottom, really giving it an old-fashioned purification. What could be more natural than to transform the old custom of spring cleaning into a religious devotion!

May 24 through 28

THE MOTHERS OF ARLES (FRENCH)

This unique festival celebrating the triple goddess is still alive and well in France, celebrated mostly by gypsies. The "Three Maries of the Sea" recall the ancient goddess of life, death, and beauty. The gypsies gather from all over Europe and carry on their annual celebrations of the triple goddess. Three women dressed up as Mare, Tavobe, and Mary impersonate the goddesses, reaching the shore in boats. In modern times, Sarah and Salome are the companions of Mary in this trinity. Fancy processions, gypsy weddings, trading of all sorts, fortune-telling, the leaping of cows (a survival from the ancient practice of bull leaping), dancing gypsy style, and candles give these days and nights their wild beauty.

May 25

CELEBRATION OF THE TAO, MOTHER OF THE WORLD (CHINESE & JAPANESE)

In Taoism, a great spiritual tradition of the East, the Goddess is perceived as the mother of the world, the Way to the heart. On this day, burn incense to the Goddess and meditate on Divine Harmony. The whole philosophy of the Way (or Tao) in Chinese mysticism is essentially a respect for the truth in nature and her ways. It is also a belief that people must live in harmony with the Way and not destroy or interfere but, rather, flow with it. This, as they say, is

holding fast to the Mother. She is the origin of all things and beings, born before heaven and earth. Silent and void she stands alone, does not change, goes round and does not weary, and is capable of being the mother of the world.*

May 29

AMBARVALIA: CORN MOTHER FESTIVAL (ROMAN)

The Goddess Ceres, the food giver, now has her corn festival, which was the cause of a great deal of festivity. Celebrants gathered to walk around the freshly plowed fields in joyous processions, wearing crowns of oak leaves and singing hymns to the Earth. Three times they circled the fields and blessed them. In Hungary, young women dressed as the goddess in colorful skirts and wore the *parta* on their heads (the crescent decorated

with shining beads). They danced a certain sacred dance in the entrance to those fields of corn in order to protect them from hail and pestilence. Sacred dances have been used as a magical device by groups all over the world.

May 30 and 31

FEAST OF THE QUEEN OF HEAVEN (EUROPEAN)

Queen of Heaven, lovely goddess of May, fully grown and gloriously enthroned in pagan and Christian times. May honors the Blessed Virgin Mary, who is the modern-day Queen of Heaven, though somewhat demoted in status from her original divinity. But have you noticed that it was always Mary who caused the miracles, who appeared to children (as at Lourdes and Fátima)? The Queen of Heaven is a hard-working woman, and we light white candles to her. Praise active womanhood wherever you are and all will be well.

In Roman times, May 31 was the date of a celebration for the Queen of the Underworld, Proserpine, and her consort Pluto, in whose honor people held what we think of as Olympic games, not on Olympus, but near the river Tiber in a place known as Tarentum.

---

*Tao Teh Ching cited in Lawrence Durbin-Robertson, Juno Covella, 121.

The May Story:
My Kirstin

M
Y KIRSTIN WAS BORN IN Columbus, Ohio, an often-rain-brushed, green, bushy, soft countryside. The only child of a bright couple, my Kirstin had a special childhood in those green hills. During the summers she would hunt with her father or go and watch illegal cockfights. During the winters she went to school, got very good grades, and made lots of friends.

Kirstin's first public appearance was at the age of seven when she was playing navy. She loved the navy and knew the names, types, and colors of all the United States ships. But, most of all she loved the uniforms—yes, the uniforms. One day, young Kirstin dictated a letter to the navy via her mom, Marie, asking for her very own uniform. She included her small size, age, and a picture. The letter was soon forgotten by her parents, but potent karma lay in Kirstin's hands even back then and she touched the navy. Her letter reached the hands of a capable public relations man who immediately recognized the potential for goodwill. He wrote back to Kirstin and invited her to Virginia, along with her parents, to visit the ship and get her own small-sized uniform that they'd custom made for her. Young Kirstin's adventure made the national news and made her a local celebrity. She still has the newspaper clippings of herself sitting in a boat being diligently rowed toward the big navy ship. A proud mom and dad sit alongside her. I have seen the tiny uniform and the newspaper clippings; I loved Kirstin for this story.

I loved Kirstin for many other stories as well. Once, when she was about fourteen, she had a long involved conversation on the telephone with her best friend Annie. Afterward, she found out that her mother, Marie, was listening to the entire talk and that for some reason she had disapproved. She said to Kirstin, "You talk too much to your girlfriends. You never talk about boys. I may have to take you to the doctor." Kirstin heard a death knell in this pronouncement. She watched her step from then on, making sure Marie was not around when she called her friends.

She was happy when she finally left the cold winters of Columbus—the unheated house, her father's heavy drinking, and her mother's loneliness—for North Carolina. Now, grown and of age, she could leave behind the fear of the "doctor," but she still had no clue as to what she had done wrong. She loved college. She lived in dorms with other young women, played softball, went on field trips, and got good grades. Marie once again became overcome by protective motherliness. She couldn't help but wonder why Kirstin didn't have dates. Much to Kirstin's dismay, she brought the topic up whenever they met or talked on the phone. The topic of men made Kirstin break out in huge, red pimples.

Then one day, Kate Millett was speaking at the college, and Kirstin went to hear her. It was a soul-opening experience, an intellectual quantum leap, a spiritual birthday. Kate's speech became Kirstin's personal Fourth of July, her favorite holiday. Millett talked about women who cared about each other, who wrote books, made music, painted, or were in sports. They were lesbians—Artemis's daughters. Kirstin's life gained clarity after that speech. She now knew what to do; she had to leave North Carolina for California. When graduation day came, Kirstin was ready. She packed up her little black VW and headed west to Los Angeles. She was going to find the women's movement and be part of the phenomenon of women coming to consciousness.

Soon Kirstin and I met. I had arrived from Port Washington only six months earlier. Kirstin came to the women's center where I was working on Mondays. A new sister, Tony, from Chicago, also arrived over the weekend, and she was so skilled at publishing that handling our newsletter didn't faze her at all. Tony singlehandedly printed, collated, and bundled the newsletters for mailing. When Kirstin came to the meeting, all the work was done and we didn't know what to do. First, we renamed Tony "Supertony." Then we went out to spraypaint feminist sayings on sexist posters and advertising. Kirstin came along without a question. I told her it was illegal and that we could get caught. She said, "Anybody who is anybody in the feminist movement has been to jail."

I liked her right away. She was electric. Touching her gave little shocks to my hands. In the car we were pressed against each other, and I casually put my hand on Kirsten's knees to balance myself. She looked at me with a look of both surprise and elation. I was keenly aware of the car's every turn and just how much my touch affected this young woman. It felt natural to touch her knees. I didn't take my hand away. At one point, she put her arm behind me to steady herself, but I felt that her arm came to reciprocate my touch. We rode silently while the others chatted. We don't remember whether we spraypainted anything; all we remember is the heat between us—a first for us both.

The six of us in the car—Katlyn, Phyllis, Emma, Supertony, Kirstin, and I—became friends. We did madcap protests and organized events together. Kirstin became an important friend. She made us laugh a lot; she played her guitar after meetings and taught us songs to sing together, such as the "Sisters of Mercy," of which she was particularly fond. She often handed me her walnut tambourine to play. I was so proud to be holding her musical instrument, an expression of Kirstin's very playful soul trusted to my hands.

I lived in a small bachelor apartment in Hollywood. A bachelor flat implied you were living there until you got married. For me, this was reversed. I had picked up my divorce papers in Juárez. It was a sad journey for me all alone in a Spanish-speaking country, getting the last of the quickie divorces available. I don't even know when our marriage had been legally put asunder. A small, bald-headed man sat at an oversized desk, stamping documents one by one and moving them from one pile to the other. There, somewhere in the midst of the buzzing air conditioner and the Spanish chitchat, my ten years as a wife had been terminated. Not even a friend was with me. I was tempted to see my divorce as a failure of some sort. But neither my ex-husband nor I really experienced it that way. We had known each other since childhood and had gone through deep uprooting changes that most Americans rarely experience—leaving home and country. Divorce was something we really did for each other to make our paths easier. Still, it hurt like hell.

From Mexico I called my friends back in Hollywood, but Katlyn, Phyllis, and even Emma were out. Kirstin was home—young, twenty-four years old, enthusiastic, ready to laugh—Kirstin. When I heard her voice on the phone—cheerful, expecting me home—a new sense of security returned to my heart. My new life was real; it was filled with emotional, practical, and historical

importance. I mattered. Kirstin promised to pick me up at the airport.

My new life was demanding. I was now a revolutionary. I had articles to write for our newsletter "Sister." I had to research homelessness by going out at night and counting the homeless women on the benches, talking to them about where they ate and slept and reporting this in our paper. There was a growing need to speak out against rape, so we formed a group called the Anti-Rape Squad. I studied self-defense. We escorted women to the police and made sure they were not harassed. We formed food conspiracies, where we got up early in the morning, about 4:30 A.M., and went shopping for all our friends wholesale at the L.A. market. Our small cars were laden with the green vegetables, red apples, and yellow and white cheeses we were bringing home when the commuters just started clogging up the freeways. Meetings had to be attended; Robert's Rules of Order (we renamed them Roberta's rules) had to be followed. We feminized our world by supporting women musicians, organizing concerts of women's music, and believing little girls who said they were molested. We wrote letters to the Olympics committee and the TV networks when they called the women's events the "girls' events." Artemis was working us in her most devoted fashion.

Kirstin shared my passion for revolution and added her cheerful enthusiasm to all of our ventures. But there was another life we also lived, our personal courtship, which grew, day by day, into a relationship. For about four months, Kirstin would knock on my door and insist on waking me up with a cup of coffee every morning at 7 A.M. She offered neck rubs and morning jokes. On our days off, we would talk till 3 A.M. about everything that had ever happened to us. To be with Kirstin meant that you were intently listened to. Every detail in my life gained importance because Kirstin cared. She encouraged me to write; she applauded my feminist dedication. These were also the mornings where I learned all her mythology. Kirstin was very close to her mom, yet not close enough. She couldn't tell her mother the truth about her sexuality. Kirstin received weekly packages from Marie—nighties, blouses, high heels, and makeup—the carefully planned ammunition of the heterosexual girl. They all landed in her trash.

At this time, we were all nonpracticing heterosexuals. We were not willing to put up with men anymore, and to change them seemed to be their job, not ours. There was one thing we noticed. As we worked side by side at the women's center with lesbian women, we realized that lesbian women had more fun.

They were always so full of plans and emotions—laughing, crying, dating, making phone calls, and talking deep into the night.

We, too, talked politics until the wee hours; we printed the newsletters, and we even sometimes risked our lives in peace demonstrations for all womankind. But when the weekend came, we retreated alone to our apartments for a rest, and that was that. We had no dates. We had lost our interest in men. There was something we didn't acknowledge in spite of all our political bravado, and that was love. We saw each other not as sexual beings but as minds and ideas—as respectable revolutionary women who were going to create a better world. Then the worst fear of our male critics came true. We began to fall in love with each other.

First, Delphin, a lesbian I knew from the consciousness raising group, fell in love with me. I suddenly had dates again! Then Katlyn fell in love with me! This was very difficult, since she was my best friend and I didn't feel the same way about her. Then, as if this was not complicated enough, I fell in love with Kirstin, and Kirstin fell in love with me.

For nonpracticing heterosexual women, we waded deeply into the realm of Artemis, the goddess of woman love, and we didn't know what hit us with such elemental, primordial force. Delphin, who was more experienced than most of us, decided that she had better leave while the going was good, leaving me to deal with Katlyn. Now I had to be lovers with my best friend, otherwise it would seem as if I were rejecting her. In order to protect my friendship with Katlyn and to have a chance of getting close to Kirstin, I told Katlyn that Kirstin would be lovers with both of us.

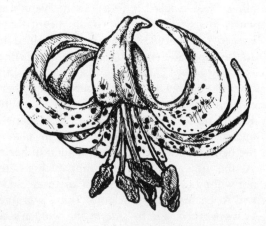

In this way I hoped to have my cake and eat it too. Big mistake! I was so miserable; I wanted to sleep through the three days Kirstin spent with Katlyn, waiting for my turn. What a fool! As soon as Kirstin had her initial encounter with Katlyn, Katlyn cut me off and acted as if she were married to Kirstin. "Sisters can be lovers" proved to be impossible—for us, anyway.

Nothing was ever the same after that. My year-and-a-half-long honeymoon with sisterhood temporarily bit the dust when confronted by adult sexuality. For six long, unbearable, stupid months Katlyn and I shared Kirstin. We all lived in the same apartment house that I managed at the time. Footsteps above my head meant at least that Katlyn and Kirstin were not in bed. Silence meant to me that they were making love. Jealousy seared into my being as I'd never felt before. I played loud music so they could not talk or sleep in peace. I took reds to sleep through Kirstin's absence. Our political work declined, and the women's center suffered because of our confusing relationships.

Finally, I decided to go home to Hungary and cool off. My mother had been asking me to visit; she had much to tell me, and I needed to get away. I told Kirstin that when I came back, I wanted her to choose between us. I'd had enough. I was casting love spells in Budapest, using my mother's method of whispering on the winds, calling up the ancestors and asking them to stir things my way. My ancestors were very nice people with no homophobia. One moon into my vacation, the phone rang and it was Kirstin. She was coming to see me! She was already in France with her aunt, visiting relatives!

I was beside myself with happiness. I threw my brother out of his bedroom and took it over for us. I told my mother all about my girlfriend. Mother knew a lot of lesbians in the art world, yet she had never talked about them before. My family received Kirstin with great hospitality and kept a sly eye out for flaws. The first night, Kirstin went to the bathroom, but on the way back, she missed the door and stepped out into the cool summer night of Budapest, closing the door behind her. She had to knock on mother's window to be let in. It became a running joke, how Kirstin stood on the street, half-naked in the middle of the night, knocking on mother's window like a bird.

But the rest of the time we had an old-fashioned, fun-filled honeymoon. Nobody I was friends with in my new life in the United States knew anything about where I came from. Kirstin was here! In big Budapest! My joy was boundless. We tasted wines in cool cellars and got sick together on spicy foods. We shouted each other's name into the echo in Tihany on the Balaton. We photographed large white storks nesting on the rooftops. We went horseback riding in the Puszta and found real gypsies to tell our fortunes. We made love in my brother's bed until all the sheets were wet. All my misery was wiped out in this magical wonderful week. Redeemed and forgiven, chosen and celebrated, I was home. I had found my mate! When Kirstin finally left, I knew I could come home to Los Angeles without having to share her love.

The price for our happiness was high. No more the innocence of pre-sexual days; no more the camaraderie of old friends. All our friends had taken sides. We had grown as women. We learned to respect ourselves, our sexuality, and each other. We were no longer just "kids" who played for fun; we were women and we had to be careful. None of the original six of us gave up the struggle for the liberation of women. We branched out and pursued different goals; I took on women's spirituality as my contribution.

Kirstin and I found a place together in Santa Monica, where we set up our household—two cats and a dog. Kirstin didn't get much public recognition, but whenever I was teaching women's rituals, giving classes, or conducting sabbats, she was there. Kirstin was the first priestess who took on the clergy mantle. She understood right away that religion is the highest of politics in a time when spirituality was not taken seriously by feminists.

Kirstin and I stayed together for seventeen years, sometimes as lovers, but most of the time as friends and roommates and all of it as priestesses of the goddess. We live separately now. I enjoy seeing Kirstin in her forties. We have gray hair and move more slowly than back then, but Kirstin is still twenty-four to me and I am thirty-one to her. She still thinks I'm beautiful. She hasn't played her guitar in years and years, but I still have her tambourine. I hid it from her so she wouldn't take it when she moved. It is her joyous woman spirit that lingers in its bells, and the memories, the treasures of our youth.

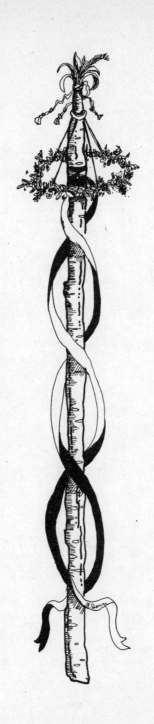

June

Hera

I AM HERA, MY VERY NAME MEANS courage. My title "Lady" refers to my sovereignty. My mother is Rhea, who squirted milk from her breasts to create the Milky Way. I manifest as a triple goddess: Hebe as my virgin self, and Theria as my crone self; I am the kingmaker and destroyer; I am the Queen. It was I who owned the apple tree that was guarded by my faithful servant, the wise serpent; it was my holy tree.

Every spring I still submerge myself in the regenerating pool of springwater in my old paradise. It was I who gave the drink of immortality to my children, the gods—the tasty ambrosia. On my head, I wear the crown of millions of stars, for my home is in heaven, and sometimes I wear crowns of cities, with their towers, landmarks, churches, and homes of my people, because my domain is also on Earth.

I protect the young and the weak; I control the powerful and mighty. I protect women especially, because they do my divine job—creation of new citizens. When women take consorts, I am there to bless the union. When they conceive their children, I am there to bless the seed so that it will be healthy.

If you call on me when you use power in the world, I will bless your ability to lead and I will send you good counsel. If you abuse that power, I will take it away from you. In my destroyer aspect, I have brought down haughty men with scandals, lost health, and lost loved ones. I lay low the proudest when my gift is used against the weak.

Some of you call on me for help in surviving. I bring you opportunities and am glad to aid. I am a gracious and generous queen—my main job is to exercise power. Without vision, you cannot aspire, you cannot grow. I bless the ones who give vision to those who lack it. I am the queen who moves the hearts of the prosperous to use their wealth in socially responsible ways, for all power originates from me. As queen, I rule human societies; I formed order out of creative chaos.

In Rome they called me Juno, the swarthy queen from the Mediterranean. So what is your business with me? Do you feel forgotten by power? Do you feel discarded, pushed aside, given the shaft? Meditate on me; visit me in your temple.

My season is midsummer, the height of the year. I delight in the orchards laden with fruit, and I adore the summer flowers that can drink deep from my rain. I am the summer queen, pregnant with the harvest, hopes, and opportunities of life on earth. I even appreciate the heat of cities, the flowers in flowerpots in concrete jungle windows. In this, my season, take time from your modern life and jump into my rejuvenating lakes, oceans, and rivers.

You can find me in the prime of your life. I shall pose to you disturbing questions in your middle age. "What have you done?" I will ask relentlessly. "How have you used the gifts given to you?" Fullness of power is my blessing. The queen is always just and well attended. Her touch is healing; her blessings are redeeming.

June's Aspects

The month of June received its name from the Goddess Juno, protector of women and marriage. This is where the custom of June brides originates. This month has many flower festivals, rose parades, weddings, and dances. Midsummer Night is a major international holiday for lovers, for divining the future, for building bonfires, and for jumping them for good luck.

Full moon aspect: Mead moon, strong sun moon

Universal event: The sun is moving away from the earth, but the constant moon prevails. The summer is peaking out, all ripens and gets ready for the harvest.

Communal event: Midsummer Night and Day. This is usually a three-day festival featuring dancing in the woods, with religious ecstacy. This is a time to gather all the tribes together, travel home to the old homestead, visit family and kin. All restrictions of chastity were lifted at this time; marriage proposals and weddings are lucky now.

Message: To bond, to lead, to rule

Activity: Endurance and triumphant fulfillment

Emotional mode: Bonding, loyalty

Healing properties: To make strong, to cleanse; prevention and protection

Appropriate spells: Celebrations of womanpower and loyalty to one's own sex, hexes against murderers and rapists, blessings on upcoming endeavors, money spells, love spells, weather spells, protection spells

Color: Purple, indigo

Tree: Oak and mistletoe, symbols of the male principle. This is the time for ritually cutting mistletoe (for later magical use) and catching it in a white cloth so that it never touches the ground (this practice was later resurrected for Christmas). Mistletoe is used in love spells (kissing under it).

Flower: Rose

Creature: Wren

Gem: Pearl, moonstone, alexandrite

Anna's Spells, Rituals, & Celebrations for June

CHANTING FOR PERSONAL POWER

Find a place under the full moon where you can chant without being observed. Go there and take with you some food, especially apples and pears (sacred to Juno) and some incense to offer her. Juno, who is the goddess of personal power, is within you. You simply must stimulate her. Close your eyes after viewing the moon and meditate. When you open your eyes again, imagine her standing in front of you as a kindly and beautiful matron, tall and draped with dazzling jewels. Chant now:

> *Juno, Hera; Queen of the Powers,*
> *Bring me, bring out my own, my own.*
> *Let all that is needed be done well, be done well.*
> *Let me sing of your glory under the moon.*
> *I am ready for my personal power.*
> *I am the arm that does your work.*
> *I am the mind of your thoughts.*
> *I am the will of your achievements.*
> *I am the conductor of your power.*
> *Hera, Juno, Hebe, Theria,*
> *I am the heart of your love.*

As always, invent your own chants and rituals. I am only offering a pattern. Hera has listened and you shall receive what you've asked for. The universe is aware, not asleep. The spirits grant what is needed. Under full moons, always light a white candle for strength and honor.

SPELL TO MAGICALLY DEFEAT A LAW

This is a spell to do if you run into an unjust law, regulation, or practice, such as a company policy that prevents a woman from getting equal pay for equal work or becoming an executive, or an ordinance that prohibits a woman from using her psychic talents to prophesy or counsel, or judgments under which a child is placed in the custody of his or her abuser. I am sure you can find your own examples of injustice.

Perform this spell during the waxing moon. Take the page (or make a copy of it) from a law book that contains the law you are working to defeat and soak it overnight in vinegar. Assemble any paper links—descriptions of cases involving this law, appeals, briefs, memos, pictures of individuals who support the unjust law, or anything else you can come up with. To work the spell, you will also need some fresh honey in a comb and brandy.

Create your magic circle and invoke the four corners of the universe as described in the naming rite in March. Place the page from the law book on the altar along with the paper links. The woman acting as high priestess addresses the Goddess:

> *I invoke thee, Dark Mother of Erebus, to sit in council regarding a great injustice being done to me and to others. I invoke thee, mighty crones Tisiphone, Alecto, and Megaera, and all the gracious company of the queen of the witches. I invoke thee, Hecate, to grant me power to rectify this great injustice. Hear the facts.*

Here give a short but passionate account of this law's oppression. Take the copy of the law and the paper links and pass them around the circle with a pair of scissors so that all can snip into them, saying, "I weaken you, I cut off your strength, I cut off your power to oppress women," and so on. Throw the copy of the bad law into the cauldron along with the offering of a lock of your own hair (the "cauldron" can be any dish that can safely contain the fire) and set it aflame. Pour a little brandy into the cauldron to make the flames jump high.

Then everyone dances slowly counterclockwise around the circle at least three times. After the spell has been danced, sit down for the feast but be sure that three places are set for the Furies. The Furies are the "enforcers" of the Goddess, who hunt down wrongdoers and wrongdoing. Offer them honeycomb, barley, apples, and wine. After the feasting, thank the Furies and the spirits who have guarded you. Continue organizing and fighting the unjust law.

SPELL TO STOP HARASSMENT
AT HOME, WORK, OR SCHOOL

Unfortunately, the life of a woman or child is not safe in the patriarchal United States, no matter where she lives or walks or studies. There have been many cases of harassments on the phone; in school, where professors sometimes will block the career of a student if she won't give him sex; in the streets where we must walk; or in the home when women are asleep. Women are attacked every two minutes by men. It is a national shame.

Practice this spell during the waning moon. Prepare your altar with white candles. Use a black candle to represent the person who is harassing you. Anoint it with your urine and write the name of the person doing the harassment on the front and back three times. If you do not know the name, write "whoever is oppressing me." Roll the candle in black pepper and leave it on your altar for three nights in a row. Burn a little of the candle each night, chanting:

> *[Name] or [whoever is harassing me] will stop. In*
> *Aradia's name be this done. By his own mistakes, by his*
> *own fault, he will bring himself down, down, down!*
> *According to my word, so mote it be.*

Aradia is the queen of witches; she will protect the innocent. After your candle is finished, there will be some drippings. Throw them in the path of your harasser. If you know where he lives, throw them in his yard; otherwise, cast them into a living body of water. The Goddess will know for sure where to deliver your spell. Eliminate all thought of fear from your mind and turn this matter over to the higher power. Remember the Goddess is within you. It's your duty to stand up for your own integrity.

THE HOLIDAYS

June 1

CHILDREN'S FESTIVAL (CHINESE)

What a fine idea it is for a nation to celebrate its children! In China, there are posters advertising this fine day weeks ahead, many circuses open their shows, ice cream is priced low or is free, and the whole day is devoted to catering to kids of all sizes.

The Goddess Carna (Roman) also rules this day. She opens what is closed and closes what is open. She is the hinge of life. One of her powers is to unlock the door to information that has been suppressed. This is a good day to start investigations, research, discoveries.

June 2

JUNO REGINA'S DAY (ROMAN)

This is a day to celebrate women who are in public life. We have seen how hard it is to combine the soulless public life of a leader with the inner life of a woman. Find out who in your area is struggling to take political power back into the domain of the feeling world. These can be both male and female officials. Send them good luck, and if a woman is running for office, send her money.

June 3

SECOND FESTIVAL OF PEACE: PAX (ROMAN)

Pax, the goddess of peace, is the protector of persons and property, the essence of safety. Light a white candle for yourself; pray for the safety of your own life and your loved ones. There are three holidays a year for Pax. Imagine what it would be like if we actually celebrated peace with processions and demonstrations, not just protests. Singing contests, writing contests, and musical performances would fill the day; people would run around crowned with olive branches! What a sight! Budget cuts from defense would be spent on the poor of the cities. How blessed! Do we dare to wage peace? How scary is peace, really? Ask the men in power, they will tell you—very. Make an effort today to write your official representatives to take courage and use diplomacy instead of escalating the arms race.

June 4

ROSALIA: FESTIVAL OF ROSES

The rose, so fragrant and varied and beautiful, has been a symbol for the Goddess for millennia. The worship of the rose was the worship of Aphrodite, the goddess of love. The red rose represented full-blown, mature, fertile womanly sexual love. The form and meaning of the rose have gone through many changes, like the Goddess herself.

The rose originated in Arabia, and was brought back by the Christian crusaders. In the twentieth century, the symbol of the rose was reassigned from Aphrodite to Mary, Mother of God. The Goddess Mary is often called Rose Garden, Mystic Rose, Queen of the Most Holy Rose Garden. This still means that the rose is the symbol of the life-giving vulva. Its male counterpart is the wild briar rose, that "pricks" and draws blood from the maidens. The rosary is organized in multiples of five for the fivefold petals of the rose. This is the number of the five-pointed star on our flags and the pentagram of the witches.

Tend your garden today, pick your roses respectfully, and meditate on the tree of life as a rose or apple tree and the sexuality of the Goddess as the source of all life.

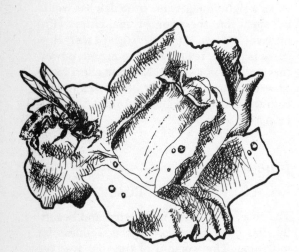

June 7

VESTALIA: PURIFICATION (ROMAN)

The Goddess Vesta, a fire goddess, was celebrated on this day. On Vestalia, priestesses traveled to the rivers to throw from a wooden bridge small images of men into the waters. This was done as a sacrifice to the ancient ones to protect the living.

The temples also received vigorous attention during Vestalia. Priestesses (vestal virgins) swept and scrubbed and washed and beautified the house of the Mother. (See March 2 for discussion of vestal virgins.) During the festival, the innermost sacred space of the temple was opened to all priestesses. This was a space where no man was ever allowed to set foot. Here the priestesses would crowd together, standing barefoot, for prayers and rituals concerning their own order.

Vestals prepared the first fruits of grain and offered it in the temples, while all millers and bakers were garlanded. There are parallel customs to Vestalia among the Creek Indians of North America, usually in July and August, when their first corn is ripe. They, too, maintained the ritual purifications; bathing of sacred images; sweeping public plazas, temples, houses; and fasting before partaking of the new first fruits, putting out the old fire and rekindling a new one and solemnly and communally eating of the first fruits of new corn.

Other fire goddesses—such as Pele (Hawaiian) and Heartha (German)—should be remembered. It is the fire of life they represent, the fire in our bodies, of our passions, the purifying fire of love. This is a good day to barbecue or do other fiery things. Court a lover; make love; go dancing.

June 11

MATRALIA (ROMAN)

Not only do we have holidays for women who are mothers, but this day we celebrate those who are motherly without having borne children. Mater Matuta, the Goddess of Dawn and Death, and also of harbors and the sea, received homage from women who were not mothers themselves. Honor your aunt or friend who is childless. They are our support system.

June 13

FEAST OF EPONA (CELTIC)

From the Iron Age in Britain through Roman times, the worship of the horse-headed goddess Epona was celebrated on this day. In ancient Hungary, she was portrayed as a magical white horse, a *táltos*, and her worship was practiced by many other central European tribes. The horse represented mobility, agricultural power, and sadly, also a warrior's tool. The Goddess would appear in the form of a horse to transport her shamans to other magical realms of existence, such as the world of the spirits.

June 14

BIRTHDAY OF THE MUSES (GREEK)

Yes, even the Muses had a mother. She was the Goddess Mnemosyne (memory), who was herself a Muse. Her daughters brought humanity the joys of inspiration and, in a way, the age of technology as well. The nine Muses are Calliope (epic song), Clio (history), Euterpe (lyric song), Thalia (comedy), Melpomene (tragedy), Terpsichore (dance), Erato (erotic poetry), Polyhymnia (sacred hymns), and Urania (astronomy). The creativity of women is the food of the spirit. Support the arts today; stimulate your own creativity. When was the last time you went to see a play? Do something cultural today that you have never done before. Break the chains of your old habits.

June 17

MARRIAGE OF ORPHEUS AND EURYDICE (GREEK)

This day is All Couples' Day, gay or straight—the celebration of married love, loyalty, and faith in each other. The following story captured my imagination, since there isn't really any other holiday that celebrates not the individual but the joint act of being married.

Orpheus was a great musician who loved his wife so much that when she died of a snakebite, he followed her into the land of the shades, where the dead live on, and asked the Queen of the underworld to let her return. He used his artistic power to play his lyre with such beauty and called forth such sweet notes that he charmed the dark spirits below. Eurydice was released to him on the condition that he should lead her back into the world without ever looking behind him to see if she was really there. He obeyed until he was almost to the surface, but just before he reached the world of the living, he lost faith and looked back. The spell was broken, and Eurydice had to go back to the land of the dead after all.

Let this story demonstrate how deeply lovers can bond with each other, and also how overprotectiveness can ruin the whole thing. Celebrate by taking a vacation together, exchanging gifts, giving a party—and making a reality check on your possessiveness. Leaving a space between yourself and your true love where "angels can dance" is the secret of having a long-lasting relationship.

June 21

SUN ENTERS CANCER

Cancer is the sign of the crab. Take some time off to pamper yourself. Slow down; pay attention to your home. Look within and be aware of your feelings and honor Yemaya Olokun, Yoruba goddess of the depths of the sea.

June 21

SUMMER SOLSTICE

Happy midsummer to you all! Now the Earth has reached the midpoint on her journey around the sun. From this time on, the daylight hours will begin to shorten again. This peak of the summertime is Midsummer, Summer Solstice.

The goddess of this season is Litha (European, North African). She is abundance and fertility, power and order. If you wish to conceive a divine child (and whose child isn't!), lie with your lover tonight. Tonight is lovers' night all over the world. Renamed by the Christians as St. John's Day, Midsummer is an excellent time to perform divinations about affairs of the heart.

For protection in the coming year and purification from sorrow, jump over a balefire or a candle (or your trusty hibachi) in your backyard. If there is something that bothers you a lot, write it on a white paper with red ink, smear it with honey, fold it gently and burn it in the flames, saying:

I give my sorrow to the flames, the Goddess of Fire will consume my pain. It is done.

If you are single, it's a good night to cast a love spell. (See April.)

Another goddess associated with this season is Cerridwen, who usually has her cauldron of rebirth handy as she brews the ingredients of our lives. Her sacred animal is the sow, so eat some pork tonight if you are not a vegetarian.

Ishtar (Babylonian), Astarte (Canaanite), Aphrodite (Greek), Yemaya or Oshun (Brazilian) are all love goddesses who may be celebrated with fires and fruit offerings tonight. The fiery goddess Aine (Irish) is honored with torchlight processions around the fields; cattle are driven through fires to purify them from sickness. The wheel of the year is turning; from the high point of summer, we now face the coming winter, even though its first signs are far away.

Summer Solstice is a magical time for wishing. Walk to the nearest river, ocean, bay, brook, or lake and, chanting to yourself (the Muses will tell you how), float a flower with your kiss on it—traditionally a rose— into the waves to carry your wish home. It is a message to the Cosmic Mother (whose symbol the rose is) on the waters (her life-giving element) to send something to her daughter or son—yourself.

Here is a chant to make a midsummer wish:

Yes, you are here in the soft buzzing grass.
Yes, you are listening among the flowering
*   gardens.*
Yes, you are shining from the most royal blue
*   sky.*

*Yes, you are granting me what I wish
    tonight:*
*Grant me a healthy life rich with high
    purpose,*
*A true partner to share my joys and my
    tears,*
*Wisdom to hear your voice giving me
    guidance,*
*Wealth to give to others as you have given it
    to me.*

June 24

LADY LUCK (EUROPEAN)

Lady Luck, Fors Fortuna, she who rules chance—today we light her green and orange candles to stimulate her lucky power and to be lucky enough to receive her favors. But Fors Fortuna is really a trinity of goddesses, the Three Fates. Think how often during your life you have prayed to the Fates. "Oh, if I only got a chance!" we say. "Opportunity only knocks once!" "Don't offend the fates with too much praise!" warns an old Hungarian belief, so we underplay our enthusiasm when praising a newborn baby. "Not a bad-looking baby!" we say, carefully protecting the new child's luck.

Who are these crotchety old ladies who control everybody's chances? The Old Ones indeed are fussy. They are almost forgotten by most people except when we are in trouble, at which point we all get "religion." But what kind? The Old religion! In her neutral aspect, the Triple Goddess, as ruler of fate, consists of Lachesis, who controls the length of the threads of life; Clotho, her older sister who spins and weaves the tapestry of our lives into a beautiful work of art; and, finally, Atropos, the oldest of them, who controls

endings with her shears and cuts the threads of life when she feels it's time. When the fates are not honored, they reveal their dark faces—the Furies Alecto, Tesiphone, and Megaera.

The three of them share one life, since without ending, there is no beginning. They are pictured often as old maids spinning in a dark cave (in our deep minds), sharing one eye among them; thus the saying "the fates are blind." But the fates can be brought up from the forgotten crevices of the old mind into the brilliant sunshine, where they can see much better and be part of our modern lives, where we need them. So remember the three maids—the Norns (the Norse goddesses of fate), the Fates, the Furies—and turn them back into the three Graces—three lovely naked women entwined in a dance. Light three candles (gold, green, or silver) and pray to the Fates for good luck.

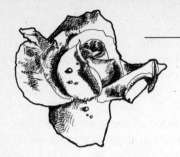

The June Story:
Motherhood
Is a Goddess Issue

HURRAY FOR MOTHERHOOD, for we create like gods. Think about it. Every powerful man, right- or wrong-doing, every sainted man and every genius, every evil man and every lover, every bigot and every murderer, every rapist and every good guy, even the pope, came out from between a woman's two legs.

"What do you mean you create like gods? What about us men? We had a little something to do with it didn't we?" I hear my critic's voice. "Sure," I answer, "but there is a long, long, long road to travel, from the naked little squiggly sperm that provided the impetus for the egg to divide all the way to a tax-paying citizen. This adult, in the end, is woman's product. We women are the people makers who create the economy. We're the ones who create countries, villages, communities, families. We are humanity. Even in the Christian creation story, giving life to Jesus is an act that takes place between God and woman; man had nothing to do with it."

We women are surrounded throughout our fertile lives by a multitude of souls asking to be born. Pictures of the Virgin Mary demonstrate this concept. She is crowned by her cherubs, those rosy little winged babies who always accompany the Holy Mother, those unborn souls in waiting. She is the archetypal Mother Soul, the great Reincarnator, the cauldron of our rebirth. The cherubs are the baby souls that flutter about us while we have no intention of getting pregnant. And if we slip and have sex without protection, these little souls are ready and waiting to snatch a nice body for themselves from our wombs. These are souls in a hurry, filled with impatience and vigor. They like to hang around young, fertile women, who are apt to hop into bed with somebody and give the little souls a chance for rebirth.

But where does it say that every little soul that manages to land a fertilized egg is entitled to occupancy? Abortion is the prerogative of the Dark Mother; she aborts us monthly; it is called menses. The shadow of motherhood is abortion, which is also our responsibility, making the choice of life and death as much a part of the Goddess as her life-giving good nature. The Fates take into consideration woman's choice when they decide how and when we come into this life. What good is it to be born if you never have an opportunity to thrive, only to suffer?

And what have we ever done together as mothers politically? When did we take our awesome divine power and protest effectively against wars? We get together when there are children's bodies to bury; we protest in parts of the world for peace and an end to war. Have we ever threatened the patriarchy with a moratorium on births? No! We have the most potent of tools for protest—ending the production of people! Think of it—for five years, only five years, no more babies! Hold up the conceptions. Go easy on the fertility. I don't mean an end to sex. No. Just a pause in baby making, a five-year generation gap. The peace warriors, little unborn souls, would always be remembered as the ones who never came. What would happen? Imagine the mothers of the world actually deciding to do this to protest war. We would say, no nukes, no bombs, no nothing. Abolish the military. Create the flowering countries the world has never seen before. End hunger. End child abuse.

If a moratorium on babies went into effect for five years, industry by industry, business would go way down. No babies, no nurseries and no baby clothes, no baby foods and no baby showers, then no elementary school kids, no teenagers for five years, no college kids. Like a reminder of what is important in life, the quality of life, the generation gap would move like a ghost across the age spectrum, perpetually providing a focus for people to remember what happened when the women were pushed to employ such drastic measures to get the men off war. Think about it.

How about paying mothers for the years of production they spend to create a society? Not welfare—wages for creating life. Each child ought to be worth money to the state that takes it for a consumer. The market value of a fully-grown, well-turned-out new citizen should be calculated and awarded to the mother. There must also be a pension fund for aging mothers, not only married women, but the single ones as well. Women must be protected in their old age.

I was very young—nineteen—when I became a mother. It was during the time right after the Hungarian revolution, and I was waging a private revenge against the Russians by trying to replenish the lost Hungarian lives all by myself. The first birth was long and hard, and I felt very alone during it. Nothing had prepared me for the changes it made in my body and life-style. I was a student at the University of Chicago with an international scholarship that required high grades to keep. Pregnancy and childbirth drained me of all energy and made me too tired to study. After the second birth, I gratefully dropped out of college. Two kids were enough for me.

I named my boys after my favorite people. Låszlò I named after a legendary king of Hungary who had magical powers and could get water from a rock if he struck it with his magic wand. Gåbor I named after my favorite humorist, whose books had entertained me so many times. They were good kids. Not pleasant kids, because they were always screaming or fighting—only good kids. They were honest and gentle and talented.

They were spitfires, according to my mother, who taught them ceramics and exhibited their first works along with her own in her shows. They liked to build rockets or, with their little long skinny fingers, silently make clay dinosaurs for hours on end. After their prehistoric phase, they moved on to airplanes. They built model airplanes, thousands of them. I hung them all over the bedroom. They hovered gracefully when the breeze went through the room. Låszlò never got out of his airplane phase; he became a pilot. Gåbor moved on to study the stars and made photographs of the planets. He became a scientist. And now they are both pushing thirty. Isn't mothering a wonder?

There was one thing I did more than any of my other motherly deeds that influenced my boys as future men. Of course, I provided superior motherly services, including teaching them how to swim in the Atlantic Ocean, and how to bicycle, or taking Låszlò up in a private airplane for the first time to look around among the clouds. But the hardest and most important thing I did was to teach my sons positive attitudes toward women.

I don't agree that boys should talk to their fathers about girls. A father could communicate a sexist attitude and ruin a perfectly good boy. I think mothers know infinitely more about boys and girls than fathers do. Mothers keep up to date on the changes, which is crucial, since boys will be approaching contemporary girls, not the kind their fathers used to court.

The incident I remember happened on a warm summer afternoon, the kind on which I liked to go to the beach and then come home and submerge myself in a bubble bath and soak out all the pebbles from between my toes. These were my quiet times. The boys were about seven and eight years old. They would watch TV or fight with each other or eat. I didn't care. There are times when a mother has to stop saving lives and just have a good soak in the tub.

This was what I was doing when, quite politely, there was a knock on the bathroom door. That alone was suspicious. The boys were never polite. "Come in!" I said. "What's going on?" As a mother, I had developed a scanning device within my psyche.

Just by looking at the boys, I could tell all kinds of things about them—what they were up to and whether they were lying to me. But now all seemed to be fine. They were acting shy. But it couldn't be my nakedness underneath the bubbles; they had seen my naked body often enough before. This was the sixties.

They snickered to each other and giggled, and I realized that something was up after all. "All right," I said. "Come here and talk to me." They both sat down on the edge of the tub and dangled their skinny little boys' feet in the warm water, splashing a little but not enough to get chased away. "Mom," said László, the older, "we want to ask you a question."

The boys stared down at the bubbles and then at their own toes. "Well, we don't really know what it means, but we heard that girls have a . . . clitoris." "No, a cliptomis!" Gábor corrected the older one. "Cliptomis? No—critomis?" László was looking insecure. They were obviously worried that if they didn't communicate precisely, they might never get an answer.

So that was it. I bet some boys made dirty jokes in school when this word surfaced. It was embarrassing for the boys even to bring it up. "I see. And what do you want to know about the clitoris?" I asked. László threw a victorious look at Gábor; he had won on the identification of the mysterious word. Emboldened, he continued. "Mom . . . where is it?"

At this point, they both stopped being shy and openly looked to me for answers. They were accustomed to being able to ask me about anything at all. I never hit them, never told them they could not inquire about sex or anything else. But this was my moment of truth. Was I going to behave as I always preached a good Aquarian Age mother should, honestly and openly? Or was I going to throw the little ones out on their ears and tell them never to talk to me like this again? Even as I lay in the bubble bath, I could hear their attitudes forming. I thought, "If I am hesitant, they'll think it's dirty. If I just talk about it, I'm not really answering the question." I took a deep breath and reached down between my legs and opened my outer labia with my two fingers to expose my clitoris. My heart was pounding and my breath was short; this was not easy. "There!" I said, managing not to betray my flustered state. "That's mine!"

I shall never forget the two small bodies leaning toward me over the water and peering into the door of life, the very door through which they had come into this existence. The moment was mercifully short, but to me it seemed to take longer than anything I had ever done before. I tried to stay calm and nonchalant. The thought crossed my mind: "I am doing this for all those future girls in their lives, for all those little girls who are now in diapers who will grow up to date my sons. I hope that one day they will thank me for this."

Then it was over. The little skinny bodies relaxed, and László said, "It's cute!" Gábor thought it over and agreed. "Neato!" This was his big "good" word at the time. I let go of my breath. Ahhhh. Back to normal, thank heaven! The issue of my clitoris was never brought up again. In fact, the boys don't even remember this incident; it was just one of those days when they learned something new. The rest of their sexual information they must have put together themselves. My husband contributed many things that were useful for their manhood. But I think that they are good lovers of women today because of that summer afternoon in Port Washington when they acknowledged and declared a woman's private parts "cute" for the first time.

July

THE GODDESS SPEAKS

Athena

ARE YOU CALLING FOR ME? Is it time to write or sing or create or invent? I am the inspiration that wins you self-esteem; I am the accomplishment for which your world will give you recognition. I am the flawless leadership you all aspire to; I am the cooperation of your peers, the celebration of unity. My origins are African, not Greek.

I am Athena, daughter of Metis, not of Zeus, who used to be the tribal god of patriarchal raiders before they made him into their king of heaven. How like him to steal my good name and story and force my lore to support a male-glorifying system! But know this, I have never betrayed my women, women who loved me the world around. I am not a "scab" who crosses over to the enemy; I never endorsed matricide. I never preferred men to women; I have never abandoned you.

I am strength of body and mind in females and males. I am loyalty to a cause, or the arts and sciences. I am talented, powerful, and a curious scientist. I am increasing the number of women politicians so they will manifest my powers of reasoning and of resolving conflicts without violence. I am stirring in the hearts of little girls who renounce marriage as the only way to make their living in the world. I am the bold plan and the scholarship and later the success for those daughters and sons who have listened well.

I do not advocate a cold bed for my followers; that is another lie about me. I want you to love wisely and give of yourself. Love and excellence are compatible sisters. I require no price for my gift of ambition, but keep a clear head, follow your common sense, and attend to the deep mind and all will be well.

Have you ever noticed how ambitious nature really is? Have you seen ants ever just rest? Have you seen trees take a week off? All nature hustles, works, strives, builds, and destroys. That is my energy—this everlasting striving, this ecstasy of new goals and ideas, one project after the next. And I am nurturing the new inventors, from their cradle to the moment of discovery. There they are, still babies, but the cures for your horrible sicknesses will be made by their tender little hands, and my protection will allow them to reach their moment of contribution.

How do you find me? Each time you help somebody succeed, you have made an offering to me. I will notice it when your time for good luck is near and repay you. Every time you give your sister or brother a break without jealousy, you are making an offering to me. When you give money for scholarships, establish centers of learning, acknowledge those who have helped you, give someone needed information, and support the sciences and the beloved and necessary arts, you have made Athena stronger.

I am the chief Muse, the One before the Nine, the future of the world depends on my efficiency. My hands have to keep the hands of the madmen from destroying the earth. My magic has to shield life on this blue planet from the fools who dominate it. Use your personal power to be my partner in strategy, and Athena will lend you her mighty arm when you need her. Grow and protect, dare and discover—share, share, share what you find; teach and sing and write and make music to the glory of life. I am she who holds the scepter of sovereignty, and my best friend is Lady Victory. She stands on the palm of my hand, and together we never fail. Join us.

July's Aspects

This month is named after Julius Caesar, who reformed the entire Western calendar in 45 B.C.

Full moon aspect: Harvest moon

Universal event: This is the month of increase, the beginning of the barley harvest. The days are starting to get shorter. It is a time of reversal, of overthrow of the old order.

Communal event: Lammas Sabbat, the Festival of the New Bread (end of July/beginning of August; see August 1); celebration of the Lady of Plenty— Habondia, Freyja, Hulda—goddesses of nature and fertility

Message: To invent, to know, to succeed

Activity: To prosper, to enjoy, to grow in wisdom; ecstasy in nature

Healing properties: Prevention and protection

Appropriate spells: Blessings on the fields, love spells, health spells, money spells, and all activities that are positive and nourishing

Color: Green/gray

Tree: Oak

Flower: Larkspur, water lily

Creature: Starling

Gem: Ruby

Anna's Spells, Rituals, & Celebrations for July

Voodoo Spell for Wealth (American)

All of us would like to improve our lot, to use our goddess-given talents better—to gain wealth, improve our love life. To do all these things, we use a special part of our being called the subconscious—yes, the very same thing all the New Age studies are making millions of dollars on.

This spell is one of those attempts to manipulate the old unconscious, that repressed part of our brain that ultimately controls everything from success, to making money, to health and love. This part of us is stimulated by prayer (to whomever your higher power happens to be). And in the old days, we influenced the unconscious by casting spells. The unconscious responds to moonlit landscapes, candlelight vigils, misty incense clouds, and the sounds of howling wolves at night. In order to speak to this part of us, we have to consciously retreat from the twentieth century and create a symbolic language that can attract and seduce it into listening to our modern minds.

Do this spell for three days during the full moon. Make a doll out of green cloth to represent yourself. Stuff it with bay leaves or clover (both represent wealth). Tie some of your own hair around the doll's head; give it eyes and a nose and mouth and generally try to make it you. Make it a little scarf from something that you wear a lot.

On white paper with red ink write the amount of money you need, or the kind of wealth you seek. Pin the paper to the doll and place the doll on a clean white cloth on your altar; anoint it with cinnamon oil and sprinkle it with gold dust (pyrite). Take a green cord (string, thread, or ribbon) and tie it around the doll's middle three times, saying:

> *Thus do I bind you, thus do I tie you to wealth!*
> *You shall know no rest until you have captured*
> *the desired and the best!*

Imagine now all the abundance that you described on the paper coming into your life. Dwell on it, visualize it, breathe deeply, feeling it. Before you put away your doll, say:

*Old unnamed mind, murky and dark, keep my spell
strong, keep my spell tight.*

Fold the doll in the white cloth and hide it in a dark spot where
no one will find it (your chest of drawers?). This spell must be
repeated either during the three nights of the full moon, or nine
times on consecutive nights (repeating the same steps each night).
When the nine nights are completed, hide the doll until the desired
results manifest.

When your spell comes true, take your doll and burn it
in a lovely herbal fire, then scatter its ashes into a living body of
water. If you want to go after another goal, you need to make a
new doll.

SELF-BLESSING FOR HEALTH, WEALTH, LOVE, OR WISDOM

Get hold of some powdered mountain ash leaves (or pulverize
them yourself). Legend tells us that the ash tree can be used to
cast a powerful blessing (or curse). It is believed to be the Tree of
Life—the legendary Yggdrasil, which figures so prominently in
Germanic lore. If you carry a leaf or bit of wood of this tree in a
red bag on your person, it is believed to protect you from all kinds
of harm. I recommend it for car charms. If you were born under
an air sign (Aquarius, Libra, Gemini), you are a natural for this
spell.

Walk into your favorite spot in nature; take a handful
of the ash tree powder with you. Establish which way is east, west,
south, and north. Then take the ash tree powder in the palm of
your right hand and blow it toward the east, saying:

*East wind, carry this offering to the guardians of the
east, that they may bless me with [whatever your reason
to do this] and protect me.*

With the fingers of the left hand, place the ash tree
powder in the palm of the right hand and blow it toward the south
and say:

*South wind, carry this offering to the guardians of the
south, that they may bless me and protect me.*

With the fingers of the left hand, place some ash tree powder in the palm of your right hand, blow, and say:

Winds of the west, carry this offering to the guardians of the west that they may bless me and protect me.

With the fingers of the left hand, place some ash tree powder in the palm of the right hand and blow it toward the north, saying:

Winds of the north, carry this offering to the guardians of the north, that they may bless and protect me.

Now turn back to the east and say:

The magic circle I have turned.
Powder of the sacred ash I have offered.
Now, Diana, send my wishes true to me.

Listen and wait a little while to see what will happen. An idea might come to you or an animal may manifest. Then go home in peace, knowing that Mother Nature has heard your prayer and will grant it within a moon.

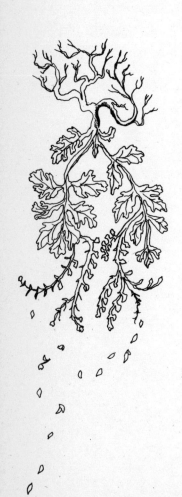

THE MAGIC OF MUGWORT (*Artemisia absinthium*)

Add a little mugwort to the dinner your are cooking for a friend or lover, and it will make the most frigid one amorous. Those who are impotent will find they are virile again (central Europe).

PRAYERS FOR PEACE IN THE FAMILY

I learned this ritual from a woman from India who lived in West Africa. During the new moon, the women fast all day, though they give food to little girls. The women have slept with henna tied to their palms. In the morning, the henna has made a yellow mark on their skin, which is part of the ritual.

The women then bake a shell from wheat flour and fill it with butter-soaked cotton balls. They wait until the moon is visible to them and then set fire to the cotton balls. They pray over them, reciting the names of their spouses and asking the moon to grant peace in their homes. They pass the tray of lights around their circle. After all have prayed over it, they have a great meal, chatting and laughing with each other. Some women put the cotton ball lights on leaves and float them down the river as offerings to the goddess of the river. This is said to bring peace at home. (This is, however, not a cure for battered wives or violence at home. See your women's center for referrals.)

A MARRIAGE CEREMONY FOR THOSE WHO FEEL ───── IT IS TIME FOR TRYSTING

This is a ceremony for natural people, gay and straight alike, to glorify and witness the commitment the two lovers are making. For the ritual, you and your love should buy two chalices (to represent pleasure and feelings). You may want to inscribe the date on them so they will serve as a future memento. You'll also need two flower crowns to represent respect. Finally, and most important, you'll need a tray of food to represent the Tree of Life. Arrange the foods aesthetically on your tray so that they represent roots, stems, flowers, seeds, and fruits. For example, you might use carrots for roots, celery stalks for stems, cauliflowers for flowers. For fruits, use melons or grapes and, finally, almonds for seeds.

Gather together your friends, your community—people from work, from your childhood, from the important times in your life. To begin the ritual, both you and your partner should extend your hands over the tray with a friend, or if you are lucky, with a priestess. Now invoke the Goddess of Marriage, Juno/Hera, on the tray.

> *We invoke you, Goddess of Life, by these roots, so that this relationship may be deeply rooted in the community and in the two who are joining their lives today.*

> *We invoke thee by the stems and branches, that this alliance may reach out to others and gather a rich community around it.*

> *We invoke thee by flowers, that this relationship may make the respective talents and desires of both partners grow.*

We invoke thee by the seeds, that this love may create new love and our devotion bring forth new discoveries in each other.

Now you answer these questions put to you by the priestess:

Do you [name] take [name] for your lifelong companion, in sickness and in health, in richness and.in poverty, as long as you live, even if you love others?

You answer, of course, "I do."

The question is repeated, and you must think about what it means. It isn't sexual ownership that is promised here, but loyalty until death. No matter who else might occupy your heart, you have to look after your trysted one, show up in emergencies, make sure your friend is all right. Act as family. You are not allowed to hold a grudge or to stay away from each other. No matter what life may hold, the promise is to cherish and be there for each other.

Finally, present each other with crowns of flowers, saying as you place it on the head of your beloved, "Thou art Goddess," "Thou art God," recognizing that the creator is present in both of you, so you will continue to respect each other. For lesbian trysting, each woman says "Thou art Goddess"; gay men say "Thou art God."

After you make your vows, feed each other from the tray of food and say, "May you never hunger." Offer each other your beautiful chalices filled with champagne or juice and say, "May you never thirst!" When the ceremony has been performed and you are ready to "jump the broom," place on the ground a branch of myrtle, oak, rowan, or willow (whatever you can find) and, holding hands, jump over it toward the east, the direction of beginnings. When your feet touch the ground, your vow is in effect, and the shared future begins!

THE HOLIDAYS

July 2

FEAST OF EXPECTANT MOTHERS (EUROPEAN)

Here is a gem of a women's holiday. Women's clubs, attention! Gather together all the moms-to-be and give them a big honoring dinner! And you, moms-to-be, collect baby-sitting pledges from your sisters now while the going is good and fill up your calendar for the next year. You may find that you are getting a lot of attention while you are big with child, but once the baby is able to cry and make noise and smell up the house, non-moms and nondads tend to stay away. Beware of the gifts of doilies and "cute" gifts—they are useless! Tell your friends to give you time off. The most precious gift a new mom can have is a little time for herself. If you are not pregnant but wish to be, drink licorice root or raspberry tea every evening at sundown.

July 3

FESTIVAL OF CERRIDWEN (CELTIC)

Cerridwen is the fertility goddess of the Celts. What a joy it is to gather in the fruits of your harvest, be it from your humble back-yard garden or the large fields of a farm. The ripeness of the cherry trees or the sweetness of the plums and peaches all depend on the rays of the healing sun. The yellowness of corn and wheat's ripe seed are the work of the sacred sun and the sacred earth together.

Cerridwen's symbol is the clever and fertile sow, yes, the pig, which is a symbol of good luck in Hungary and elsewhere and is connected with prosperity. Why did the lowly piglet achieve such high status among the ancient folk? Try a lovely Hawaiian luau, and you will know what the earth-baked sweet meat is like—you'll never dream of steaks again. The pig loves the earth; she wallows in it. Her meat is delicious, and she produces six or eight or sometimes thirteen little ones, which are easily transportable if necessary. She is the wealth of the people. Cerridwen shares this symbol with other goddesses such as the Greek Demeter. Be thankful for the harvest, enjoy a good pork feast or, if you are vegetarian, eat what the pigs love best—corn.

July 4

INDEPENDENCE DAY (AMERICAN)

Here you can see how the fire festivals of the ancients gained new meaning while maintaining the old practice of making fires, explosives, and fireworks. The actual signing of the Declaration of Independence, which Americans celebrate on this day, occurred in early August. Honor Lady Liberty, who protects our freedom to practice our religion.

July 5

SUN DANCE FESTIVAL (NATIVE AMERICAN)

In a Sun Dance, traditionally, the Assiniboine Indians of Montana fast and then undergo all kinds of heroic tests, some painful, some ecstatic, in order to take the pain of their people on themselves and thus liberate the tribe from bad times. This was predominantly a men's festival; women were believed to have done this spiritual service for their people every month when they bled and when they gave birth. How true.

My advice to white folks who want to imitate Native Americans is—don't. Learn from them, but do not imitate. It is not respectful to take up their spiritual practices. Moreover, the Native Americans don't want us to. My friend Janet McCloud says:

In the beginning we had the land, and the white man had the "book." Today he has the book and our land. Spirituality that we managed to keep for ourselves we don't want to share. We want the white folks to give us something, not just take, take, take. *

She calls those white people who are trying to be Indians "wannabees." The Natives would rather see us reclaim our own spiritual

*Personal communication, 1983.

practices, such as the Native European practices written up in this book, for example.

July 7

TANABATA (JAPANESE & KOREAN)

Once upon a time, there were two lovers, represented by two stars in the sky that today meet once a year in the sky. The star Vega, near the Milky Way (in Virgo), represents the weaver girl; on the other side of the Milky Way is Aquila, the shepherd boy. The lovers, who fell in love long ago, met once a year on the seventh day of the seventh month, to consummate their love and to help other lovers in the world become one. People in Japan and Korea write the names of their beloveds on fine parchment paper and tie the papers to trees and bushes for the stars to see.

July 13

CELEBRATION OF OUR LADY OF FÁTIMA (PORTUGUESE)

The universe is busy on this day. The Queen of Heaven appeared on this date to children in Portugal and gave them instructions to build in Fátima her shrine for the healing of the sick. It has been consistent with the miracles of the world, that Mary, the Mother of God is the one who comes back to help personally when the sickness is killing us. Our Lady of Fátima is celebrated in Portugal this day.

The festival of Demeter, also on this day, is from classical Greece and was celebrated with flower-garlanded processions, feasts of foods in season, and dancing barefoot on the good earth.

For Obon, this day's holiday in Japan, the folks remember the departed souls, who are believed to come back and mingle with the living today. So think of your loved ones who have been received back into the good earth, where the Goddess takes good care of them.

July 17

FESTIVAL OF AMATERASU-O-MI-KAMI (JAPANESE)

In Japan, this is the great festival of the Sun Goddess Amaterasu-o-Mi-Kami. The sun is the symbol of Japan, and street processions go on all day. We usually think of the female deity as being connected with the moon or stars, but the sun is often honored as a female deity. According to the Japanese legend, the Sun Goddess Amaterasu was saddened because of her brother's insensitivity. To show her sorrow she hid herself in a cave. As a result, darkness and great disasters fell on the earth. The remaining gods plotted to trick her into coming back out by staging a great party outside, laughing and carrying on. When the goddess attempted to find out what the merriment was all about, the gods captured her face in a mirror, fascinating her, and drew the goddess back into the world. What does this mean? If you are displeased with anything, confront it and do not hide, because passivity lends itself to trickery. Or perhaps it means that the sun must hide once in a while, so don't lose your cool over it.

July 19

THE MARRIAGE OF ISIS & OSIRIS (NORTH AFRICAN)

This is still the season to celebrate marriages, sexual unions, and commitments. As June was favorable for unions of a lasting nature, so is July. On this day we celebrate no less than the marriage of the Goddess of Love, Isis/Aphrodite, and her consort, Osiris/Adonis. Their holy sexual union has always meant good luck for natural folk. Under the rule of Cancer, kiss and make up and make commitments. The season ripens, summer is raging, go outdoors, make love beneath the stars, picnic, and carry on.

July 19 and 20

FIRST WOMEN'S RIGHTS CONVENTION IN THE UNITED STATES, 1848

On this day the most important love gift to both sexes was conceived—equality. The Goddess moved our sisters Susan B. Anthony and Elizabeth Cady Stanton to begin the liberation of women then at Seneca Falls. I made a reverent visit to this site and saw the giant oak tree they planted to witness their hope for the future. There is no doubt in my mind that with all that politicking, they instinctively called on the higher powers to fuel their struggle by planting the tree of sovereignty. Plant a tree today yourself in memory of them to inspire future generations. Read up about the American Women's Movement.

July 22

LA FÊTE DE LA MADELEINE (FRENCH)

There is an interesting myth about Mary Magdalene. On this day, women come from all over France to a holy cave in Provence, which was a traditional sacred place of the Goddess, her vulva in the earth, to ask her to find husbands for them. I think that here we have the ancient goddess of love and fertility performing the matchmaking for those French maidens.

July 23

SUN ENTERS LEO

Leo is the sign of the Lion. The woman in the sun, who is she? She is Leona, the female lion, she who hunts, she who rules. It is a very queenly sign. She is Sekhmet, the lioness-headed goddess from ancient Egypt. She is Cybele, whose carriage is drawn by lions. She is Freyja from the north, whose carriage is drawn by black cats or rams.

Cats in history have been closely connected to magic and the Goddess. Bast, the goddess of medicine and the arts, symbolized the kindly aspects of the sun, whereas Sekhmet was a goddess of war. The cat's image is on the sistrums (sacred rattles) found in the temples of Hathor, the Venus of the North Africans.

Black cats became hated by the Christians as symbols of witchcraft, exactly because they were held in such high esteem by the ancient religions of the Goddess. When the black plague was brought back to Europe from the Middle East by the Christian crusaders, the witches were blamed. They burned women and cats, as familiars of the witches, in great numbers. This killing of cats naturally increased the numbers of rats in the cities that carried the plague, so the madness continued. But the cat has returned. In China she is the symbol of good luck and good fortune. In the United States, she is the most beloved of all pets, in numbers exceeding those of dogs.

July 27

HATSHEPSUT'S DAY (EGYPTIAN)

Today we honor the great Queen Hatshepsut of Egypt (ca. 1490 B.C.), a remarkable ruler of the eighteenth dynasty who built incredible temples to the Goddess, who ruled without a consort, and who embodied the admirable qualities of a great queen incarnate. This strong-willed pharaoh's forte was the peaceful art of government. She was more interested in architecture and commerce than foreign conquest. Contemplate the significance of women as rulers. Support your local lady running for office, or why not consider it yourself? Send in your dues to women's organizations. They depend on you.

The July Story: Interview with the Goddess

AFTER MANY DAYS OF TRYING to get an appointment with the Queen of Heaven, there were signs, finally, that such an opportunity might be granted. For example, in my dream last night I saw a tall Amazon woman approaching me. Looking deeply into my eyes, she said, "Come this way; my boss wants to talk to you!" However, I was so frightened by this sudden success that I woke up, and the interview went to pieces. But now, just walking by Bay Street and College Avenue, I saw a young woman like the one in my dream. She was walking past me, and as she came closer, she did look into my eyes, but then looked away. She is probably still mad at me for waking up.

Tonight is the night. I prepared my altar so my bed was part of it. All around me were the tiny flames of candles all yellow and white, the colors that invoke her presence. Now I had a new problem: I knew I wouldn't be able to sleep at all—I like to sleep in complete darkness. My solution was to get really tired. I walked my four miles around Lake Merritt; I ate little so as not to go deep into sleep. My object was to enter that twilight zone where the consciousness can visit with spirits, the land of overlapping reality.

At first I felt happily floating, like becoming water, peaceful and fluid. My body dissolved like angel cookies in milk. It was gray and cozy; then I saw the Amazon coming toward me again. She was one of those women who work out regularly and build up their shoulders. She was taller than I remembered from the last time; this time I was ready for her. "My boss wants to talk to you!" she said matter-of-factly, just doing her job. "Yes ma'am!" I answered eagerly.

We walked past cities, and parks, and freeways. My Goddess! I thought, overlapping reality was getting to be modernized. I expected to see high snow-capped mountains. I expected to fly past scenes of the past, to see people dressed in flowing Grecian robes, but no. The Amazon didn't seem to care much if I followed her or not. She took a couple of turns and led me upstairs to a high-rise restaurant. I'd never been in this building, but I had seen it before; it always looked too ritzy for my budget. The elevator came, and we took it to the top floor without her even touching a button. There the door opened, and she led me to a booth where a middle-aged woman was sipping her water through a straw.

The woman lifted her face to me, and opened her eyes. Her eyes were the double image of the rolling world. Two globes, one showing Eurasia and the other the Americas, complete with clouds, were rolling slowly in her eye sockets. Yet she looked serenely beautiful. Her face was deeply sunburnt and slightly lined with laugh lines and a few crow's-feet. Her skin was swarthy; her body, full and generous. Her arms were strong.

"I was expecting you the other day," she started, with a voice like that of my own sweet mother's.

"I know, Your Highness, I am sorry." I felt a deep shame having made her wait for me.

"That's all right. I am not often interviewed. Have you got your questions ready?"

"Yes, ma'am."

"The last time I was interviewed, we called them trances. My priestesses would inhale the smoke from slabs of hashish they burned as offerings to me. I gave them answers, but they always forgot half of them by the time they were saying it back to the folks." She smiled, amused.

My heart was pounding in my chest so hard that I could see my blouse heaving up and down. "My first question is . . ."

"Just call me Hera."

"Yes, Hera; what does it mean that you are the Queen of Heaven? What are your duties, what do you do all day, how do you rule?"

"Oh, dear." She cast her eyes downward now, featuring the Southern Hemisphere. "I guess it all began when I gave birth to things. I was much younger then. I was bored. All that existed was my ability to create. Just that. Ability. So I started by creating photons and neutrinos, charged particles, electromagnetic waves, gases, small stuff. Giving birth to things delighted me, so I did a lot of this for a very long time. These creations took life from me and later created their own; they organized themselves into stars and nebulas and galaxies, exploded into supernovas and created new worlds. Nowadays I am not making anything new; the stuff that I made is more than enough already. Does this answer your question?"

"Yes, ma'am," I said obediently, "but what puzzles me is how come people always took you for a man?"

"Ahhh, that!" She closed her eyes and a little tear formed in the left eye as it turned Africa toward me. "That is just the newest attitude. My dear, people historically knew I was their mother; who else can give birth to the universe—a man??? When they die, they always call me Mother. Nobody ever dies saying 'Father,' did you know that?"

"What interests me most is why you allow the crimes against nature to take place. Why don't you come down hard on those who pollute your waters? Why don't you make earthquakes to sink big companies who violate your laws?"

"My dear, I would have to wipe out two million years' worth of evolution if I acted rashly." I could see she was not pleased with this question. The water in her glass was boiling now, although she was still sipping it.

"Look, there is a big difference between us. I am immortal; you are not. It is up to you who are not immortal to maintain your home, your planet. If you fail to do so, you will wipe yourselves out. There will be no big profits from a dead population. Eventually, you must take responsibility for your own survival. I have other jobs I cannot let slide. I am still making brand new earth with my volcanoes, for example. I have to adjust the temperature of the entire Earth each and every day so you don't freeze to death or fry. Do you think that's an easy job?"

"No, no, ma'am! I don't think that's easy at all."

"Your species will have to get used to Mother's rules." She continued, "I don't send down beloved sons or daughters to die for your sins; I don't use any cruelty against your own kind to save you. If you want a savior, you have one at the end of your own wrists."

I realized she was steaming quite a bit over this topic. I tried to calm things down. "Is the universe as you imagined it would be? I mean, when you created all those charged particles, did you ever think that human beings would walk the earth?"

She took a deep breath, and looked a little forlorn. She toyed with her straw. The water stopped boiling in her glass. "Please don't take this personally, but your species is not my most favorite of all. I really prefer your Dopplegängers. You know, the species that is also human but is in every way just the opposite of you. They live on the other side of this galaxy, and that's where I like to hang out. I come this way only for work."

"Dopplegängers? Humans, but the reverse of us? I thought we humans encompassed all."

"Hardly. Take my humans from the other side. Their highest value is to enhance life. They have no war business at all. All their resources are used in building a high quality of life for all."

"What about their security? Who defends them? Who saves them when they're in trouble?"

"Oh, they don't get into trouble, because they have no concept of the 'enemy.' They think they are all one happy family living on their happy planet."

"But isn't that unrealistic? They must be childish to assume all people are nice and friendly." She shook her head, and in her eyes the night sky was showing considerable meteorite showers.

"They even know about you here on this planet," she continued. "They include it in their prayers daily, saying, 'Thank you, Goddess, that you have not created me as one of those paranoid, fearful humans of the other side of the galaxy.'"

Now I started feeling really depressed. My throat was locking up and tears were pressuring my lower eyelids. She noticed. She lifted my chin with her warm hands and spat into my eyes like a snake. I felt warm happy feelings spread about my brain as my skin absorbed her fluid.

"Thank you," I said, "I needed that."

"That's all right." She was playing down her help.

"How do you do that? You spit something magical on me, and I feel better. What is it?"

"Euphoric saliva . . . my own. I exist in a state of happiness. All my parts cause happiness in others. The spit is just the fastest way to cheer you up."

"Thank you. Let's talk about happiness. What is it?"

"Happiness is your own creation. When you are in balance within yourself and not divided by self-hate and self-loathing, when you love your life and who you are, you create happiness. It is an ongoing process." Both of her eyes were now totally dark; nighttime has fallen over half of the world.

"What about love? Love brings ecstasy and also pain. Did you design it this way?"

The goddess thought long and hard about this. "I designed love to bring me together with everybody. It is my personal calling card. I programmed it into your genes, into your hormones, to make sure you will never be able to get away from it. As long as you need love to survive, love will be around and will be experienced. But if you ever learn how to suppress love within your nature, as humans often try to do, you will know no happiness."

Then she added, "It is true that I bring you pain when I leave you. The pain of knowing that, however, is what humanizes you and continues to temper your hatred toward each other. Love is not a yoke. Love is the point. Love is my gift. My other humans live for love. They worship love as they worship me. They devote weeklong festivals and celebrations to it. Nobody speaks ill of love; that's a capital crime. Offenders are sentenced to take a sitz bath in my spit."

"Goddess, I want to move over to the other side of the galaxy. Is there anything like relocation allowed?"

"There have been no known cases of relocation. If you were to go, I would have to let millions of other humans emigrate also. This planet would fall to the forces of death and false prophets. You are the reason this planet has a future in the first place."

"What do you mean, false prophets?"

"I mean those men who are waiting for the world to end. Those leaders who think that Armageddon is near and that they have no responsibilities anymore—that a savior will come and fix things up. But I have long-term plans for this blue planet. If your species cannot survive itself and the bad dreams it learned from its prophets, I will turn this planet over to another species—a more peaceful and positive one."

"Cockroaches?"

"Cockroaches . . . why not? They are much older than humans!" The goddess started laughing. This idea of insects taking over our proud world made her giddy—a cosmic joke. She gave a final giggle and fell silent.

"Don't worry," she continued, "life will go on. I promise you that."

"But what would you have us do? I mean, we don't want to self-destruct. There are a lot of people who love you on this planet. What is your advice to us?"

"Look . . . it's quite simple." She leaned forward and her eyes showed the blue of the skies encircling Antarctica. "Life is a process. I take care of the beginning, and I take care of the end. You will all die, and I will ask no questions about what book you read to get religion. So, your challenge is to fill in the time in between, the time between birth and death. Fill it up with some good living and loving. Fill it up with giving and taking. Fill it up with responsibilities and power. Now, is that too much to ask?"

"Yes, but . . . w-w-what about the purpose of life?" I stuttered.

"What purpose? I just detailed it for you. Were you not listening?"

"How about transcendence? Isn't that what we should work for?"

"Transcendence? Do you mean denying yourself food so that you can have visions of me flying around with you in trance? Go ahead, if you like. Do you mean denying yourself earthly pleasures for some big payoff at the end, after death? I give the same payoff to all my dead people—eternal peace. It is a good gift. I don't ask you if you loved too much. I may ask you if you hurt some people, but I forgive all equally. I have no hell and no heaven. Believe it or not, I run an egalitarian ship."

"Then there is no point in transcending life."

"As long as you are alive, it is pointless. When you die, you automatically transcend, if that's what your desire is. You get a good long sleep after death. You get to wake up whenever you like. You get to watch your relatives live their lives to the end and to help them with the crossover. But if you get bored, you may want to be reborn again. Just come and talk to me. I'll help you choose a new mother and a new destiny."

"Is that the time when I can get relocated to the doppelgänger planet?"

The goddess smiled. "Sure. That would be the appropriate time."

I felt quite happy now. It wasn't a bad deal; she was fair, she was on the job. I didn't get the impression that this goddess was complacent or mean. She was a working mother. She had her own agenda, but she has not ruled us out. She laid down the laws, and those laws had to be obeyed.

"One last question, ma'am, a little personal. How do you relax? What do you do for a vacation?"

The goddess finished her glass of water, which now emitted a sulfurous smell and looked a little yellow. "I have been toying

with small particles again, you know, little ones, like the ones I played with at the beginning, when I first created the universe. They fascinate me. I like to fool around and make things happen, experiment."

"You mean you have a hobby, you are making new worlds again?"

"I don't want to run ahead of myself, but I think I want to duplicate myself—not just parts of me, but my whole being—to see if I can. I also search for myself.

"Do you know when I felt like this before?" she asked now.

"Hmmm?"

"I felt like this before when I created my male counterpart, my Pan. Who shall it be this time? My twin?"

"I thought that's what you were aiming for. I would love to see that, too."

"I'll let you know. Something cosmic is happening. It may take two of us to keep things together."

"Could you make sure one of you visits here often, please? We are badly in need of supervision from the Goddess."

"You worry too much," said the goddess. "Go home, now, and live. I'll see you soon enough."

The Amazon woman appeared again and silently took me to the elevator. I decided to address her; after all, I had been interviewing the Force of Life all afternoon. I should not be too timid to talk to her assistant.

"She is going to create another one of herself," I told her.

"Hera likes creativity," she said simply, without being fazed.

"What about you?" I pressed on. "Who are you? What is the purpose of your life?"

The Amazon turned to me, revealing her strong body that knew no shame. "I am alive and living in Buffalo, New York. I have a job teaching disabled children how to use their bodies. At night, I take classes at the nearby university, in women's studies. I have been active for the environment; I teach courses in self-esteem; I lead women's groups. Otherwise I serve the Queen of Heaven in whatever is necessary at the time. I hope you pleased her."

"But I thought you were a spirit like her."

"Oh, yes. I was created when she needed relaxation and attempted to create another one of herself."

"So she did . . ." I completed her thoughts. I could dissolve again into my weightlessness. The Amazon left an address where I could reach her if I needed anything.

My feelings were of hope and more hope, and on awakening, I realized that the skies were filled with clouds and it was about to rain. I could still see her eternal eyes—what they must have looked like as the two globes turned around and around, laced with the gray streaks of the coming storms.

August

THE GODDESS SPEAKS

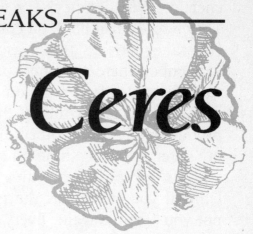

Ceres

YOUR MESSAGE WAS HIDDEN IN the middle of an apple this month. Did you find it? Did you see my clever design, the five-pointed star hidden inside its flesh? I love designing my foods as I grow them. Have you observed my barley? I have hidden in it all the vitamins and minerals your body requires. I also gave it that cute cunt shape so that you would enjoy eating lots of it. Did you chuckle at my cleverness? How about my wheat and corn? Thank you for your sacrifices of freshly baked bread on my altars—so sweet of you! The glass of wine next to it is just the right touch; you know how I love to dunk my bread into ruby red wine.

Yes, this is Demeter, the Earth Mother herself. You may think I just look pretty in photographs, that I cannot speak to you or lead you to me. Ahhh . . . of course I can. I am the only Goddess who knows where in space we are at all times. My mantle is the universe. Darkness is my sensor, set on eternity, and my life is bound together with yours. I nourished you, developed you. What do you say?

I wonder why you are so obsessed with the concept of

enemies. Who are they? The folks on the other side of my body? They wrote a bad book on communism that you hate. For heaven's sake, kids, is that reason enough to blow us both up? Remember, there are other species that will perish too. But I am warning you, life can go on with just insects and mice, even through a nuclear winter. If that happens, I will have a rest from producing the fruits you eat. I can grow nothing if you don't let my sister, the sun, shine on all my seedlings.

And you, sister, sitting there thinking this isn't your problem—if you say it was the men who made the nuclear mess, not you—think again. Every day that you are not working for me, you are allowing destruction to be forged in your name. Women must act as my activists. For you, nurturing is automatic, but it is not so instinctive to take the power and responsibility for the world that go with it. Learn it, sister, learn power fast.

Mothers—all children are your children. All hunger is yours to feed. As I receive your homage, you must receive my warning. I am Earth, the most ancient of prophets, and I say, "Women, rise and unite and use your powers together to save Earth, your mother, me." I'm telling you, it's not too late. I love you, but your ticket to live on my back is not guaranteed. Cleanse your mind from the hatred of the "us" versus "them." Cleanse your mind from believing that any one of you has got "The Answer" or "The Religion" of salvation.

You were all born saved, in case you were wondering! Suffering on Earth is all your doing. I, the God, have created all the cures, along with all the ills. You need only to look and find them. My body, the blue planet, is the only Holy Book you need to study for your well-being; its natural laws, the only set of laws to follow. The rest are your fantasies; don't blame me for them!

I have given your kind two million years to develop and learn how to fit into my holy world. Yet, you still fight me like an adolescent who needs to rebel. Would you grow up already?!! You are on the verge of global suicide! I wish you well as I feed you, but if your self-hatred, sin/guilt thinking, and love for destruction is what you are manifesting, I'll have to let you go.

Mothers must be wise. I yearn to share with you my infinity and wisdom in eternity. There is so much beauty yet to create. Won't you take more responsibility to protect me, your home? Say yes to living, say yes to life. I really want to embrace you again in my paradise.

August's Aspects

This month received its name from the oracular Juno Augusta. The term *augur* was later applied to priests, and *august* to the Roman emperors. An august person was filled with the spirit of the Goddess (the Holy Spirit). To augur means to prophesy, to see, to increase.

Full moon aspect: Barley moon

Universal event: Lammas (Loaf mass), the festival of the bread

Communal event: Festivals to honor the food

Message: To gather, to appreciate, to nurture

Activity: Concentrated wisdom, meditation

Healing properties: Awareness of time and patience

Appropriate spells: Any that deal with higher awareness—spells for wisdom, learning secrets, learning truth, prophesy, psychic development, astral travel, better interpersonal relationships, nonpossessiveness, trust

Color: Yellow

Tree: Hazel

Flower: Poppy, gladiolus

Creature: Crane

Gem: Sardonyx, peridot

Anna's Spells, Rituals, & Celebrations for August

SPELL TO INCREASE YOUR BUSINESS

It may not feel like the yuppie thing to do, to go back to Cro-Magnon times and behave like our foremothers and forefathers, but the universe has not changed all that much. The herbs are still here, thank heaven, and we still have the same need for favorable winds to blow at our backs.

Gather together these herbs: *Echinacea, augustifolia,* cubeb berries, and yellow dock. Mix a little of each into some sandalwood powder and burn some each morning and each night on charcoal, saying:

> *Augusta, Increaser, make my business grow as you grow your best corn! I am doing business in the universe, and I am willing and ready to receive your wealth.*

If you don't have time to gather the herbs and burn them every day, just do this ritual once a month under the full moon. Your business will flourish.

SPELL FOR HEALTH & AGAINST ACCIDENTS

There is an herb called feverfew that, when brewed as a tea and taken warm once a week in the morning, will keep one healthy. How about that! It is said to alleviate fevers, hence its name. If you carry a little of this herb in a red flannel bag, it acts as a protection against all harm.

SPELL TO SEE VISIONS

This spell may tax the most ambitious among you. But here it is. Gather together the following: sandalwood incense, anise seeds, myrtle, and Indian hemp. The true Indian hemp is illegal in this country, but you can obtain a kind that is called Indian hemp that is not marijuana and that is legal (although the real thing would work even better). Mix three pinches of each into a handful of frankincense and myrrh; work it into a good smooth mix with your mortar and pestle. Feeling Cro-Magnon yet? Burn a little of this before meditating or retiring to bed. In your dreams, visions will come. When you see unusual beings or animals, do not be afraid of them. Ask them for their blessings, no matter how frightening they might seem. This makes all visions friendly. You might even ask them heavy-duty questions about life and death, but be prepared to receive their answers.

SPELL TO END HATRED BETWEEN TWO PEOPLE

Locate an herb called ironweed. Soak a teaspoonful of ironweed in a quart of whiskey for seven days. Strain the vegetable matter out, and arrange for the two people who are at odds to drink your doctored brew. You could drop a little of it into tea, coffee, cocktails, or soft drinks. They will soon forget their differences.

THE HOLIDAYS

We will see an abundance of the holidays of the Blessed Virgin in this month under the constellation of Virgo.

August 1

LAMMAS: FESTIVAL OF THE NEW BREAD (CELTIC)

Lammas (Old English "Loaf Mass") is a festival of regeneration dedicated to the inventors of agriculture. Women and men celebrate the Goddess as the source of life and offer her the first ears of corn. In Hungary, public tables, on which are placed lovely new loaves of white bread and glasses of wine, are set up on the crossroads.

The festival is connected with the movement of the soul between the worlds. Our Lady of the Gates is the goddess who guides our souls from one life to the next. This is one of the witches' high holidays, opposite the feast of Brigid on the wheel of life.

August is the month of fulfillment, the first harvest of the year, and the manifestation of abundance. Since anthropologists believe women invented agriculture, this is a very feminine festival. The planting of the seeds and harvesting of the grain is a wondrous achievement. History changed when woman planted the first seedlings.

August 1

GREEN CORN CEREMONY (NATIVE AMERICAN)

Rituals such as the green corn ceremony were characteristic of Native American harvest festivals, during which certain tribes of the South, notably the Creek, gave thanks for their plentiful harvest and beseeched the gods for continued prosperity. This joyful celebration was held each summer when the roasting corn ears were ripe enough to eat.

Among the Hopi, who use corn pollen and corn meal extensively in their rituals, the corn mother is represented by "a perfect ear of corn whose tip ends in four full kernels."* She is not only present at what are called "maize festivals," but also at childbirth, standing there for the Mother Goddess herself.

August 2

LAMMAS (CELTIC)

The old festival of Lammas has a special meaning for witches. It is the cross-quarter holiday commemorating the miracle of rebirth, the everlasting grace that follows when the Goddess is remembered properly with gifts of the harvest—corn, apples, grapes—and with feasting. The county fairs with their competitions for the largest zucchinis or pumpkins are all remnants of the ancient celebrations of prosperity and the wealth of the earth.

---

*Ake Hultkranz, "The Religion of the Goddess in North America," in *The Book of the Goddess*, ed. by Carl Olson (New York: Crossroad, 1985), 212.

August 2

FEAST OF THE VIRGIN OF THE ANGELS (CENTRAL AMERICAN)

The Virgin of the Angels is the patroness of Costa Rica. This is a national holiday giving the Lady her due with a pilgrimage to the basilica in Cartago, the site of a black stone called "La Negrita," the Dark One.

August 4

FEAST OF THE BLESSED VIRGIN MARY (EUROPEAN)

The Lady has a habit of reinstating her own ancient pagan temples and holydays through miracles. If your background is Catholic, celebrate her freely, for she is the Christianized Great Goddess of pagan times, despite her status as a nondeity. Make a big feast and crown all the women and girls as the manifestations of the Lady.

August 8

TIJ DAY (NEPALESE)

This is Women's Day in Nepal, when women stop working and celebrate themselves as the Goddess. What a good idea!

August 13

FESTIVAL OF DIANA & HECATE (ROMAN)

On this day, women of Rome whose prayers had been answered held a torchlight procession to the temples of Diana and Hecate, the triple goddess in her bountiful aspect. The harvest ripens earlier in the warmer countries, and this was the crucial time when farmers would either gather in a good harvest or lose it all to hail and early storms. This was such an important holiday that the Christians had to rename it, dedicate it to the Assumption of Mary, and continue the festivities as usual.

While Diana was the soul of nature who protected the living and the young, Hecate also protected the dead souls, or those who were about to enter the realms of the dead. She was worshipped at the crossroads. Hecate was pictured with two torches in her hand, one pointing to the earth and the other to the heavens. The meaning of this was, as above so below—the ancient wisdom of reality. This is what transforms the practice of religion into a political act. As we imagine heaven to be, so we will try to arrange earthly affairs. If we accept a wrathful father as God, we will accept wars and punishments from men on earth. If we insist that God is a mother, we will mother the world we live in.

Give a party honoring your friendships with women today. Light fires of loyalty in the form of candles. Discuss your lives; maybe use the evening to read fortunes (Tarot, runes, I Ching, and so on) for each other. On your altar, offer apples to Diana and a garlic bulb to Hecate, the Witch Queen.

August 15

BIRTHDAY OF ISIS (NORTH AFRICAN)

The Goddess Isis was said to have been born on this day, which is also called the Festival of Lights or the Blessing of the Boats. In her temples in Egypt, many candles and lights were lit in celebration of her life-giving powers. If you own a boat or are about to travel on the sea, take a little incense and encircle the smoke within your boat (frankincense and myrrh are traditional). Bless your property with this incense, and yourself as well, in the name of Isis of the Sea.

August 20

SUN ENTERS VIRGO

Virgo is the sign of the Virgin. The constellation Virgo rises into view in the northern skies. This is one of the biggest constellations in our solar system. It's the time to make wishes on shooting stars, a time of vacations and heat waves, the grain harvest, baking fresh bread. This is the only constellation whose symbol is a human woman. She is pictured gathering grain or holding a sheaf of wheat. The age of Virgo is said to be the time when women invented agriculture and developed grain with the help of the Goddess Ceres, the Roman counterpart of the Greek Demeter.

August 23

VULCANALIA (ROMAN)

Vulcanalia is the fire festival in which the Goddesses Juturna (goddess of fountains) and Stata Mater (the goddess who puts out conflagrations) were invoked along with Vulcan in order to control his fires.

This day is also an important one for Moira, the goddess of personal fate. Today we consider the direction of our lives. Moira drew all things and people together to honor her with meditations and incense. People used this time to take a good look at their souls. Don't confuse it with guilt, however—guilt is an acquired weakness.

If you live in fire hazard areas, it is a good idea to observe the holiday of these protective goddesses. Take a small bottle of good brandy and pour it on the ground around your house clockwise, all the while asking the goddesses of Vulcanalia to keep destructive fires away from your home.

August 24

MUNDUS CERERIS (EUROPEAN)

We honor the Goddess Ceres. Three times a year, the ritual pit (the *mundus*) representing the underworld was symbolically opened for three days to allow the souls of the dead to come out and visit with the living. While the *mundus* was open and the spirits were being allowed to roam the cities, no regular business was conducted. Plant something in the good earth today.

August 25

OPECONSIVA (ROMAN)

This is the first holiday of the Goddess Ops, Lady Bountiful. On her altars flowers and wine and fresh-baked bread were displayed. This is the standard altar for the Goddess in many religions, even today. Ops is the planter and reaper. However, you can honor her today by going outside and touching the earth, saying these words:

Ops of the earth, planter and reaper, plant for me a long life. Plant for me a happy life. Reap, Ops, the plenty of your blessings.

August 26

ILMATAR'S FEAST DAY (FINNISH)

This was the festival of Ilmatar, the Water Mother, the Creatrix of the World. She brooded on the waters and laid six golden eggs and one iron egg; from this she created the world. The Finns celebrate her as the Great Mother of the Cosmos. On this day they eat special foods and dance and stay up all night. Here is how Ilmatar created the world:

Oldest of all women,
Loveliest of all women,
First of all mothers
Then formed the pillars
That held the sky in place,
And upon the rocky cliffs
She engraved the forms and figures.
Still Ilmatar remained in the ocean waters,
Owner of powers too numerous to count,
Possessor of magic too deep to comprehend
And perhaps she lives there still. *

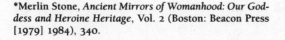

*Merlin Stone, *Ancient Mirrors of Womanhood: Our Goddess and Heroine Heritage*, Vol. 2 (Boston: Beacon Press [1979] 1984), 340.

The August Story:
Spiritualizing Michigan

M Y EXCITING TRIP TO THE thirteenth Michigan Womyn's Music Festival is in process, and I am at the Grand Rapids airport, wondering what's next. I am apprehensive, sweaty, and sleepy, since I flew in on the red-eye special from Oakland, departure time 4:45 A.M. This small suffering is part of the price of entry into this utopian woman's country. But I can tell I'm not the only one in a state of exhaustion. I can see other women sitting on top of their piles of luggage, reading or talking, waiting for the bus to take us to the land.

I am not quite sure what I'm supposed to be doing. It's been ten years since my last adventure at this event. My bags, my tent and sleeping bag, and some groundcloths have been spat out by the long twirling tongue of the rotating luggage claim machine. I collect them triumphantly; everything arrived! I walk into the sweltering heat outside to check on the rumor that our buses have arrived, and indeed, there they are—two huge buses, ready to take in all the women with their lawn chairs and portable hibachis. This is indeed the great American women's tradition by now; it is advertised very little, by direct mail mostly, but women show up for the festival from every corner of the earth.

I get a seat in the performers' bus, an unexpected blessing. The air conditioner is working, and I begin to feel normal again. I am keenly aware of my new improved status as a "worker." Back in the early seventies, workshop givers were not considered or treated like staff workers. We were let in free, and that's where the privileges stopped. I remember days when I couldn't eat because by the time I had time, there was no more food left. Women would ask me questions about rituals and spells, and I missed mealtimes because I was chatting with them.

For the next hour and a half, many things cross my mind, especially how time flies and how things have changed. One of my fellow passengers is a friend's young daughter, comely in her budding womanhood, raised free in the woman's community and sixteen years old. I remember her much younger. She makes me realize how much time has gone by and the length of my voluntary self-exile from woman's land in Michigan. When I last was here, pop stars ruled, and goddess blessings were not permitted to be made from their main altar, the night stage. Thousands and thousands of women were tenting, living, eating, making love, and learning together, and no blessing was ever pronounced on them. The priestess in me was outraged, so I vowed to come three years in a row to plant the seeds of the goddess movement. But after that, I vowed not to return until the festival got more spiritualized.

"Every time a few men gather together, another man appears and blesses them," I argued. "Why do you think men always bless their events, pledge allegiance, have a ceremony before a sports event even? Because it is empowering, that's why. Why can you not see that a blessing from the stage before any music begins would enhance the evening, give it class, heighten self-esteem of those present, and maybe even help us get nice weather for the weekend, as Mother Nature blesses us?"

The organizers didn't hear me back then. I never got to tell them about my ideas in person, because they didn't return my phone calls. I was seen as too demanding. I asked mutual friends, friends of friends, and finally performers to get the message to the leadership. The collective always listened to performers. Finally, the answer came. "No. There are too many atheists out there," was the reason they gave. "We cannot let the representative of any one religion on stage, because then all kinds of religious representatives would want to do the same." I looked long and hard at that letter. I didn't think there was anything wrong with members of many different traditions blessing the women. Imagine women rabbis and Protestant ministers along with witches and Brujas and Yoruba priestesses blessing the women in a ceremony. Why not?

I came to Michigan three years in a row, as if I were doing a spell, to accomplish this one goal—to spiritualize Michigan. For three consecutive years, I paid my own round-trip fare from California for the fifth, sixth, and seventh annual Michigan festivals. I knew that the women "out there" were not atheists. The people who supported the festival from the start were the spiritual community, who also happened to be the music lovers and nature lovers. You could already see goddess images on everything, from the ceramics of the artisans to T-shirts and buttons and jewelry. But it was just beginning.

I brought along copies of *The Holy Book of Women's Mysteries*, the very first book on the Goddess and how to call on her in our lives.* It was published by my coven. No "real" publisher would touch it—it was too radical, full of spells and mysterious doings under the full moon. I dragged my books in a green plastic bag across the grass to the workshops. Women bought the book as if it were food for the hungry, and it was.

There is something so good about time, I thought to myself on the bus. She can do what few of us can—make people change. She can make generations wake up and act with power. There are always women and men who are living in the future before the rest of us get there. Those are the pioneers, the inventors, the originators of new social customs and belief systems. In the seventies and eighties, I was such a pioneer.

Now we gather in Michigan, nine years later. The land is unfolding gently past the bus windows, like a movie. Farmers are selling raspberries and blueberries on the road. I yearn to stop and get some, but we are behind schedule. We're almost there now, and I'm thinking of my friend Rhiannon, from California. We had celebrated a few full moons together three years ago in Tilden Park. One night she said, "You know Z, my act is going to be the very first one on the night stage in Michigan this year. I can do whatever I want." Immediately, I thought of my project to spiritualize Michigan. By now, I had given up on it. It had gone on for too long without the Goddess being acknowledged. I had no communication with the present leaders. But hope eternally rises, and I looked at Rhiannon, almost believing again.

"Would you do it, Rhiannon? Would you do an official opening blessing?" "I sure would," she grinned. Rhiannon had always been a priestess. Even before she acknowledged it herself,

*Z. E. Budapest, *The Holy Book of Women's Mysteries*, 2d ed. (Berkeley: Wingbow, 1989).

I saw it in her. "It really should be you, Z." Rhiannon was reading my heart. "I admire you for being able to step aside and let somebody else realize your dream." There is nothing as powerful as recognition of your feelings from a friend you respect.

But I was just as happy that it was going to get done at last. It was embarrassing to me that I had been able to give the goddess tradition to straight women but not to lesbians. Most lesbians pretended that they didn't need the Goddess; it was just another religion, and religions have hurt lesbians all through history. Privately, at the grass-roots level, they often turned to her worship joyously, but larger, mainstream, more visible gatherings of lesbians avoided recognizing the spiritual dimension of the women's culture. But now it was going to happen. Rhiannon was going to call down the powers and transform the Michigan Womyn's Music Festival forever.

I didn't go that year, but even before I was told all the stories, I could see it so clearly—At the festival, the entire audience of seven or eight thousand women burst into tears of joy and jubilation during the goddess invocation and procession. A teary mass homecoming happiness enfolded the women when the Goddess was finally acknowledged; the deep hunger was assuaged as the daughters of the divine life giver were finally, for a time, satisfied. There is something to having this be a public, not just a private, experience. It has more meaning, this mass experience. No longer the orphans of society, discarded and labeled as loathsome sinners and untouchables by the patriarchal gods, lesbians finally could experience the feeling of being sanctified women. Like stars, loving like the goddesses, they would rise in ecstasy as Rhiannon, with her shamanic singing. Like the warm heartbeat of the audience, she invoked the four corners of the universe and asked the blessings to come on all. I saw a carved, wooden statue of Diana brought through the crowds by the women in the procession, while Edwina Lee Tyler, the best drummer in the world, elflike, followed in the religious ecstasy she always seems to have when she strokes her drums into a prayer to the universe. It was a wonderful and heady night. I visited that night often, years before it actually took place. I knew it was done and it was done well.

"Z, why is this so important to you?" I was asked sometimes when I described this project to others. "Because the true strength of any revolution is spiritual strength. Because women have a rich heritage to reclaim, a cosmology to create, which can empower us." On a personal level, just before my first visit to the

Michigan festival, I had been arrested and tried in court for reading Tarot cards for an undercover policewoman. Where I lived, the L.A. Police Department kept current photo files on all the psychics in the area, especially the feminist ones.

And now we have arrived at the festival, three years after the first blessing by Rhiannon. What is the reality going to be? Ever since I came on the land I have heard women laughing. The laughter never stops. One group takes up the laughter and passes it on to the next, completely instinctively, I am sure. It fills the air. I hear women laughing before I fall asleep and the first thing in the morning when I wake. It reminds me of heaven.

I get lots of recognition. "Welcome back, Z!" Women greet me like a wanderer. "I'm so glad you're here!" Boo, coproducer of the festival, greets me in the hot showers. We look at each other; we have both aged well. She is radiant; I am wet from my shower and feeling great. "Thank you, Boo." "Welcome to the land!" says Lisa, who started the festival thirteen years ago, when she was only nineteen years old. I feel like a returning matriarch coming back into the future, where I had gone alone ten years earlier. This annual musical event has been to the growing women's movement what the Haight Ashbury phenomenon was to the sixties. It helped our revolutionary concepts jell, making us identify the different oppressions we as women had to work on—internalized sexism, racism, classism, self-hatred, the works. And it gave us a golden chance to get down and boogie!

In my tent, I open my brochure for this year's events and read the incredibly long lists of concerns we are now addressing. A dazzling inventory of feminist sensitivities unfolds. Women's music on the land is the first tenet of this credo; no males are allowed to enter here, not even their voices on tape. This is to ensure psychic separation from the overwhelming male culture in the "fake" world. To women who live constantly in the patriarchal world, this may sound absurd, but just once in your life, challenge yourself to abide in an all-female energy environment, to read no male writers, to listen to no male voices, to pray to no male gods. An incredible flowering of your own energy occurs.

The festival goers—the festies—are coming; they are pouring in. The land fills up with tents as if invisible elves have put them up. The tents are brown and yellow, rainbow and blue,

tall and small. There is always a hushing wind in the trees, sighing and heaving deeply as you wake beneath them. It helps with the heat.

On opening night, Nan Brooks, dressed in a flowing purple robe and bearing the staff of a summoner, greets the crowds and puts out the first Goddess vibes. She makes no passionate invocation, no prayer that raises power in the audience; she leaves that to the musicians. Gently she explains that our names, the names of women, come from Goddess's names and that they all mean wisdom. She has the audience, which has swelled to five thousand souls, repeat the names—Sophia, Ma'at, Mary, Anat, Ishtar, Inanna—and then their own names along with the sacred names. It works well, the women are reminded that they are inheritors of a distant past, and their self-images incorporate this past glory.

Brooke Medicine Eagle is dressed as a Native American priestess. She blows on her eagle-bone whistle and invokes the four corners of the universe with a song by Kate Wolf. Brooke's voice is beautifully resonant and deep; it easily glides over our heads and envelops us in her reverence. All goes well, until she comes to the quarter of the north, and there she does the unthinkable. She invokes Grandfather Sky, the spirit of the fire.

Suddenly there are hisses and boos from the otherwise-cooperative audience, and I see many women who were in the ritual begin to sit down and get angry. The taboo has been broken! No men on the land! Not even in a prayer. Brooke, who is straight, didn't really know, and nobody told her to make changes in her song.

Now my "daughters" are up in arms. They come to me to complain. "Z, what can we do? She invoked a male god!" I am relaxed—not quite as bothered about it as they are. It is hard to maintain a pure female consciousness, isn't it? However unwittingly, we have been reminded of our own denial of the Goddess for so many centuries.

To give the Goddess her own space, especially for lesbians, isn't easy. All through the festival, I will be hearing women discuss the importance of controlling what has been identified at the festival's opening blessing as our spiritual experience. They are all involved; the old denial has been taken over by a new sense of responsibility.

But for the moment, all wounds are healed when Rhiannon sings her shamanic moving song, "Spirit Healer," which more than makes up for Brooke's slip. To make it even better, she also sings a song traditionally done by Maxine Feldman, "Amazon Women, Rise!," which is enough to gladden any historically proud lesbian's heart. The song certainly does something magical to me. It brings tears to my eyes, hope to my heart; I can see the future when I hear in the song that Amazon women must rise or nobody else will. Peace returns to the audience. The women are laughing and giggling again. This is their own space. Validated by their own history and mythology, they feel their power. The evening dissolves into dancing under the stars.

The next day I have to choose from more workshops to attend. What shall it be—Asian Pacific Lesbians; Women Filmmakers Today; Daughters of Holocaust Survivors; African Dance,

Drumming, and Songs; Real vs. Ageist Aging; Feminist Wicca Philosophy (taught by somebody I don't even know!)? My own workshop is on a brand-new topic, European shamanism.

We gather under the whispering trees, about two hundred and fifty women, scattered on the grass. Only a few are my age; most of the women are from a new generation. The Grandmother of Time must be hiding those ladies with white hair; I hardly see them among the audience. This always frightens me. Don't they go out anymore? I begin to talk about a time when white people were not Christianized and we lived in tribes all over—in the great forests in Europe and Asia. In this distant time, we loved the she-wolf as our role model and totem animal for bonding in tribes. The she-wolf was the key to our survival. We emulated the wolf's compassion toward the young and the weak and sick. We emulated the wolf's resolve to follow a single strategy when hunting. We told stories to our children about how she-wolves rescued humans from exposure and brought them up as their own. Europe is filled with such stories, which have survived even in modern times.

"What kind of system did they follow? The path of the gray she-wolf?" they ask, intrigued. "How do you get your information, Z?" They are testing my sources. "Where do I find out more about this?" They hunger for more. The spiritual hunger in women that I had sensed before is still there, as familiar to me now as an old hound. I stroke its head and scratch its ears; I feel needed again. I lean back and let the sun bake my shoulders; my white priestess gown is rolled down. The faces around me are turned upward with grace and interest. I go on and on about the Path. I love to teach.

Later in the program feminist spirituality and the more recent New Age spirituality come to clash. Melissa challenged some New Ager workshop leaders who were telling women that they always create their own reality. She asked them if abused children created their own abuse. The New Age teacher had no answers, of course. One of them, however, ventured to say that maybe the child had some issues to work through this lifetime. Fury erupted like a volcano in response to that. "You are blaming the victim!" the women shouted. This is a hot topic; the New Age influence on feminist spirituality is blocked with all of our political savvy.

"Do South Africa's blacks create their own apartheid? Are blacks to blame? Do we blame the victim?" Many voices mingle as the ideas get brought up and argued.

"We create our reality to a degree; there is some small truth in this, but this karma business from India is not to be trusted," says another woman.

"Look at the status of women in that country, where the karma philosophy comes from. Is ritual clitoridectomy the fault of the little six-year-old girls it is directed against?"

"I don't care what new good stuff came along in the sixties about spirituality, I take it all with a grain of salt. I like the vegetarian food, I like the yoga exercises, I like burning incense and practicing meditation, but I don't buy the rest!"

"Good!" I am thinking to myself. "This is great! This is what developing our own spirituality is all about. Question everything. Challenge everything."

You create your own destiny when you are true to yourself, when you strive to reach your dreams, yes. But if a woman is raped on the streets, was that her karma? No way! That was not her fault; she didn't create patriarchy and woman hating!

Suddenly there is consensus. No women and children and blacks and Native Americans and oppressed peoples in general are the creators of their own oppression. We create societies together, and it is the fault of those who perpetrate the crimes. No victims shall be blamed here. Women learned this long ago. The New Age teachers have to grow with us and give up their preset ideas; they are a little bewildered by the reception they are getting. No automatic obedience here, no unquestioning bowing down and assuming guilt. The Amazons are not in the mood to support anybody's oppression by blaming the victims.

We ferment the new ideas; we argue the old ones, we struggle, we grow, and we gather women friends like a rich harvest. We also make out in the shade—those who are lucky because the goddess of love is playing with them. New couples who just fell in love are all over, and you can see the women practically lighting up the dark with their own loving. The rest of us measure our loving by the kisses we get from friends, and bless our starry nights with a good sleep undisturbed. All of it is wrapped up in the sound of laughter, which, like music, is always around us in this rare and special woman/land/space. This moment in time is ours, this five days in the calendar of August snatched from patriarchy, annually and triumphantly and with the summer's high passion.

September

THE GODDESS SPEAKS

The Muse

HAVE YOU FELT THE HAND OF THE Creator touch your soul as you gaze upon my colors in the autumn? Have you felt a poem forming on the tip of your tongue, or has the urge to dance come over you? Did I challenge you to a creative act—such as giving a speech—or invention—maybe some lovely prose or a drama? Have you ever wanted to be on stage?

If yes, it is I who rule your heart, I am the Muse. My powers of inspiration are manifold, not just nine. I appreciate it when a child of mine begins to enrich human culture with originality. I delight in that which is new and entertaining, because I am the greatest artist of all. I am the sculptress of the translucent crystal clusters and the designer of rocks. I painted the malachite green and the pearl silvery. It was my hand that dipped the ruby red and copied turquoise from the color of the sky. I carved the mountains into shapes of pyramids with snowy peaks, my winds made mounds and caves, my waters deepened valleys. Even the flight of birds and the lumbering walk of elephants has been choreographed by me. It was a challenge to make tall giraffes graceful, but I have solved that artistic problem too.

I have hidden art in everything. In the act of creating art, you worship me. I will respond to you if you ask for my assistance. I'll come in the middle of the night if you are finishing a play on deadline. I am in the studio if you are sculpting a statue. All art proceeds from me. I am the true occupation of your species. You are all supposed to be creative and fill your hearts with beauty. What nonsense to waste consciousness on war! If there were enough creativity in the world, you would live as artists, and the jobs you hate today would be replaced by better ones.

I look at your wars and often cry. It's not good to make your Muse cry. Don't forget; I feed your inner selves after your bodies have been nourished. I am the part of you that goes on to survive and take other forms. I am your invisible humanity, the divine spark you have been given to use, the light with which you shine. I am the truth as you perceive it. I am the teacher of higher goals.

Why don't you visit me more often? What are you saving yourself for? Security is an illusion, for nobody is ever secure in the world. Death may come any time, whether it rescues you from your misery or stops you in ecstasy, there is nothing to lose. Free your weary hands and be creative, look at nature all around you, and receive inspiration from me. Now, in the season when I paint the leaves those brilliant autumn yellows and crimsons, don't you long to participate in this ecstasy of beauty?

September's Aspects

This month took its name (*septem*, Latin for "seventh month") from its earlier position in the calendar. It became the ninth month when Julius Caesar changed the calendar and made January the first month.

Full moon aspect: Harvest moon

Universal event: Autumn Equinox; nature comes into balance

Communal event: Autumn Equinox, September 21; Mabon (the Sacred Son) Sabbat. In central Europe, three-day revels were held; there was much drinking of wine, mead, and fermented mare's milk. This was a time when priestesses ate the sacred mushroom, *Amanita muscaria*, which gave such muscular strength that they could dance tirelessly for days. (Note, however, that this mushroom can cause death if the dose is wrong, so don't try it!)

Message: To create, to prosper, to appreciate

Activity: Arts, crafts, courting future mates

Healing properties: Prevention through tonics

Appropriate spells: Thanks giving, presenting to the Goddess the most perfect fruits of your harvest this year. These can be intangible things: personal growth, strength, obstacles that have been overcome. To give thanks, present your gift in physical form as a poem, a small statue, a dance, a party in the name of the Goddess, whatever you can think of. Giving thanks for gifts received always multiplies them.

Manifestation: The new vine, which stands for inspiration and ecstasy

Color: Brown

Tree: Hazel

Flower: Aster

Creature: Snake

Gem: Sapphire

Anna's Spells, Rituals, & Celebrations for September

SPELL THANKING THE GODDESS ————————
FOR FAVORS RECEIVED

From time immemorial, acacia flowers have been a legendary favorite of Diana, the Goddess of Nature and therefore of all life. The sap of the acacia can be burned as an incense. Its proper name is *Acacia senegal*, or gum arabic.

Take a little of this and burn it in your fire-resistant incense burner on special charcoal (not the kind you use to barbecue). Burn a little bit in the morning and a little bit at night before you go to sleep. This practice opens your psychic centers at the times when you are most relaxed and makes you more receptive to blessings. Almost any prayer can be sent up on the acacia's fine curling smoke: thanks, or more prayers for good luck, or health, or whatever is needed. You may want to say the following prayer:

> *Diana, lovely goddess who runs in front of the winds,*
> *You who grant the wishes of your children*
> *And tend to their needs like a mother,*
> *Thank you for the blessings you have bestowed upon me,*
> *And thank you for the blessings yet to come.*

SPELL TO DRIVE A POLTERGEIST ————————
FROM YOUR PREMISES

There is no need to go through terrors and call an exorcist. If you really think a lost soul is bothering you in your home, try this first. Poltergeists are souls with unfinished business who died in terror and can't find their way over to the other side. This little herbal spell might help them across.

There is an herb called bistort (*Polygonatum bistorta*). Boil a pint of water with just a teaspoonful of this herb in it for half an hour, then strain it; the next time you clean your house, add this water to your floor wash, saying:

> *Out, out, out, restless spirits go, only the good can stay, the rest of you must be gone!*

If you have wall-to-wall carpeting, sprinkle this water on your carpet with your hands. The poltergeists will be so impressed that you found their very own herb, they will leave you alone henceforth.

SPELL TO HELP ANGRY COUPLES TO KISS & MAKE UP

Here is a situation all too common in our lives today. How often we take fights to bed with us instead of leaving them behind. When a couple has quarreled, it is very hard to smile in bed and make up. But here is an ancient problem-solving method.

Get hold of an herb called black cohosh, otherwise known as *Cimicifuga racemosa*, and sprinkle a little bit around the bed where the couple sleeps, saying, "Angry soul and painful heart change into white doves and fly!" three times and visualize the couple smiling. It's worth the try! If this doesn't work, tell the couple to get counseling.

SPELL TO KEEP A WANDERING LOVER AT HOME

Oh, I've got your attention now! When you have a lover or husband or wife who doesn't want to spend time with you (and what a fool that person is!), just trust your old herbal charm. This time the herb's name is yerba maté (Paraguay tea). You take one cup of boiling water, put in one teaspoon of the herb, and let it simmer. Add a little pure honey and try to have your mate drink it. If he or she is protesting too much ("What is this concoction anyway?"), get crafty and hide it in wine or coffee. But before you offer it to the wandering beloved, you whisper these words over it (three times, of course):

> *Warm seed, warm heart [name] and [your name] never part.*

Legend says it will make all his or her desire to wander without you simply stop. If this doesn't help, get a more faithful mate.

SKIRA: CREATIVITY FESTIVAL

Skira, the ancient Mediterranean festival of creativity, is an attractive addition to the list of women's holidays. On one day in the year, gather art supplies—clay, paints, glitter, gypsum (if you want to go traditional)—and create images of the goddess just by sitting down and giving yourself over to this sacred task. You don't need to be an artist to create a mother goddess figure, and it doesn't even have to depict a goddess. If you've ever tried this, you will know the peace that comes from doing something different yet familiar. Creating images projected from the soul lets us feel the satisfaction of the artist in all of us.

What happens when it's all done? The ancients used to parade their works of art through the streets. Skira obviously charmed everybody, and art was created in great numbers by everyone, not just by the few professionals.

We in modern times should do the same thing with our Skira images that we do when our children bring home their first ashtrays fashioned in art class: Display them and hold on to them. If a piece is very beautiful, place it in the center of the table, place flowers around it, and use it as the focal point in your meditations. Have Skira parties for your friends.

THE HOLIDAYS

September 1

THARGELIA: FESTIVAL OF FIRST FRUITS (MEDITERRANEAN)

For northern cultures like our own, the harvest festival would be held in September, but in the early days in southern Europe and Asia Minor, as now, harvest began with festivals in May or June. The first of three such early harvesting festivals was the Thargelia, which is placed here to coincide with the northern growing season.

The road on which our feet are set
Is in a harvest way.
For to the Fair-Robed Demeter
Our comrades bring today
The first fruits of their harvesting.
She on the threshing place
Great store of barley grain outpoured
*For guardian of Her Grace.**

September 1

RADHA'S DAY (INDIAN)

Lakshmi is the Hindu goddess of fertility and prosperity, and Radha was famed as the lover of the God Krishna. Lakshmi brings cheerfulness and health, and in her golden aspect, she brings the wealth of the world. This day celebrates the shared love between couples.

---

*Theocritus *Idylls* VII.31 (trans. Jane Harrison) 7.31.

September 8

NATIVITY OF THE BLESSED VIRGIN MARY (ROMAN CATHOLIC)

This celebrates the day on which Mama Anne gave birth to her divine daughter Mary. This is one of Christianity's few concessions to celebration of the female side of God, and it is observed with great pomp and circumstance. Even Pope Innocent IV ordered the faithful to hold an octave, eight days of remembrance.

September 13

BANQUET OF VENUS (ROMAN)

This feast day is very good for conception and making merry. Burn pink or red candles and visualize for yourself health, wealth, and wisdom—the divine three. Make love today to have a healthy baby or just to make love.

September 13

CEREMONY OF LIGHTING THE FIRE (EGYPTIAN)

The people created a festival of lights, with candles and lanterns and lamps of all kinds in front of their gods and goddesses and the statues of ancestors, who were stimulated by the light to journey back to the loved ones for a visit.

September 21

FEAST OF THE DIVINE TRINITY:
RITES OF ELEUSIS (GREEK)

This is the beginning of the celebration of life, beauty, death, and rebirth—the Feast of the Divine Trinity—Demeter, Koré, and Iacchos. On this day, the altars are decorated with flowers, golden apples, cider, and seed cakes. Divine life, as experienced by us all, becomes the mystery of the life cycle. We celebrate the essence of life, the abundant outpouring of the spirit of the Goddess who creates and sustains everything.

September 23

SUN ENTERS LIBRA;
AUTUMN EQUINOX;
ELEUSIAN MYSTERIES (GREEK)

The sign of Libra is the scales, signifying balance. Mother Nature establishes, once again, equality between the forces of light and darkness. From now on, the days will shorten and the nights get longer. The Goddess descends into the underworld, the world of darkness, where she tends to her dead souls. This act of going down into the underworld and defeating death is celebrated by the many rituals and processions of the Eleusian mysteries.

The Eleusian rites were the most famous goddess festival in all of Europe. Men and women came from all over the continent to participate, because it was believed that those who went through the mysteries gained good luck and insights; they became sanctified by the goddesses.

From the time of the Autumn Equinox until the end of the month of September, a different ritual, a different theme of the proceedings, was observed every day. The festival started with processions from Athens to Eleusis. Participants deposited sacred objects at the feet of the Goddess Demeter, then went to bathe in the sea, put on new linen, and poured libations on the Earth. The women and some men gathered together for Torch Day, when processions began to form again, going through the temples and the town in the search for Persephone, Koré.

For the celebration, matrons carried baskets filled with the goddess's belongings, such as a comb, a symbol of Aphrodite, a mirror, a snake figure or live snake (for rebirth), wheat, and barley. The women came in oxen-drawn carriages, and they called to each other, using "loose" language. One can just imagine it: "Hey matron Althea! Your ox looks weak as a lamb, and your baskets have holes in them!"

September 24 was the second day, the day of the grand purification ritual—a bath in the sea! The initiates washed away ignorance and assumed new grace. On September 25 the people built an altar around a tree. They burned incense and poured libations of wine and juices on the good earth, symbolizing the reverence they felt for our planet. A big procession took place on September 26, celebrating the goddess of the earth, Demeter. Her representative was carried around on a cart, while people shouted enthusiastically, "Hail, Demeter!" Everybody dressed up in their best finery; the day was raucous and filled with dancing.

On September 27 people marched day and night, carrying lit torches. This marked the true start of the mysteries.

September 28

THE HOLY NIGHT (GREEK)

All the people lined up behind the solemn goddesses represented by two veiled, mourning matrons. On the bridge approaching the city, they met another goddess, Baubo, the jester. She tried to make the goddesses laugh and draw them out of their sadness. At this time they drank *kykeon*, a hallucinogenic brew the women brought with them. The comic old woman lifted her skirts and exposed her sex to make Demeter laugh. It worked, the goddesses rested, and all were bidden to take a refreshing drink.

Don't believe it? Here is Orpheus's poem about it:

She drew aside Her robes and showed Her body all unveiled. Child Iaccus was there and laughingly plunged his hands below Her breasts. Then smiled the Goddess, in Her heart She smiled and drank the draught from the shining cup. *

There was a second bridge to cross the salty Rheitoi, and here the Mystai (the purified ones) had to identify themselves with the traditional words. These passwords were required for admission into the sacred place Epoteia:

I have fasted, drunk the kykeon, *and taken things out of the big basket. After performing certain rites, I put them into the little basket whence I put them back into the big basket.*†

---

*Orpheus's poem quoted by Clement of Alexandria, *Protrept.* 22.19, in Carl Kerenyi, *Eleusis* (London: Ron Hedge & Kegan Paul, 1967), 62.

†Jane Ellen Harrison, *Prolegomena to the Study of Greek Religion* (New York: Meridian, 1955), 569.

The people thronged toward the place where the great fire was built. The hierophant invoked Koré, and her real presence was felt. Painted in dark colors, she was seen enthroned as the Queen of Hell. The Mystai bowed at her feet in the temple. Her image was the vision of the feminine source of life. The corn, which is the eucharist of the Goddess, was silently reaped. Barley and wheat have very close resemblances to female genitals, and their display evokes veneration of the female. Men who went through these rites gained a deep understanding of their part in nature. They were "regenerated" men who received Demeter's life-giving powers. For women to behold the real presence of Koré and to venerate things female reinforced their sense of self and promoted self-esteem, responsibility for the world and her affairs, and a kinship to the deity of life.

Holy Night was a most important time; people confronted the idea of death as they watched Koré, the Divine Maiden, turn into the Crone and then turn back into the Young Queen of the underworld. The presence of the Goddess gave people a chance to see their own death as part of their lives and to remove fears about the afterlife.

On the seventh day of the mysteries (September 29), there were sports, games, and footraces. The winners were crowned with laurels and measures of grain were given to them.

On the eighth day (September 30), initiations were performed again, this time in the deep caves of the sacred temple. One fresco shows us a scene with three women: one dressed in dark colors, one naked, while the third is having her hair cut off. Cutting the hair was often a symbol of spiritual rebirth.

The September Teaching: Rites of Passage

I N OUR MODERN LIFE, all celebrations of passing from one stage of life into another have been erased. The intricate web of relationships, and their even more intricate shifting positions, have been ignored and hence devalued. We live our lives from birth until death with just a few markings to guide us.

First, there is birth, which is just too involved for a baby to truly appreciate, because there is so much to do. You have to learn how to cope with breathing air, solid foods, being away from mother, sometimes for hours. Next you get to be a toddler; you have to deal with kindergarten, soon going on to school and meeting your peers in a competitive system where you have to fight for good grades. Then you graduate and go on to more school, or take a job and settle into a society you inherited but did not invent. All this time, you get only birthday celebrations to remember the importance of your own existence.

As an adult, your only time of celebration is marriage, when you take a mate. This is the first time in your life that your family gathers and takes notice of your adult self. This also may be the last time you see any community celebrating your pleasures. After the marriage ceremony, there are anniversaries to recall the only moment of glory you achieved (never quite the same, of course). Your mate even may forget the date soon, so then the anniversary times become a series of hurts.

When you die, there will be a burial ceremony of some sort, but again, you cannot truly enjoy it because you will be busy adjusting to an existence without your body. There will be all your loved ones to visit who passed on before you—and even some heroes and heroines you admired in your lifetime with whom you will now be able to meet and commune. (I know John Lennon must have lots of visitors; Janis Joplin, too.) But your burial is not going to be your high point in dying.

What do these kinds of lackluster rites of passage communicate to us? They say, simply: We don't count. There is nothing remarkable about our growth from cradle to grave except when we marry. Even then, all the symbolism points to making babies, so the social message is, in fact, that propagating our own bloodline is the only contribution we have made to the world. We do deserve better.

The human psyche undergoes remarkable changes along its path, all of them important in building happier lives. Happy lives are not a dominant value in our culture. Money is. I have nothing against money, but I know too many people who have money and feel miserable. Money does not get us happiness; this is an old and true dictum.

I'd like to suggest that you celebrate the following rites of passage, despite the social message that you don't count. Answer back to those old tapes—shout it back to society with your determination to retrain your own mind—and see your own life as a shining miracle.

Birth

This is a most blessed event, but the attention must be equally on both mother and child. It has been shifted over too much to the celebration of the baby, forgetting the source of life—the new mom. This simple ritual is designed to minister to the new mother's feelings and to banish the deadly postpartum blues mothers are so vulnerable to.

BANISHMENT OF THE POSTPARTUM BLUES   After the birth, let a couple of days go by until the new mother feels stronger. You can visit her and bring soups and food so she doesn't need to cook. Help bathe and feed her baby; assure her often that all is well.

Then on the seventh day, sacred to Artemis, the protector of women in childbirth, perform this ritual. Gather together three gifts: a gown for beauty (or material for it), an herb that heals the tired womb (such as red raspberry leaves), and, finally, invitations to parties or a ticket to a theatrical event—some cultural experience in public.

Friends of the new mother come to visit, all dressed up to denote the specialness of the moment. A little sage could be burned to purify the home from the old vibes, from the ordinary. The first friend says:

Welcome to the circle of mothers, dear [name]. Please receive this gown [her favorite color] to honor your body. Your beauty is shining; your new life is approaching. Be strong and be honored!

(If you feel like improvising on this, please do so; let the moment teach you what to say.) Other friends can present her with the herbs, which immediately can be shared as a tea, and, finally, with the tickets to a public event. This is to encourage the new mom to think of herself as an individual, not just as a caretaker of her baby.

Then, if you think there is good cause to banish post-partum blues or just to be sure they will not attack your friend, repeat this banishing prayer from ancient Europe. With sage or artemisia burning as incense, encircle the head then the whole body of the new mom. The first friend says:

Into the dark night, take away the evil spirit!
Over the night's mountain, scatter the evil spirit!
Into the Mother's night, drive it in punishment!
Draw it into the invisible river!
Drive it further into oblivion!
Drive it across the threshold of the darkest night!
All the paths leading back into life be barred
With twice seven arrows barbed with knives!
Depression depart! Depression depart! Depression depart!

Now light a snow-white candle (in a jar) that will burn safely a whole week. The dancing fire will remind the new mother of your good wishes.

Before you leave, let the friends pronounce a blessing on the new mother as they feel inspired to do so, such as:

I bless you with cheerful disposition!
I bless you with health and strength!
May you find joy and happiness with the new soul!

BLESSING OF THE NEWBORN BABY   This should take place when the baby is ready to be in a public ritual (but always after Mom has already had her own ritual). Gather friends and relatives under the full moon for a lovely supper. After all have eaten to satisfaction, the new baby is brought out, undressed, and held in a snow-white cloth made of silk, cotton, or lace, according to your resources.

You need two friends holding two white candles and one friend holding an incense burner with some fine temple incense in it, such as frankincense or myrrh. All step outside, where the moon is fully visible; the candles are lit to the full moon and so is the incense. The mother takes her child in the white cloth and holds it up high, presenting the baby to the moon, saying:

> Queen of the heavens
> We brought you here.
> The fruit of my womb
> For joy and for fay.
> Bless this child with golden luck.
> May her or his heart have the silver touch.
> Health and wealth shall be her or his lot.
> Never sickly, nor unhappy!
> Thanks a lot!

In fairy tales, you remember, on this occasion relatives or good witches pronounce blessings on the child; now is the time to practice family magic, urban shamanism, and bless the little lucky one with all sorts of splendid futures.

> You shall have a robust immune system!
> You shall have tremendous thirst for knowledge!
> You shall have great capacity to love!

If you'd like to substitute something else for any of these lines, feel free to do so. My belief is that prayers live within us; these are just examples.

RITUAL AFTER ABORTION OR MISCARRIAGE   It is not enough to protect a woman against laws that force her to bear children against her will; it is equally important to take care of her soul after the trauma of abortion or miscarriage.

The ancients believed that a fertile woman is constantly accompanied by hundreds of souls, ready to reenter human existence, waiting for a body to slip into. When the woman decides that she is not ready to take on the responsibility of developing and bringing to life and adulthood this fertilized egg with the soul in it, the soul is sent back to wait a little longer. Not all souls get bodies, but being without a body is not a tragedy. There is no pain and there is no aging on the "other side."

After an abortion or miscarriage, when you feel stronger, create a small white altar for the little soul who got sent back to wait longer. Put some flowers on it; put pictures of your ancestors on it, people who loved you and were related to you, and who now also abide in the realm of the other side. Ask these ancestors to take in the little soul for safekeeping until you are ready to call on him or her again to enter your egg. Light a snow-white candle and say:

> Good-bye, my friend, until we meet again! Seek your relatives among my own! When the time comes, you will know! Good-bye, my friend, good-bye, my own!

Chances are the little soul will not hang out with your relatives unless she or he is very attached to you but will instead find some nubile young maiden on an off night when she doesn't think she can get pregnant.

Puberty Rites

When a girl reaches puberty, there is the onset of menses. When a boy reaches puberty, the time is not quite that clear, so we can just set it for boys around age 13.

PUBERTY RITES FOR GIRLS: CELEBRATING THE BLOODS
Young women are entitled to honor for enduring this monthly inconvenience. However, our culture hushes up the importance of menstruation, its holy meaning, and the ancient rituals that used to be remembered along with it. Today the goal is to keep menstruation so secret that people cannot even tell when we bleed. Young girls go through a lot of shame and pain and expense taking care of their bloods.

A sensitive parent of a girl in puberty should talk to the youngster long before the menses occur to prepare her psychologically for the event. I know young people don't want to hear about it; they get fidgety when asked to listen. You may have to endure your little girl squeaking in protest, "Mom, that's gross!"

But soon after her first period, there should be a rite of passage created for the young girl. (See March for this ritual.)

PUBERTY RITES FOR BOYS   When your son is struggling with having his voice break when he talks to a girl; when he breaks out in bright red pimples; when he cannot make up his mind if he wants to be a hermit and live in the jungles alone or have a harem of his fantasies; when you find he is reading girly magazines in his secret place and you know he is masturbating—it's time to acknowledge the man he is about to become.

Give a party for him and his peers and call it something attractive like "In Search of the Lion" party, because if girls are squeamish about impending womanhood, boys are allergic to any overt acknowledgment of manhood. It has to be symbolic. Make sure that the boys play games and eat well. Then propose a game called "In Search of the Lion," which goes like this. All lights are put out; only candles are burning. An image of the lion is hiding in one of the party presents, but the boys have to answer riddles in order to get to the presents.

The first riddle is: What is manhood without violence? The boys might want to give quick-fix answers, but that won't do. Allow them to contemplate this by candlelight in the dark for a little while. Chances are there will be no clear-cut answers; the point is not the answers—the point is the search. If the celebrant gives a good answer (any attempt without joking would rank as a good answer), he can open a package. The lion image itself will be hidden somewhere, and he will need his buddies to find it. Let all the boys try to answer the riddle. When the lion image is found, lights go up again, and normal partying resumes. The presents themselves should address his pending manhood, such as books about his interests, about biology, and so on. This occasion is a good time to bring up sex and talk frankly about sexual practices. If you don't think he is ready to listen, just make sure there is at least one book about it among the presents. Finally, before leaving, gather the boys into a friends' circle and bless the lion, your youngster.

> *The lion is blessed today, my friends.*
> *The lion who grew from the little cub.*
> *The lion is blessed today, my friends.*
> *The lion whom I love so very much!*
> *The lion will grow up and roar and roam.*
> *The lion who grew from little cub.*
> *The lion is blessed with courage and love.*
> *The lion that I love so very much!*

If you find a better verse to express what his passage from childhood into manhood is, please substitute it. Having raised two sons myself, I found they are not very interested in direct ways of dealing with rites of passage ("Booor-ring!"), but if you make it like a game, they are grateful to tie in with it.

Crowning Ritual: Rites of Middle Age

This time called middle age is the bulk of our lives. Society despises us in this flower of our lives. Women, especially, suffer from neglect in this age group; we are supposed to have outlived our usefulness and roll over and die. In the old days when women were not part of the work force, we could actually be herded into invisibility, but not anymore. Work is the great common denominator: Women and men—young and old—work side by side. For women, middle age is always more painful. There is a sense of defeat around this time, our beauty fading, our bodies aging, our role as mothers often ended.

CROWNING RITUAL FOR MIDDLE AGE   Debbie, who has been best friends with Maggie, wants to do something special for her. Maggie has been promoted to manager of a large software firm and will have a lot more responsibility. Maggie needs some confidence and assurance of support from her friends. So Debbie sends out an invitation to all the people she feels Maggie would be comfortable sharing this step in her life with. The promotion becomes more than just a little thing, a "step" ahead; it becomes a symbol of all the powers that are inherent in ruling; it prompts the occasion for Maggie to accept her role in life as queen.

Being a queen means that in the middle years of her life, Maggie will treat herself with respect and use her powers as a mature woman to take care of business. Being a queen means that she will not minimize her own importance, that she will consciously affirm her own role to lead. The archetype of a queen is Hera, the goddess of cities and governments, she who rules civilizations. Hera wears a crown of all the towers and castles and landscapes she rules.

In Maggie's case, Debbie has a silver crown designed with a crescent moon in the middle to represent in a tangible way this queen age in Maggie's life. The partygoers know that they will be honoring Maggie as queen today, honoring the power of middle age. The tables are set for a party, and people gather and chat about whatever they like, but at one point, Debbie calls them all together in a circle and says:

> *Welcome, welcome to Maggie's crowning ritual. As you know, our friend has been promoted [or, in other cases, started her own business, ran for office and won, and so on], and now it is time to give her the necessary support to manage her queenhood successfully. Dear Maggie, are you ready to accept the mantle of the queen and all that it implies?*

Maggie says, "Yes, of course." And Debbie continues:

> *Then in the name of all of us who know you and trust you well, I present you with the crown of middle age, the height of our lives. Please wear it every time you want to get in touch with your power.*

Debbie places the silver crown on Maggie's head. Her friends applaud.

Now, one by one, the friends bestow a blessing on Maggie, sprinkling her with gold (iron pyrite) dust or sparkling confetti.

> *May your new position evoke no envy from your coworkers! May it evoke only a wish for cooperation!*

> *Let the spirits be gentle around you; let you rule like a gracious queen!*

> *Let power never isolate you from those who you love and who love you!*

(I am sure each of the guests will know what to say; I only offer these lines as an example.) Maggie wears her crown all evening long; at the end, she is so used to wearing a crown that it has become part of her.

RITES OF PASSAGE FOR MENOPAUSE This is a real time of change that hardly anybody celebrates. A little girl is born with a hundred thousand eggs in her body; she sheds quite a few in menses; she gives birth to even fewer as babies; and then at one point in her life, the egg factory wants to rest. At times like this, she feels totally at the mercy of her hormones. If we celebrate this event, it will become a source of strength to us. Taking power over the hormonal changes also means doing a bit of study on it. Don't just swallow pills a male doctor hands you. He doesn't know that, for example, eating a sweet potato a couple of times a week will help balance the hormones in your diet; doctors are not taught common sense or natural medicine.

Gather your friends together for a meal. When the mood is high and you and the guests are ready for the ritual, bring out four red candles on a tray or have a friend do it for you. All pay attention to the celebrant. The first friend says:

> We gathered here together to celebrate the withdrawal of the flowing bloods from our friend [name]. We ask the Great Mother to bless our sister with good health, vitality, and gladness.

All toast with glasses filled with juice or wine, saying: "Health! Vitality! Gladness!" The celebrant now lights her first red candle, saying:

> I light this first candle for the flowing bloods that are gone! I light this second candle for the children and the health the flowing bloods have brought me! [Omit this if not applicable.] The third red candle I light for the flowering of my womanhood, the fourth, for the labors the bloods required, which ended in glory!

The friends toast again, saying: "The bloods ended in glory!"

Now, the first friend can play priestess, and she lights a yellow candle and says:

> I release you, says the goddess of the red! I accept you, says the goddess of the yellow ray. I call you into my wisdom to grow in. I call you like a new maiden into my sciences, into my knowledge, into my dreams to manifest!

The celebrant replies:

> I have completed my journey of the bloods. I have come home now to rest. I thank you, goddess of the yellow ray. Hold me and protect me and help me grow again!

The symbolism of this ritual is very simple. Red candles are symbolic of menstruation and the flow of life. Number 4 is the number of completion. Yellow is a higher vibration; its color is associated with spiritual growth, skill development, and transcendence.

RITUAL AFTER REMOVAL OF WOMB, BREASTS, OVARIES

Why do we celebrate operations like these? Why not? They save your life, don't they? You would not remove parts of your body unless it was important, and, of course, you obtained many opinions about your decision before you made it. But now you have come home from the hospital, and everything is wonderful; you are healing. Only the psyche is unattended in this matter; that requires a ritual.

Create a party where there is a chance to jump over fire. (Candles will work just as well and are easier to jump over.) As you jump over the fire, you may make a wish; since you jump over the fire three times for good luck, that makes three wishes. The first friend calls together the others and explains:

> We are gathered together to purify our friend [name] from her sense of loss, her sense of not being whole, her sense of depression. [Omit if not applicable.] Dear [name]! Welcome back! We feel fortunate that you have returned among us. Now we ask you to jump the fire, and each time you do, make a wish so your future can begin.

Now you jump over the fire (without getting your gown caught in the flames!), making your wish each time before you leap.

CRONING RITUAL—ENTERING THE WISE AGE

When the great planet Saturn spins back for the second time in your natal chart, you are fifty-six years old. This is the age we recognize as the doorway into the age of wisdom. This time in a woman's life is really devalued in modern society. A very unkind treatment is allotted to those of us in this age group. Watch out, because soon most of America will be in this age group, and it will be fashionable to be old—just wait and see!

Gather friends together. The first friend should secure a purple jewel we call the Crone Jewel, which will be given to you. The color purple is a high-power color; it also stands for fame and fortune and hard work. She should find a bell, which is used to ring out all those brave years you have been alive! Go ahead with the party, and when the time is right, call your friends in attendance into a circle. The first friend says:

> *Hello, everybody, welcome! Today I would like to tell you what I know about crones. Crones start to be crones at the age of fifty-six, because crones are cosmically created by the return of great planet Saturn into the natal chart. In ancient times crones were more powerful than younger women. We were asked to arbitrate, settle disputes, act as judges. We were everybody's older sisters; we were the wise ones. In ritual, we had always an honored place to sit. Today society forgets about us, but we do not forget our own history. Today we celebrate [name], because now it is her turn. I would like to present you with the magical Crone Jewel, to remind you that you are our beloved sister, teacher, and now honored crone of the Goddess.*

The celebrant crone answers:

> *I traveled the road from my mother's breast to cronehood. I thank the Goddess for the seasons that have passed, and I thank the Goddess for the good seasons yet to come!*

Now the first friend rings the bell fifty-six times, each time for a year in the life of the celebrant. It will be very impressive as the chimes ring on and on. You will gain a sense of importance and a sense of continuity of life and be impressed by the numbers of years experienced.

After the last ring falls silent, let loose a loud cheering and applause for the woman who achieved such longevity. All members of the party now say:

> *Bless you [name of the new crone] with health, happiness, and long life!*

It is done.

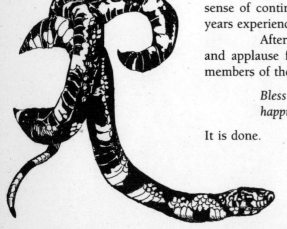

VARIATION FOR MEN When it comes to aging, men around this age also start getting heartless messages from society to step aside and let the young bucks in. The time to be sages is now. The Saturn cycle happens to men as well. It may not be a value for men to focus on their spiritual side at this time, but I'll bet there are growing numbers of men who would welcome not having to be the great providers and "hunters" and instead settle into their spirituality.

For men, the symbol of spirituality is a wand. Today you can get little ones, large ones, crystal ones, and plain wooden ones; find one that suits the person the ritual is for. Collect all the man's friends who would contribute to the celebration and not treat it as a joke. Create a party, and when the time is right, the first friend addresses the party:

> *I would like to tell you about the great medicine men who were serving our ancient communities. These men were called the sages because their advice was sound and their judgment clear. These medicine men taught the spiritual values of courage, wisdom, compassion, and peaceful arbitration. They were our fathers and grandfathers who entered the wise age. Today we honor [name], and we would like to give him this magical wand to remind him of his spiritual heritage and to celebrate this occasion of his reaching the age of the sages.*

The celebrant should accept the gift with a little speech, improvised or otherwise, saying, for example:

> *I traveled the long road from my dear mother's breast into the age of wisdom. I toast the good seasons that have passed, and I toast the good seasons yet to come!*

Now, the first friend will ring out the sage's fifty-six years with the bell, and all listen and appreciate the art of living. When it's over, a great ovation follows; then proceed to feast and celebrate as usual. These are just a few ideas on how to elevate the passages of your life into memorable occasions. For further information read my books and check out some of the other books in the bibliography.

October

The Goddess Speaks——

Hecate

I HAVE BEEN WITH YOU FROM the beginning. Don't you remember my voice above your mother's birth cries? I, the priestess of the Earth, midwifed you and all your kin. Silently, I watched you growing, and I was at all your rites of passage. I was the priestess holding aloft the torches of life in each hand, one pointing up to heaven and one down to the great below, for it is said, "As above, so below." Even the Earth herself calls on my services. I am the queen of the crossroads, witch queen, the transformer. I have come again this season to scream my frightening banshee yell and scatter pumpkins in your backyards and your living rooms like so many orange balloons.

The ancient primal season of the witch is here, and you welcome me. Yes, you love to be frightened by me. I force you to laugh at your own death, to dress up your children in ghostly guise. Now comes your first sense of the coming cold season, chilling to the bone. I bring the harvest, and if you haven't harvested your apples, I'll nip them with frost. After Halloween, all that's left in the fields is mine!

If you wish to honor me, I will show you my magical ways. I take away your fears of death and make you glad. I am the keeper of the altars, outdoors and inside. I am speaking in you when you feel the desire to stand alone on a hillside or in a clearing in the woods and talk to the full moon. I am the wild part of you, your sixth sense, the one that gives you your hunches, premonitions, dreams. I am the priestess immortal. My face is threefold—young, old, and in full bloom. I see ahead and behind; I am the hinge of reality. I am your primal goddess. Into your lives I bring these feelings, even now, in the artificial forests of your urban concrete world. My witches are flying on their broomsticks, and the ghosts are quaking in your windows. All is well, Halloween is here; souls come to visit, and the living world throws a party to mingle with the dead. I share in your merriment and warm my cold hands at your hearth.

— October's Aspects —

This month received its name from its earlier position in the Roman calendar (*Octo* means "eight" in Latin). In the Gregorian calendar it is the tenth month. Just shows how rulers like to mess with time by changing its name.

Full moon aspect: Blood moon

Universal event: October 31, Samhain (Halloween), summer's end; one of the high cross-quarter days in the journey of the earth around the sun

Communal event: Halloween celebrations, the Spiral Dance

Message: To let go, to clean, to remember

Activity: Preparing for winter

Healing properties: Sedation of nerves

Appropriate spells: Protection spells, uncrossing spells from bad luck, memorials to the departed, evening of scores, paying back debts

Manifestation: Ivy, plant of resurrection

Color: Blue

Tree: Yew

Flower: Calendula, cosmos

Creature: Mute swan

Gem: Opal, tourmaline

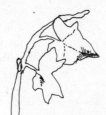

Anna's Spells, Rituals, & Celebrations for October

TO DESTROY AN ENEMY'S POWER TO HARM —————

Sometimes people hurt each other, and it is necessary for good people to put up a defense. Take four ounces of the herb called ague root (*Aletis farinosa*) and cut it up in small pieces. Add the same amounts of crushed patchouli leaves, myrrh in small lumps, olibanum tears, and wood betony. Mix all these together in your wooden bowl (or any other) and burn a little of it on self-igniting charcoal, which you can get in gift shops or occult supply stores.

As the smoke rises, say three times the name of the person who is harming you, and then say:

> *Burn fire, rise smoke,*
> *Hecate's attention now I draw!*
> *Let the evil sent to me be returned to its house.*
> *Burn fire, rise smoke!*

Do this seven nights in a row before you go to sleep. Your enemy will be weakened and will not harm you.

SPELL TO STOP SLANDER & GOSSIP

If you are sure somebody is really damaging you with bad gossip and slander, you can do what our ancestors did to stop it. Get some powdered cloves (you may have this spice already). Write the name of the person who is slandering you backward nine times with red ink on a very small piece of white paper. If you don't know who is doing it, just write "whoever is slandering me." Burn a little of your powdered cloves in the morning and a little at night for seven days in a row. On the last night, burn the piece of paper with the name on it along with the powdered cloves; then cast the ashes into a living body of water. The gossiper will stop or will not be believed.

SPELL TO TRAVEL IN SAFETY

When you make travel plans, casting a little spell to make sure that your investment in the journey is protected is not much bother. For this, sprinkle a little of the herb called Iceland moss on the bottom of your suitcase, or in any other luggage you are carrying with you. Cover it with thin paper; then put your clothes on top of it. You'll see how Mother Nature will keep her eye on your things—airports won't lose them. Your plane will not be hijacked, fall out of the sky mysteriously, or be harmed by any other terror that lurks in the skies.

RITE TO HONOR THE DEAD

This meditation is the oldest form of worship. I believe the human race invented religion because of the awe death causes in us, the emptiness we feel when loved ones depart and we wonder where they have gone. If they send us a vision, if they return in a dream, we know they haven't gone away, they have just passed over to the other side. In October, this other world comes very close to the world of the living.

Create an altar for your ancestors by decorating a table with a white cloth, flowers, and a small bowl of water. Sprinkle some herbs on your candles. Put pictures of your departed relatives in the middle. Light your white or yellow devotional candles in front of them. Burn a little incense for the ghosts—one of the oldest of customs. Put out some food, such as red fruit or hard candies. Use your own words to speak as if you were talking to your own mother, father, aunt, or child, saying something like this:

> *Dear [name], hello! This is your [relative—daughter, sister, whatever] talking. Happy Halloween! I have set out food for you to eat and water for you to drink. I honor you, my ancestor, because what you were is who I am today, and I am all that you could give me. I thank you for my life and ask you for more protection on the street, in my home, and within myself, so that I may reject negative ideas and will not internalize oppression. Rest in the holy beauty of the Goddess; rejoice in your nearness to the source of all life. Extend your powers like wings over the family you have left behind, and we shall remember you with reverence on this night every year.*

If your parents or relatives are buried where you can visit them, go to the cemetery as well. Make sure all your loved ones' graves are well tended, and pay your dues to the cemetery caretakers. Do this on Halloween for sure, or November 1, the feast of the dead.

SPELL TO LET GO

Somehow, our modern lives make us feel that we have to accumulate things—people, phone numbers, contacts, books, newspapers, tools, stuff! Most of the time we are right, for there is always need for a new idea, an old tool—the old and new together save us time and money. However, this principle doesn't hold in all areas. Sometimes we need to divest, to let go of the collection of things and feelings that have already served their purpose.

October is a good time to tidy up the soul. First, make a list of things that have got to go, such as resentment of friends or enemies, anger at yourself (potent and common garbage). Just think through your life to see what you no longer need. Go through your soul as if it were a long-forgotten attic and see where cleaning up is way overdue, then write down what you find. I am not talking about resentments like those you feel if you're just divorced, if you got ripped off, if you had to leave a job due to harassment, if you lost a promotion because you were not a man. These oppressions are not your own doing, so please don't blame yourself for them. Find groups with which to work them through and channel your anger into political activism, which can give your life more meaning.

Create an altar with black cloth, the color of the universe, the color of chaos, where everything comes from and to which everything must return. Place on the cloth some fallen leaves, representing the natural order of the seasons and the discarded past. The fallen leaves are beautiful, but they are meant to become compost; to compost is where all our bad garbage is going as well. Place your list of psychic garbage on the table, light two black candles, one on either side, and burn some dispelling incense. If you can't find incense specifically made for this purpose, use sandalwood, frankincense, myrrh, or cedar.

When you pray to the Goddess, always talk normally, as if to your own sweet mama. You can say:

> *Dearest Goddess, I have come a long way this year,*
> *carrying my burdens. I would like to take them off my*
> *shoulders and give them back to you to recycle, to bury,*
> *to compost. Here, I offer you my resentments against*
> *friends, family, and [fill in your own needs here] and ask*
> *you to absorb them into your black universe. Relieve me*
> *of them and allow me to walk more lightly.*

Burn your list in the flames of your candles. Now imagine all these feelings evaporating into smoke, and say something like:

> I feel all light, happy and cleansed now. Dearest
> Goddess, you are my true strength and guide. I thank
> you for being accessible and answering your children's
> call. I honor you and thank you.

Gather all the things that were part of your meditation and cast them into a living body of water. When you cast them off, don't look back. Even let go your thoughts about the ritual.

THE SPIRAL DANCE

In the San Francisco Bay Area, the Spiral Dance has become one of the most popular and significant public festivals. Holding large rituals is a long-standing tradition for many pagan groups in the Bay Area. Starhawk and the Reclaiming collective began the tradition of the Spiral Dance in 1979 to celebrate publication of Starhawk's book *The Spiral Dance*.* Since I had been doing Spiral Dances in Los Angeles since 1975, when I moved to the Bay Area I continued the same tradition for women.

This is what it's like to celebrate the old rites in a modern community. On Halloween night, we gathered at about 9:00 P.M. in the Women's Building in San Francisco. Considering how cold it can get this time of the year, the night was a warm one. The audience filed in wearing colorful costumes—goblins, fairies, and the like. Someone brought a giant python that rested patiently across three people's shoulders.

When everyone was ready, three women, representing the three Fates, entered the room, chanting blessings to create a sacred space.

> Three times around with smoke I purify the ground.
> Three times around with sound I purify the ground.
> Three times around with water I purify the ground
> From all evil and all harm.

---

*See Starhawk's description in *Truth or Dare* (San Francisco: Harper & Row, 1987), 306.

As the Fates exited, eight priestesses came forward, representing the eight major sabbats of the festival year, the holidays celebrating the stations of the Earth in her journey around the sun—the solstices, the equinoxes, and the high points in between (Winter Solstice, Candlemas, Spring Equinox, May Eve, midsummer, Lammas, Autumn Equinox and Halloween). Each priestess faced the assembled audience (which totaled about three hundred people) and addressed them:

"I am winter. I bring you introspection; I bring you the snow. I bring you germination of the soul, preparation for the future. I am old, and I am young," said the priestess representing Winter Solstice and danced around the circle once with her lighted candle. "I am Brigid of Candlemas," continued the next priestess. "I bring you inspiration, bright ideas, the sap rising."

"I am Spring Equinox. Here are my flowers—smell them," said the next. "I am May Eve," a sultry priestess purred, "I love my body. I love the woods."

"I am midsummer," said a woman who reflected the ripeness of summer. "I gather in my kin—we feast and dance." "I am Lammas, of the fresh-baked bread. Come and eat at my table," said another as she passed out wonderful fresh loaves.

"I am autumn. Look at my beautiful decaying leaves," said the seventh priestess. "I am the mother of the dead," said the Halloween crone. Since the night belonged to her she spoke softly.

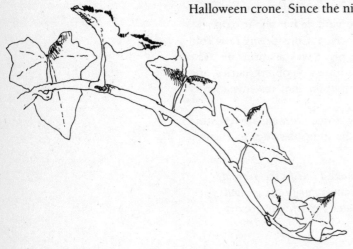

She was dressed in black and her head bore a crown with bones. "Did you lose somebody this past year?" she asked. "Are you mourning? Who was it? What is her name or his?"

One by one people said the names of their departed ones. Voices were choked; some cried freely. The names of the dead flowed from their lips; there were so many we were stunned. It had been a sad year in San Francisco. Many people had died of AIDS, as well as from other causes. We held each other and howled and let the pain burn itself out like an old flame. When the Halloween crone finished interacting with the people, she entered the center of the circle and shrouded herself in stillness.

Then the rest of us began the journey to visit her in the underworld. We all started from the outside in a line behind the dancers, curling inward in a spiral toward the center. "Down, down, down, decompose, recompose," we chanted, our line constricting in even smaller circles, until we finally arrived at the door of the Goddess of Death. Now we were free to give her the things whose time had come to die. "Insecurities," a woman cried. "My fear of sickness," another added. "My temper," "My meekness," others chimed in.

The Goddess rose and, with a nod, accepted all our psychic garbage. To see her in her black feather hat and crown of human bones, accepting all these unacceptable things, filled us with security. Only the act of facing our mortality can set us free. When she finished it was time to ask for rebirth and return from the darkness. "Hecate, Cerridwen, Dark Mother, let us be reborn." When the chant was convincing enough, the Goddess nodded and said, "Go back and live your lives more fully. Tend to the graves and the memories of my dead. Keep your hearts in courage and bliss; love each other as I love you all."

Then we danced, this time faster, chanting, "Let it begin now! Freedom for all people! Let it begin now! Our freedom! Let it begin now! Our good health! End to oppression! Let it begin now!" Joyously we danced our way back into the big circle and continued dancing until midnight, sometimes in a line, sometimes in total confusion that always miraculously reorganized itself again. Halloween is a time of rebirth, not just drunken parties. Make it more meaningful.

THE HOLIDAYS

October (variable)

DAY OF ATONEMENT (JEWISH)

The day of atonement occurs sometimes at this time, depending on the moon. This Jewish holiday is a holdover from the Babylonian new year celebrations and rituals. This is a time to review the past year and bring harmony back to the soul.

October 5

DAY OF THE HOLY SPIRIT (GREEK)

Sophia, the spirit of female wisdom, disguised herself as a white dove, her sacred bird. Christianity tried to write her out completely, retaining only the symbol of the dove,

which is the giver of powers to Jesus at his baptism, also appearing to the apostles when they gathered after Jesus was killed.

In Gnostic tradition, Hagia Sophia, the Great Mother, was born from silence. She was the great revered Virgin in whom the Father was concealed before he created anything. She suffered great slander from the new patriarchal religions, which despised a female god but couldn't quite eliminate her worship. Eastern Christians built her a magnificent cathedral in Constantinople during the sixth century A.D., which became one of the wonders of the world.

October 11 through 13

THESMOPHORIA: FESTIVAL OF WOMEN'S RIGHTS (GREEK)

Also known as the Festival of Demeter, Thesmophoria was a major celebration, a holy day dedicated to the observance of the laws of the Goddess Demeter. Theocritus reported:

It was law among the Athenians that they should celebrate the Thesmophoria yearly, and the Thesmophoria is this: Women who are virgins and have lived a holy life, on the day of the feast place certain customary and holy books on their heads and act as though to perform a liturgy.*

The origins of Thesmophoria are ancient. In fact, in this celebration we find the roots

---

*Theocritus *Idylls* (trans. Harrison) 4.25.

of magic, blessings, curses, pronouncements, and the beginnings of binding law. A list of those whom the priestesses felt had offended community morality was read in front of the doors of the temples of the goddesses, especially Demeter and Artemis. Nobody wanted to be on the list because they believed those so cursed died before the year was done. This was a time when more gynocentric practices were reinstituted, and the people were reminded of the rights of women.

On the first day of Thesmophoria there was a ritual known as *kathodos*, or a "down-going and uprising." The priestesses for this day's celebration were women who had been purified. These women acted as the "drawers-up," bringing out of the earth the offerings of previous years. They dressed in crimson and purple gowns and descended deep into the cleft of the earth to where the shrine of Demeter stood. The priestesses carried piglets, considered sacred to Demeter because of their intelligence and the fact that they love earth best. The staple food of the people, therefore, was symbolically returned to the Goddess, the source of all food. The priestesses left the piglets at the shrine and collected the remains of the piglets left there the year before. They then replaced the sacred goddess images, snake statues, and home-made shrines.

The second day of Thesmophoria, Nesteia, was dedicated to Demeter the law giver, who ordained that "men provide with their own labors for their own nurturance."* This was an acknowledgment of the fact that women would not nurture men throughout their lifetimes; that after a certain point, men had to take care of themselves. On this day,

everyone fasted. All the things that had been "drawn-up" were displayed on the altars; prisoners were pardoned, courts closed, amnesties granted, and Demeter, "smileless," received worshippers while sitting on the ground rather than on her usual throne.

The third day of Thesmophoria was spent "sowing" all the "drawn-up" things once again in the good earth—a sort of magical fertilization. Only women who had no deaths in their families could perform this sacred ritual of the *Kallingeneia*, the "born fair," or "born beautiful." Afterward, feasting took place throughout the community, and everyone danced while the music played.

October 12

HOLIDAY OF THE GODDESS OF HAPPY JOURNEYS (ROMAN)

Her name is Fortuna Redux. Ask her for favorable times before you go on long trips. Put chamomile flowers on the bottom of your suitcase for good luck on the road or in the air.

October (variable)

SUKKOTH (JEWISH)

This harvest/wine festival occurs this month, depending on the moon. It is associated with Asherah, the Queen of Heaven. The day is celebrated by building booths and displaying the harvest's bounty. General good times and socializing with kin and friends are ways to gladden the Queen of Heaven.

---

*Jane Harrison, *Prolegomena to the Study of Greek Religion*, 123.

October 31

SAMHAIN: HALLOWEEN (CELTIC)

The new year of the earth begins. We have reached the midpoint between Autumn Equinox and Winter Solstice. This is the time to think about our own mortality. The veil is the thinnest between the worlds tonight, and dead souls visit their living relatives. The custom of going from door to door collecting sweet cakes and money came from a British custom of begging for the poor. When you let your kids go trick-or-treating, know that they represent the future. When children knock on your door, offer them sweet gifts to sweeten the future. To give poison or bad gifts to children on this night is to bring bad luck on yourself. But the true stars of Halloween are the elderly. They represent the year, now worn old and gray. Remember grandmothers, grandfathers, and elderly relatives. Give them greeting cards and food or take them out to dinner. To appease the past is also good luck for the future.

According to Celtic legend, the four great grandmothers of Halloween hold the great treasures. The cauldron of rebirth represents pleasure, the stone of destiny represents power, the sorceress's spear represents courage, and, finally, the invincible sword, about which one finds so many legends, stands for knowledge. These four older women are often portrayed in folkplays as holding their treasures and naming them. To see them and hear their voices is reserved only for the initiated and means great good luck.

This is a good day to give alms to the poor. The spirits receive these gifts with favor. In Europe, food is passed out to the poor at the gates of cemeteries. In the United States, many people go to parties dressed up in outrageous costumes representing ghosts and the dead. Leave some milk out on your windowsills or on the dining room table, with a white candle burning to light the way for the wandering souls of those who may come by. In Ireland and Scotland, people believe that the souls of the little people, or fairy folk, are about on this night. The invisible barriers are lifted, and they revel in the company of the living.

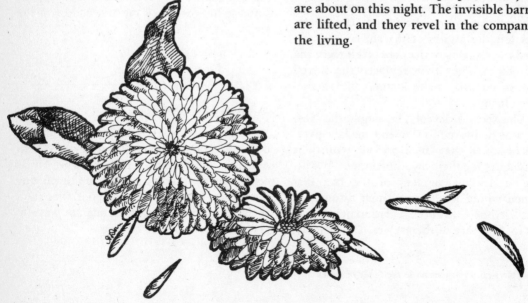

The October Story:
The Crone Moves
in Lucky Ways

THERE HAVE BEEN MANY rites of passage in my life. My first psychic experience was at age three, when my beloved grandmother died and came to me to say good-bye. This experience usually means that the dead person is signing on as your special guardian angel, to look after you until you die. My vision allowed me to cross from mundane reality into an invisible one, to kiss and touch my dying grandmother thousands of kilometers away and to hear her dying breath say my name. Because we had loved each other, I cried when she was gone. But this experience burst my psychic doors wide open. Ever since then, when the need is great, I have been able to travel into this invisible world to find her and others. Then there was the glorious moment when, at fourteen, I sold my first short story, which won second prize in a national radio contest in Budapest. The first prize went to an older man; he was twenty-one. I felt my childhood ended then, when I became a writer/money-maker. My mother baked me a cake with a single candle on it. I was born to her as an artist.

But the most shattering, exciting, and forever significant experience of change in my life was the Hungarian Revolution. It was not a revolt, as it was called in the West, nor was it the counterrevolutionary uprising, as it was called in the East. It was our own homespun, spontaneous revolution. It began in 1956, on October 23. These memories lay repressed in my mind for many years. With whom do you share the sound of the tanks ripping up the old cobblestones? To whom can you explain how the acacias must be blooming now on the streets of Budapest? How can you weave into a conversation the fact that your heart aches when you see streetcars, because in your mind they are yellow, with trolley wires scorching ahead on their rails, making sparks as their "antennas" touch the main line? Who can you talk with about your guilt because you lived when all those thousands of people died? Veterans of revolutions disperse into the world like puffs of dandelion seed, seeking to integrate and assimilate into new soil. But what are the costs? We try to deny our origins by changing our names to suit the countries we live in. And still, everybody asks, "What is that charming accent you have? Where are you from?"

When the revolution began, I was a high school student, and I was minding my grades, for I had a lot to catch up on. It was a new school for me; mother had moved me right after my last summer vacation with my friend Tünde, on the Danube. She didn't even let me unpack my things to be washed; she just announced that I was to move to the Buda side of the river to live with my father, the well-known prude. This was Mother's response to a report from the janitor's wife that she had seen me sitting in a boy's lap in our apartment while Mom was away working. Mother always used to tell me she was giving me too much freedom, and she just hoped I wouldn't abuse it. If I ever did, she vowed again and again, she would take it away. And that she did.

My best friend Tünde lived in Pest. We spent every free moment together, because we used to live so close to each other. We would talk about the world, the school, the girls, and sometimes even the boys, but Tünde and I didn't belong to the boy-crazy group. And now I had to go to a school with no Tünde. We had been in school together every day since we were nine years old. Father lived up to his reputation. A heavy smoker and drinker, he would wrap himself in a cloud and read the *Figaro*, a liberal French paper he liked. But he was very much aware of my comings and goings. I had to be in bed by 7:30 P.M. Unbelievable for a woman of sixteen! He asked me about my schoolwork, which was always done, and then he would leave for the bars, locking the door from the outside behind him. Into this life, full of the pains and discontent of growing up, I welcomed the revolution.

The revolution arrived on a leaflet—my first look at this medium—carrying the message that we were to have an authorized demonstration at 3:00 P.M. at the Bem Park, on the shores of the Danube. The leaflet was being passed out in front of our school by a college student! I took it to my class and read it aloud as if I were part of the organizing. When I read the part that proclaimed that all Russian troops must leave Hungary, that we wanted free elections and a free press, everybody yelled wildly and pounded jubilantly on their desks. Only the teacher came over and said quietly, "Let me see that leaflet." But it was too late. We had already decided to go.

Nothing can be as intoxicating as being part of a spontaneous emotional national event that involves everybody, old and young, men and women united by a passion for a higher cause, the masses achieving union with their own will. Mother and I were supposed to meet for dinner later in Buda at the Blue Peacock, around 8:00 P.M. Since she tossed me out to live with my dad, we had been sort of dating. I thought I would just go to the demonstration and then have dinner with her. It is taken for granted that you can have demonstrations in the United States. Back home in 1956, this was everybody's first one. It was new, like the first kiss.

This was the first rush of freedom. Most of my classmates came, and we made a gang of about thirty. We felt like chanting and shouting slogans; we clapped our hands and sang the national anthem at every corner as we moved toward the plaza. It was a victorious joy ride. Hungarians, who normally hate each other as oppressed people often do, discovered love for their own kind, and it moved our hearts! Being Hungarian had never seemed to matter before this day, when suddenly it became a badge of honor, membership in a distinguished club, a nation with a history of courage and bloodshed, but a nation that was always trying to get out from under the domination of others. Suddenly it meant pride. A little old lady was cutting the Soviet symbols out of the Hungarian flags in the window as we cheered her on. Workers coming home from the factories where they had labored since dawn suddenly joined us. Memory shows me pictures of streaming faces, young and old, kids and fathers and mothers suspending regular life for the big change. Daring to make history again. Last time our country had a real revolution was a hundred years ago; we were due to have another one.

It was getting late, but I just had to get a taste of what the meeting was all about, so I stayed on the outside, losing track of the rest of the girls. I was going to slip away to keep my date with my mom, but not before I absolutely had to. I heard more devastating, loud chanting, ten thousand voices yelling, "*Oltsàk el a chillagot! Foggyasztja az àramot!*" They were chanting because the red star on the top of the Parliament building was lit, but there was no Hungarian flag. The crowds were chanting to put out the red star. This chant went on and on. And then, after what seemed an eternity, the red star went out. Where it used to glow in the early evening was just a spot of darkness. The crowd went mad with victory. We were shouting and screaming, hooting and hollering, drunk on our own unity, on our own power.

I had a lot to tell Mom, and I started dropping back toward the river where it would be easier to go in a straight line. Another deafening cheer went up. Somebody in the Parliament building had found a Hungarian flag, opened a window, and hung it out for all to see! Voices started rising in the national anthem, "God bless the Hungarians! Bless them with good humor and prosperity. Extend toward them your protecting sword when they are struggling against their enemies. Bad luck has long been our lot! Bring us now a happy year!" This song was not something we had often sung before. It tasted new in my mouth, like a new food tried for the first time. And, of course, I cried each time I got to the part about the bad luck. But what words we have! What other nation prays for "good humor" as the first thing on their agenda to ask God? The Hungarian Revolution made me fall in love with my own kind.

It was around 11:00 P.M. when I finally reached the Blue Peacock where Mother waited for me. She had obviously been crying, her mascara was all over her cheeks, and her perfume, mixed with her sweat, had worn thin. She was afraid something had happened to me. It was rumored that the Secret Service had moved in on the crowd after the permit to demonstrate was withdrawn. I missed all that by leaving early. The rumors were true. My classmates Alice, Rita, Ruth, and Erzsèbet never came home. They were victims of the guns that fired into the unarmed crowds. For weeks to come, we would hear shooting from different parts of the city all night and day. My world had collapsed.

Papa also underwent a remarkable transformation. He shifted his attention from guarding my virginity to roaming the dark streets and breaking with rocks the windows of places he considered Communist headquarters. These included newspapers, offices, meeting halls, sometimes even the homes of people whom he didn't like. Papa became a regular right-wing terrorist. Now that my life was in danger, I was free to roam the streets, get shot

at, go to demonstrations; he was too busy to care. I was going to attend another demonstration against the Russian occupation of Hungary that was to be held on the Pest side in a medium-sized plaza not too far from the Parliament. There was always room for large gatherings on the Pest side. It was now a couple of weeks into the revolution, and we appeared to be winning it.

Our own military had come over to our side. They were fighting the occupying Russian troops. Some students managed to talk to Russian soldiers and found out that they were being told that this was Panama, the Danube was the Suez canal, and we were the "capitalist pigs" they should destroy. When the students explained to the Russian youngsters in the tanks that they were actually in Hungary, some of them also changed sides and refused to fight us and even turned over four tanks to us. In this changeable but favorable atmosphere, I felt safe in attending the demonstration. I got dressed and walked as fast as I could, but somehow it wasn't fast enough. My body felt like lead. I was all legs at this time; such exercise should not have strained my body, yet I could not move, could not make it to the opening of the gathering, which always was the most moving part. People would be singing the national anthem, young poets reciting their latest nationalistic poems—it was great fun. When I finally made it and was about to enter the plaza, I realized that instead of the rumbling of the voices and cheers and songs, there was a silence. I turned the corner. And then I saw. There were thousands of people in the plaza—men, women, and kids, all shot to death, lying freshly killed on the ground. Had I been on time as I planned, I would have been gunned down with the rest. My own contemporaries were the main casualties. The elders said that Budapest was reduced to a worse condition than it had been during World War II—except for the bridges, of course, which were not destroyed.

I think my grandmother has protected me all through my life, and here again, she displayed her powers of protection, making my body heavy, slowing me down, saving my life. Facing this mass death filled me with so much unspeakable pain, a pain that went so deep, that then and there I made up my mind to join the refugees and leave my country. I remember walking all over the city, saying good-bye to my favorite little streets, coffeehouses (kids drink coffee in Hungary), theaters. My love for my city was overwhelming; leaving was a painful decision. I had to cut the ties that nourished me and try to put down my roots elsewhere. But I was too young to really understand what being a refugee was all about.

I chose to leave on a full moon, November 19, because my mom and I were witches, and we believed the full moon was good luck, and besides, you can see better at night when the moon is full. I remember the moon was red that night. I prayed to Grandma, received my mother's blessings and all her extra cash for the road, and left a note to my father: "I am leaving for the West because I want a future." I visited my best friend Tünde and asked her if she would come along. Thousands of kids were fleeing; we would not be alone. Many Western agencies were taking the refugees from the borders to different countries; Hungarians were distributed like puppies. Austria said she would take a couple of thousand; Australia wanted more; England just a few and mostly the men; and so forth. But Tünde said no. "I have to stay for my mother," she said. "I am the only daughter, who would help her?" By this she meant who would help Mom make the preserves and tomato pastes, pick fruit in the orchards, and slave in the house alongside her? It never occurred to her that maybe her four brothers could put in some labor. But this was very much pre–women's liberation. I accepted her answer.

I never loved anybody as much, as deeply, and as magically as Tünde again. She was the apple of my eye. I would have sacrificed anything to be with Tünde. Anything but my life. Death was very real to me now. I had seen the thousands of bleeding bodies. I walked on streets strewn with chlorine, stepping on blown-off hands or legs of my people. I wanted a future; I was not going to stay because Tünde was not coming. This feeling is still unresolved between us. When we next met, some twenty years later, she was still angry at me for leaving. She blocked out of her mind her own part of it, how her mother was afraid I would talk Tünde into leaving. Tünde loved me as a sister and more. She gave her daughter my pagan middle name, Emese. She felt abandoned, but I know her love for her mother was always greater than her love for me. And that is how it should be. Now in her forties, she still lives at home with Mom. Losing Tünde was the highest price I had to pay for the revolution. It had to be done. My childhood was severed.

On the road to the West, I had a lot of time to think about my short life. I had always wanted to be a great novelist, and I contemplated what a fine chapter this would make one day, when I wrote my memoirs. Grandmother's protective powers were awesome. The first night, when I was too tired to walk any farther, I wanted to take a ride in one of those trucks that are constantly moving between the cities, carrying livestock or goods. I was going to catch a truck that had just passed me on the road and then stopped a little farther on. There were other refugees before me on the road who boarded the truck speedily and gladly. I tried my best to catch up. But you know the feeling when you are in a dream and you have to move and you can't? Well, that old lead-footed feeling was back. I couldn't catch that truck in time, and they were not waiting for me; that much was clear. But when the truck finally started to move, something else became clear as well. I saw it turn around and start back in the wrong direction toward the capital—or maybe Siberia. I could hear the screams coming out of the truck as the people realized that their good Samaritan was a government agent. After the truck was gone, my normal running powers returned, and I thanked Grandmother for her help. She kept me so safe that during my entire exodus I did not even see a Russian soldier!

My last night in Hungary I slept on a desk on the second floor of an office building in Györ, looking at the big green City Hall clock. From below I heard screams and cries, but by now I was too overloaded with such impressions and took them for granted. Next day, before dawn, I slipped out of the building through the side door the way I entered it. Once out on the street, I looked back and realized that I had spent the night in the police station, where the refugees rounded up from the streets were being held and turned back. The only reason I wasn't arrested was because I had taken refuge on an unused floor in the police station, the safest place in town. The last leg of my journey to the West was with a farmer who was taking his sugar beets to the commune as his yearly donation to the common good. He said he would escort me through the swamps to Austria. I gave him a watch I had saved for just such a bribe. I sat patiently while they weighed his beets and he signed the papers. He knew the swamps like his backyard. He said he went to Austria every so often through his secret paths— for a beer.

I already felt the impact of my leaving—swamps all around me, nice and mushy. No soldiers' tanks could possibly make it through here. The slim birches shaded our way, and before I knew it, though the swamps still looked much the same, we reached Austria. We entered the smoky, crowded Gasthouse. The place was loud with bilingual chatter as everybody toasted their arrival in the West with loud expectations. "To your good future!" the farmer said to me, draining the golden beer from his glass. I felt very self-conscious. All the kids that I saw there had come with their parents. There was not one other young girl of my age alone. I talked with my farmer friend and gave him all the money I had, since our money was not even registered in the world market. He politely protested, but put it away. Then he did something very unusual. He clicked his black boots together as they used to do during the monarchy and said, *A Boldogasszony álldjon meg!*"—"May the Gladwoman bless you." This pagan blessing came naturally out of his mouth. The Virgin Mary had assumed all the old names of our old goddess, the Gladwoman. Then he turned back to return to the waiting good earth of my ancestors. His traditional black vest was flapping in the wind; his black pants were now dusty from the sugar beets. He already belonged to Mother Hungary more than I did.

Grandmother was on the job that night. Shortly after the farmer went back to Hungary, I started to worry about where I was going to sleep. A woman poked her head in, saying something in German. I wished I could understand this language, but somebody translated it. She said she really wanted to help out, but had no space unless there was a young girl who could share the bed with her daughter. As her eyes swept over to me, I slowly put my hand up like we used to when we wanted to be called on in school, and she immediately broke into a smile. "Come, *schön*," she motioned with her hand to me and I obediently followed like a long-lost cousin, now firmly found and collected. I followed her to her warm, milk-smelling house. Finally I was to go to bed with the beautiful and long-gowned Ulrika, the oldest daughter in the family. She received my body into her bed with the best of patriotic intentions, as one young girl to another.

Ulrika reminded me of Tünde, not in the way she looked, for Tünde was swarthy, with jet-black hair, while Ulrika was fair, but her acceptance of me and her warmth was the same. I fell asleep, exhausted, in Ulrika's arms. She protectively enfolded me, shielding me against the enemies who had caused me to leave country and parents. As I lay looking out through the white lace

on the window into the moonlit night, I thanked Grandma. I
meditated on her floating on the winds, looking into the window
to see me safe. Just when I imagined that she was looking in and
actually making contact, I heard in the dark a familiar whisper.
"And tomorrow, you tell them you want to finish high school and
enroll with the Anglican teaching nuns—they run the best school
in Switzerland." "Yes ma'am—Grandma!"

I never did find the Anglican teaching nuns, but I found
a high school in Innsbruck where I could study in both German
and Hungarian. The school had only thirty-five students before the
revolution; now it had six hundred. Fortunately, they had a large
staff of high school teachers, who also escaped from Hungary. A
week and a half after I walked out my door in Budapest, I was
attending school as usual. The workers from charitable organizations found us foster homes. Innsbruck seemed to have many
aristocrats who were doing their patriarchal duty helping the refugees. My adoptive folks were working people who owned and
operated a respected fashion house; that was good.

Onkle Pepi, the father, and Tante Margit, the mother,
were cheerful, sporty people, with a passion for skiing and singing
songs. They had a little son, Peter, born on my very own birthday,
who was cute and curious. Hemma, a young woman a few years
older than I, was the housekeeper. I fully anticipated that I would
have to do housekeeping duties and work for my keep, but no—
all was taken care of. My only duty was just to study. I lived with
my new folks for two and a half wonderful years. Those years were
the most restful time in my life. I remember going to dances in a
shiny red gown I got from them, dancing gracefully on the arms
of all those Tiroler Burshes (young men). Every weekend Pepi
drove his family to a lovely mountaintop to hike around and,
ultimately, to eat a nice lunch in a nearby Gasthouse. There was
as much chocolate, bananas, oranges, and whipped cream as I
wanted. With these loving strangers—well-wishers, a little brother,
school—life was getting better and better.

The first time I used the name Zsuzsanna Budapest was
when, two weeks after I left Hungary, I could send back a message
to my mom, via Radio Free Europe.* It said: "Z. Budapest has
successfully arrived in the free world; Grandma Ilona watched over
me all the way. Letter on its way."

---

*I could have used my real name, but it would have been dangerous to my parents
to do so.

November

The Crone

I PUT YOUR MESSAGE INTO A spoonful of honey for your morning tea and wondered if you noticed it. I also turned on the heat. My bones are cold, my blood is thin, and I am gathering into myself that which is mine. I am gathering in what remains to be seeded; I gather in all. I gather my animals into warm caves and drive my birds south to winter. I put my bears to sleep until springtime and change the coats on the backs of my cats, big and small. My dogs are guiding me; they howl if danger approaches. My faithful hounds, wolves, and foxes are exquisite singers of the night, the crone's serenades. I said yes to life, and now I am saying yes to death. I am the first in line to go over to the other side. My wisdom about the herbs, life, and love, I pass down to you. Did you get it? I put it in your genes, in your racial memories, and in your dreams. Those are good places to store wisdom, preserved like jars of sweet jelly.

I would appreciate it if you would use this wisdom. I myself received it this way. Its purpose is to strengthen my daughters and sons. What for? To transform your realities, to hold onto happiness, to bond and dance and rejoice in the circle of rebirth. If you've resented your life, the burden of freedom, the chore of keeping body and soul together, your death will be just as unwelcome as your life has been. Death is not rest; it's hard work. You must pass over to the other side; do you know where that is? There are no highways, there are no maps; you are on your own! I count on your love of life to help you find the next life beyond this one. Only I am there to guide you. Yes, I am the crone. I shall be waiting at the crossroads. You will know me by instinct and welcome me. I shall guide you into the light once more, because you have been a good child of mine. I reward you with deep peace and reincarnation, if you so desire. Be well now . . . until we meet again.

November's Aspects

This month received its name from *novem* (from the Latin meaning "nine"), which indicates the position the month held in the Julian calendar.

Full moon aspect: Snow moon

Universal event: The dead draw near to the living, creating a time favorable for seeking guidance and prophecies.

Communal event: Feast of the Dead, November 1

Message: To secure, to root, to prepare

Activity: Preparation and protection

Healing properties: Healing overindulgence

Appropriate spells: Devotions to the dead, automatic writing, crystal-ball gazing, working with trance states and divination

Manifestation: Chrysanthemums, flower of the dead

Color: Green

Tree: Alder

Flower: Chrysanthemum

Creature: Owl, goose

Gem: Topaz

Anna's Spells, Rituals, & Celebrations for November

SPELL TO IMPROVE PSYCHIC POWERS

Psychic ability is not developed with one spell but rather through a series of events throughout one's life. Studying the stars, dream recording, and maintaining a healthy diet are good steps for development. Perform this spell during a new or full moon. To perform it, you must release your third eye; dress in yellow and place yellow candles on your altar. If you have a crystal ball, place it in the center. Brew yourself a cup of saffron tea to drink while meditating. Sit comfortably before your altar, breathing deeply. Think of your spine as a serpent uncoiling, reaching up, raising your energy. Light some incense that contains any of several herbs that are good for psychic work, such as wood betony, sandalwood, olibanum, uva ursi, nutmeg powder, or orrisroot powder.

As you inhale the smoke of these herbs, chant softly under your breath:

I am the channel of divine insight in the universe. My inner eyes see what my god sees. My inner ears hear what my god hears. My inner heart loves what my god loves.

Do not spend more than thirty minutes at this. When you retire, hold for a moment that fleeting feeling that comes just before slipping into sleep. Hold it and remember it, then let it go. Keep yellow candles burning in your room, fresh flowers by your bed, and a window open so you have fresh air at night.

STENIA: THE BITCHING FESTIVAL

One of the most remarkable women's festivities is the Stenia, otherwise known as the bitching festival. In the old days, around the Mediterranean, it happened like this: After the harvest was brought in, tents were set up and covered with fig leaves and grapevines. The elder women of the community were escorted into the tents and wined and dined by the younger ones. Men had to stay away, for the Stenia was women's business. At nightfall, younger women came to visit matrons in the tents and to also partake of drink and food, casting a wary eye on each other. First, the young ones exchanged verbal insults, calling each other names, then gradually they got as far as throwing dirt bombs. As the night advanced, dirt bombs became wrestling matches. Everything short of drawing blood was allowed. If the bitching got out of hand, matrons had the power to stop the Stenia and send everybody home. After the Stenia life returned to normal, cleansed free from resentments.

A modern version of the Stenia is when we get together and discuss our negative emotions. We pay a lot of money for these moments in therapy groups. Somehow, negative emotions are not acceptable, and we pretend we don't have them. If we are lucky and have a best friend, we can always vent these negative feelings to them. But what a joy it would be if we could safely tell off face-to-face those people we are angry with!

THE HOLIDAYS

November 1

REIGN OF THE GODDESS AS THE OLD WOMAN (CELTIC)

This period begins and extends until the end of November. The goddess is pictured as the veiled woman. Her name is Cailleach, and she embodies the forces of concentration. The festivals on this day involve building large balefires, sharing spirit cookies (shaped as people), and offering glasses of wine or milk to departed spirits. This is also the time of the banshee, who comes to visit her favorite family member. She foretells the future to those who listen and warns the family of impending disasters. In Gaelic, *ban* means "woman," *sidhe* means "the other side"—thus, woman from the other side, the ghostly white lady who brought death to her listeners. If she loved the person who was about to die, she would sing them gently over to the other side in their sleep. On the night of November 1, dances were held to entertain the spirits. At midnight, we fall silent, for that's when reverence toward ancestors serves the needs of both the living and the dead.

November 1

FEAST OF THE DEAD (MEXICAN)

On this day in Mexico, people celebrate the Feast of the Dead. Dressed in colorful costumes, good folks go picnicking in the cemeteries to share food with their departed ones. There are skeleton cookies, skulls made of sugar, and all kinds of decorations relating to mortality. But the mood is festive and playful, not solemn.

November 2

ALL SOULS' DAY (ENGLISH)

In England, the poor go begging for soul cakes, saying: "Soul, soul, soul cake, pray you mistress for a soul cake." This is where trick-or-treating—going door to door asking for sweets—originated.

November 3

FESTIVAL FOR THE NEW YEAR (GAELIC)

On this day the cattle are brought down from the mountains. The initiation of the soul starts on this day and finishes in February on Brigid's Day. It is a time to begin a new enterprise.

November 8

FESTIVAL OF THE GODDESS OF THE KITCHEN RANGE (JAPANESE)

This goddess is called the Kami of the Hearth in Japan. Housewives, honor yourselves. This is the celebration of the kitchen workers, providers of the hearth and daily food. On this day, it is a good idea to take the hard-working Kami out to eat and have somebody else in the household do all the dishes. I believe we should pay homemakers wages as we pay men who make war.

November 10

CELEBRATION OF THE GODDESS OF REASON (FRENCH)

In revolutionary France, the goddess of reason and the goddess of liberty were the same, and on this day there were wonderful and colorful processions through the city of Paris. A French woman was dressed up as the Goddess in a white frock, a blue mantle, and a red Phrygian cap. She was carried to Notre Dame de Paris. There she would receive her worshippers, who were crowned with oak leaves.

November 13

ISIS RESURRECTS OSIRIS (NORTH AFRICAN)

The good king and brother of Queen Isis disappears, and the mournful cries of Isis can be heard echoing in her temples: "I am your sister, by the same mother, thou shalt not be far from me."* The ritual goes on for at least four days while Isis searches for Osiris. She then gathers all the parts of his body together and breathes life into them, and resurrects him so that he can formally take his place next to her on the throne. What a graceful savior!

November 16

NIGHT OF HECATE (GREEK)

This is the night of Hecate, the Goddess of Witches and of the Crossroads, She Who is Three-formed. Hecate has been seen as part of the most ancient form of the moon goddess

trinity: Artemis, the virgin; Selene, the mother; and Hecate, the crone. She is the heavenly midwife, and the women most closely associated with her in the community were midwives. Hecate's worship was held at crossroads where three different roads met, for she was the goddess of transformation and ruled the passages of life. People left food out at the crossroads as a sacrifice to Hecate (although, of course, they understood that it was to be eaten by the poor). Her sacred symbol was the toad, universally used as a symbol for conception. Witches paid homage to her as the Witch Queen. From her came prophecies and cures, visions and magic. Her ancient threefold power was plagiarized by the new patriarchal priests and promptly assigned to their new God, namely, the threefold power of Christ to rule in heaven, on earth, and in hell. This is a good night for fortune-tellers, meditations, and prophesies.

November 22

SUN ENTERS SAGITTARIUS

On this day, honor Artemis, the archer, during Sagittarius, the sign of the archer, as well as the Amazons.

*"Lamentation of Isis" in *The Golden Bough*, ed. by James G. Frazer (New York: Macmillan, 1985).

The November Story:
Troubles, Troubles,
Boil and Bubbles

I SPENT MOST OF MY LIFE thinking that getting in trouble with the law was totally outside of my life-style. I always have been a law-abiding citizen. Sure, I jaywalk sometimes if I'm in a terrible hurry, and I got one speeding ticket when I was twenty-three years old in Chicago, doing 70 mph around 3:00 A.M. But by the seventies, those wild days were well behind me. After I became a feminist, especially a spiritual one, I was a vegetarian. Why would I ever be arrested?

It happened one fine spring day, when I got it into my head to incorporate feminist spirituality as a regular legal church. I called it "The Sisterhood of the Wicca." I found a feminist lawyer, who had great fun drawing up the papers; we filed with the state, and that was that. So now we were going to have the first Goddess church for women. The year was 1975. Three weeks later—just enough time for somebody in Sacramento to open the mail and start making some inquiries—a plainclothes policewoman called at our humble candle shop in Venice, California, which was called "The Feminist Wicca," and made an appointment for a Tarot reading.

This by itself was not unusual. I had read the Tarot very successfully for many different types of women: housewives, policewomen, street winos from the beach, stockbrokers, bankers, career women, unemployed women, lovers, widows, divorcées, movie stars, comics, composers, singers, writers, dancers, and a judge. But on the fateful day of this Tarot appointment, a curious thing happened at The Feminist Wicca. Just before the policewoman's appointment, a terrible stench went up in the small shop—an intense, cat-shit smell. Normally, we smelled lovely in that candle shop, with all those fine herbs and oils and incenses burning all the time. People always commented on how good it smelled in there. Nobody could explain why we should suddenly have such an awful odor in the shop, especially since we didn't have a cat— only cat shit, and only now.

The stench so upset me that I asked the waiting woman, "Please come back some other day. I cannot read the sacred Tarot and see into the future with this psychic disruption going on." I begged her to leave. But there was something very stern about this lady. She wasn't going to take no for an answer. She said, "Don't worry about a little smell of cat shit; it happens in the best of homes!"

"But you don't understand, we don't have a cat! We have only my dog Ilona. This is an omen. I have to figure out what it means."

"Oh, no," she repeated. "Let me help you clean it up, and then you can read my cards."

"I'd rather do it some other day. I'm too upset," I said.

Then she looked into my eyes and really laid on the guilt. "But I made an appointment. You said you would read my cards. I thought I could depend on my feminist sisters."

Now, in those days, these lines were loaded with meaning. How could I possibly disappoint this poor woman? The future of the entire movement might depend on it. I could not be a bad role model, and all the rest of such guilt trips passed through my mind. So I looked for the source of the stench and found it! It was right under my reading chair! A neat, fresh pile of healthy cat shit, and no cat to explain it! It was astonishing. I had to make a decision.

"I don't feel this is right," I said. "You'll have to come back some other time."

"I don't have any other time for this," she said. "I took time off from work to come here."

It was clear she was not going to go away. I had done another reading just before hers, and there was no trouble. Then I drank some water, took a few breaths, and suddenly the stench.

Why? Finally, I cleaned it up and washed the floor with lemon oil, which pretty well masked the stench. And I sat down to read this woman's Tarot cards. I shuffled the cards; she shuffled the cards; she cut the cards and handed them back to me. I laid out the first card, her significator. It was the Devil! Now we in the craft do not believe in a Devil, but the Tarot has been Christianized and has one, and one of its meanings is bondage. She didn't look as if she were in pain or in any bondage, but there are invisible chains, too. Little did I know the bondage was meant for me.

So I laid out the rest of the cards. What I remember now is that she had the Queen of Swords in her future, as if she really lived alone. She had a daughter who was a very good student. There was a mother around. A change of residence was indicated for the daughter, who was going to college. There wasn't really any great emergency, as she'd claimed. She said she had marital problems, but it looked as if she were divorced already. I gave her an oil for protection at no charge. She paid and then left. Minutes after she went out the door, two plainclothes policemen in red ski jackets came in and arrested me.

"Z Budapest, you are under arrest!" they boomed.

"What for?" I asked. I don't want you to think I was very cool and calm and took it gracefully.

"For fortune-telling! You violated the MC 43.30!" came the answer. A third policeman came with a camera and started taking pictures of all the candles and oils and books on the shelves. The omen! It suddenly came to me. The Goddess had tried to stop me from reading for the policewoman—I had been set up!

Then one of the policemen pulled a pair of handcuffs from his pocket. They glinted in the light, and something inside me turned over, like an ancient memory from the witchburnings. I pointed my fingers at them, and with all my might, I said, "Four months' worth of nightmares to the first man who touches me!" You should have seen their faces. They didn't count on a curse. They had felt so superior to me just a minute ago, busting a mere fortune-teller, discounting witchcraft as fraudulent and feminism as heresy. But now, faced with my curse, they decided not to handcuff me after all. No man dared touch me. No man read me my rights, either. The men opened the door to the police car for me, and took great care not to even brush by me. At the station, I was treated to fingerprinting with a towel. There I was, a witch accused. Hours later, my lawyer came and bailed me out of jail.

Emotionally, I felt as if I were back in the middle of the Hungarian Revolution and the Russians were firing at me. Except this time it was the Los Angeles Police Department. It felt very dangerous, the whole thing.

The first thing we had to do was to popularize the issue, which I saw as a violation of women's spiritual rights, a ban on prophesying. The entire women's community, however, was not yet educated about the importance of having our own religion. We were divided on how important spirituality really was. I also had to reach the women's audience about money—I didn't have money to pay the lawyers to defend me. We started building our case. Everybody thought it was going to be easy. I was exercising my religious rights. To "tell" fortunes, you had to use speech, and speech was protected under the First Amendment. No big deal, only harassment.

Sometime before I fell asleep that night, I remembered. According to law, nobody who has a criminal record can found a new religion. That was it! They were trying to discredit me and my dream of women's religion. To make the long and nerve-wracking story short, we managed to raise enough money to retain an experienced lawyer, who was joined by two rookie lawyers, one

of them a witch herself. Everybody thought they created a very good defense. The opposition had a woman lawyer as well. Fight feminists with the token woman. The district attorney had to dig up a woman; they found her in the research department. Nobody had ever heard of her before. This was her big chance to ascend from the lower ranks into the limelight. When we first laid eyes on her, she looked fierce and full of hatred toward witches. It was easy to dismiss her as incompetent, but she wasn't.

For four days we battled the forces of the L.A.P.D., because their evidence was all the case there was against us. There were no ripped-off little old ladies complaining that they'd been taken on a ride by a bad psychic. Against us, only members of the police testified. There was the policewoman and her phony marital problem. There were pictures of the oils and books and incense presented in large blowups. There were charts and more charts every day. Where did I sit? Where did the officer sit? What card came up when? Was that a snakeskin hanging on the wall behind me?

Then the prosecutor got into the religion itself. What kind of mumbo jumbo did I teach? Why were men not allowed to come to the gatherings? She was merciless, but with all her bravura, she couldn't say that I should be burned at the stake. In another century, she would have sent me to the pyre. By now, the press was out in front. A witch was on trial in Los Angeles, the first such trial since Salem. But the press doesn't like losers. And we were not winning. For all the pioneering work on female spirituality that had been done, this was still very, very early. There were no books out to provide examples of women's spirituality at this time. All the future teachers and writers on the goddess were still hatching from their older incarnations into their new ones. I only wrote articles for the local women's papers, and at that time the groundswell of the Goddess movement was only a low grumble.

We gave the prosecution a good lineup of credible witnesses. An anthropologist, who had been with us from the Susan B. Anthony Coven Number 1's inception, testified that witchcraft was a worldwide phenomenon before native people got Christianized. We marshalled another "credible" sister witch, who told the jury, composed mainly of Asian women who didn't speak much English, that she had seen wonderful healings happen in circles, the kind that couldn't have been explained by science. A Christian priest testified that he saw me as a peer, and sometimes lent me his church for gatherings, but there was no way we were going to convert the prosecutor, or the judge, who attended mass every day.

When it was all said and done, the only question that remained was whether I did predict the future. The undercover policewoman testified that everything I had said to her did come to pass. Her daughter moved to Florida and was attending veterinary school; by the trial's end, she was divorced and living alone; and, yes, the job she had was very demanding and she did feel in bondage about it quite often. Listening to her, you would have thought that she was testifying for our side. The jury was instructed that if they thought I had predicted the future, I was to be found guilty. The jury agreed that I did predict the future quite well. I was found guilty.

We started the long and hard journey to appeal, and appeal, and appeal. We fought for three years after the trial, until I got bored with the whole thing. The yellow pages in Los Angeles are filled with listings for all kinds of psychics—Madam This and Sister That—promising to fix love, money, and health problems. Where were these ladies when the law was battled? They were no fools. They wanted nothing to do with me. Feminism was a bad word. They liked the law as it was. Getting busted once a year was for them simply a form of taxation—cheap taxes at that. So I gave up the legal fight as well. It cost too much, it depressed me, and my old famous clients stayed away from me. I got tainted. Let somebody else fight this unjust law further. I thought that I had made the first chink in an armor that was bound to break soon enough. As Grandmother Time had it, it took nine years, but this law finally has been struck down by the California Supreme Court.

I am reminded of my visit to Rheo, a sister Dianic witch in her eighties. She understood what I was trying to do. When I saw her last in her own shop, the House of Hermetics, she took my hand in a sudden move of prophecy and kissed it! Now, older witches don't kiss younger witches' hands, I want you to know. It took me greatly by surprise. Then she looked at me and said, "Z, you will win this issue, but not the case. You will win it but not in the way you think!" I was already living in Oakland when I saw the headlines in the papers: "Fortune-telling Law Struck Down!" Nine years is just about the cycle of years it takes for the Grandmother of Time to fix something when you ask. It was well done.

Today, I read cards by appointment only, for people who keep coming back. I have books to write, workshops to teach, my own life to live. Sometimes I feel envious of those fashionable "channelers" who give themselves totally to this kind of work, communing with the spirits. They get written up in books by Shirley MacLaine and collect the very wealthy as exclusive clients. I would have fun with my favorite stars, extend my wisdom to those hard-working creative people. I can see it . . . what a plum of a job for a priestess! I feel good about the hundreds of women and men whom I have counseled in the past twenty years who have changed their lives for the better. They may not be famous media stars, but they are self-empowered and self-realized. Not even the stars could ask for more than that.

December

Lucina

NOW YOU ARE SHIVERING, BUNDLED up as you walk in snow and ice and fearing the rain because it brings colds and coughs. Oh, you poor souls! How you need me, your Sun Goddess, Lucina. My people in Sweden have not seen me in six months. My festival of rebirth there is awaited eagerly. Little girls dress up in white bridal gowns, wearing evergreen wreaths with candles in them on their heads—my own designs. They dispense cookies and spirits on the streets at dawn. Songs are ringing out from my people's hearts, praising me and my wintry peace. I like December festivities because I too am lonely for my young body and young thoughts. I, too, am longing for the warmth of my people and the lengthening of the days.

There now! I am coming back to you, little bird shivering in the winter. You already sing of me because you know I am faithful and will return soon. Winter Solstice is my birthday. My birthday has been taken away from me, but all my symbols are intact. The Christmas tree was once my Tree of Life; the holly is my symbol of rebirth. It is evergreen, of course, for in death, life still shines forth. How about the angels and star on the top of the tree? Did you enjoy seeing it as a child? It is the star of the fairy queen, she who brings magic into the newly lit world. And mistletoe, need I say, is also my symbol. The Golden Bough, as well as being medicine for the heart, is sacred to love of life as I hold life sacred. Singing and caroling all are ancient pagan customs, practiced long before my shrines were trampled and I was pronounced to be a male, a fallen angel named Lucifer. But there are places in the world where these new stories didn't take root, and my name is still the same, as you can see.

See me in my full regalia. I am wearing an evergreen crown with lighted white candles all around it, eight of them, representing the coming seasons (equinoxes and solstices and the high points in between). I, the Goddess of the Sun, shall bring you rebirth. Flowers are lonely for me within the womb of the earth; fruits are but thoughts of the trees. But I shall come and ripen them to delight again. And I shall feed the hungry people and tan the skins of the pale. I shall throw my magic on lights and make shadows and bless you all as I bless the invisible sleeping grain.

December's Aspects

This month used to be the tenth (*decem* in Latin) in the old Julian calendar. Now it is the twelfth month, but it is still called by its original number. Some things never change.

Full moon aspect: Moon of long nights

Universal event: The revitalizing of waters. Until Winter Solstice at the end of the month, night continues to increase and dominate. The Goddess of the Night reigns supreme.

Communal event: Winter Solstice Sabbat, December 21, the celebration of the birth of light, of the birth of the sun goddess Lucina

Message: To endure, to die, to be reborn

Activity: Introspection and renewal

Healing properties: Purification of body and soul

Appropriate spells: Rebirthing, getting rid of depression

Manifestation: The alder tree, which grows by the water and is often used by witches for making rain, and the helicon, the sacred bird traditionally seen only on the two solstices, regarded as the manifestation of the goddess in her life-in-death and death-in-life aspects

Color: Blood red

Tree: Alder and pine

Flower: Poinsettia, holly, mistletoe

Creature: Rook, helicon

Gem: Turquoise, zircon

Anna's Spells, Rituals, & Celebrations for December

SPELL TO HELP THOSE IN DEPRESSION

December is the month when cheerfulness is pushed on us in commercial doses, but it isn't really the mood of the season, at least not until Winter Solstice. In fact, depression is the natural mood of the month—introspection, self-doubt, questioning—it's none too cheerful. Still, too much depth is not good, so perform this spell for yourself with confidence.

The herb you'll use is called huckleberry herb. If you cannot find this, use sage. Purchase a good ounce of this, and do this spell when the moon is waxing. You will also need some high-quality temple incense—frankincense and myrrh are traditional: If you can't get it, just using sage will do fine. Create a circle about seven to nine feet in diameter and stand in the middle. The direction of the east is associated with inspiration and breath, newness and cheerfulness, eagles and flight. Call on those spirits to help you or somebody you love to fight depression.

Hold up your hands after you have lit your incense and, inhaling it deeply, say:

> I call on you, healing spirits of the east,
> That you shall attend me at once.
> I conjure you in the sacred name of Hecate, the
> Transformer and Midwife!
> I conjure you by the sage and [name the herb you are
> working with] to lift my spirit from this despair!
> Lift the misery by the smoke.
> Lift it by the fervent wish.
> Lift it by the power of the moon.
> So mote it be!

Repeat this ritual on three consecutive nights, and soon all shall be well.

SPELL TO BRING FAST LUCK

Seven Job's tears are needed for this spell. (These are common fare in occult supply stores.) Stuff these seeds in your pillow and sleep on them every night. Of course, opening up your pillow and sewing it shut again after you put in these seeds makes a bit of a mess. But it's worth it.

SPELL TO ATTRACT A LOVER

So what if it's December, these spells can be done any old time! Here is another one for would-be lovers. The magic herb is queen's root (*Stillingia sylvatica*). This herb is powerful in fertility matters as well, but first, the love spell. All you have to do is to carry this root on your person in a little red bag. It hides well in purses and pockets. If that works, one legend tells us that if you drink the tea of queen's root, it helps conception.

SPELL TO CALL ON THE ANGELIC FORCES

This spell is done best in December. If you can perform this, you can really have all your Christmas wishes come true, and then some! This is also good for asking the angelic forces, those happy spirits assigned to humankind for protection, for help in solving any problems. They can help us in matters of the heart; with mood, survival, miracles; even to write a book. The rite will require another trip to your herb shop, where you can buy an ounce each of pipsissewa (*Chimaphila umbellata*), rose powder, violet powder, and powdered vanilla. You have to crush pipsissewa into a fine mix and then add it to the rest of the magic ingredients; use a handful of each.

When you see the evening star rising, light a white candle in a jar, or a so-called seven-power candle, which has seven different colors on top of each other. This seven-power candle originates in Africa and is pretty powerful. These jar candles burn for a week without relighting, and they are safe in their fireproof jars. Meditate on the Angels of Light as you watch your candle burn (take a bath before you do this), and then light your very special incense and pray to the angels. The angels are older than Christianity by far; talk to them as you would to powerful friends. Tell them your heart's desires and your problems; bare your soul. Do this spell every seven days, seven being the magic number of the Goddess, a lucky number. The angels will get used to coming over to your place, and you will experience all kinds of miracles. Transfer the light of one candle to the next without putting it out.

SPELL TO FIND INNER PEACE

Every so often, we want to make a clean beginning and must therefore atone for the past. I don't mean we have to feel guilty; just the opposite. When you send out your Winter Solstice greeting cards, send some to people with whom you are not on good terms or to those with whom you may have quarreled. Just say, "Hey, let's forget our bad times. Blessings to you." Each time you share forgiveness, somebody else will forgive you. It's a good way to make friends out of enemies. To make sure that your message won't be misunderstood and make things worse rather than better, rub lavender buds on the card or include some in the envelope. Your credibility will rise.

WINTER SOLSTICE PRACTICES

If you make room for new things to happen, Nature, who cannot stand empty space, fills it up again for you with something new. In your home, put up a wonderful Yule Tree (any evergreen). The tree's scent is purifying, and it represents the tree of life. Decorate it with symbols of plenty—round balls in many colors and glitter of the fairies. When you drink eggnog, remember it is mother's milk you are drinking and feel her rejuvenating powers. Don't abuse your body during the winter holidays. Burn lots of candles all around your home all month long. Write in your journal; take time out for reflection. This isn't the time to be totally oriented outward. December is a truly merry month, but it is also a time for contemplation of the soul.

THE HOLIDAYS

December 3

FEAST OF BONA DEA (ROMAN)

Bona Dea is the Good Goddess of Justice. In her honor, women held celebrations, which men were not allowed to witness. Not even male cats or dogs were allowed to be near the women. Bona Dea sounds like the origin of separatism! Did men have a curfew? Have a women-only event today; start a group!

December 4

PALLAS ATHENA (ROMAN)

The goddess of wisdom, experience, and study was celebrated today by the Romans. However, Pallas was a separate goddess from Athena. Theirs is a lesbian love story one never hears about. The virgin Goddess Athena and Pallas were lovers in their youth, but Pallas fell from a cliff during Amazonian games. Athena grieved so deeply that she established Pallas's image in all her own temples. She put her name in front of her own and her image on her breast, the woman's head on the mantle called the *aegis*. Athena is not a cold-minded goddess; she is a lover who has deep feelings and attachments. Wisdom, the arts, strategies—all are her inventions. She is the weaver, the musician, and the artist. Celebrate lesbian love today.

December 5

SINTERKLAAS DAY (DUTCH)

On this day, children in Holland put out shoes to be filled with presents by the old elf, Sinterklaas. We borrowed Santa Claus from the Dutch; he brings presents to fill stockings of children later this month.

December 8

IMMACULATE CONCEPTION OF THE BLESSED VIRGIN MARY (EUROPEAN)

Originally the White Goddess, the Virgin Mary is celebrated on this day. She is portrayed as the Queen of Heaven, with the moon under her feet and the sun shining behind her. Her long hair flows to her shoulders, and all the symbols of the pagan goddess are in the backgrounds of her portraits. In her hand is the olive, rose, lily, mirror, scepter, and crown. The goddess proceeded from herself. As the Egyptian Neith states, "No man hath ever lifted My veil."* Old customs of burning incense to her suggest that the Virgin Mary is none other than the goddess of sun and moon.

In southern Mexico people celebrate the ancient Mayan mother Ixchel on this day, with processions and blessings on small boats and fields. In Japan, women take this day off to entertain and take over men's roles in the

---

*Egyptian inscription, quoted by Durbin-Robertson, *Juno Covella*, 245.

household. It is called the Hari no Kuyo. Reverse the roles; step into each other's shoes!

December 9
FEAST OF TONANTZIN (MEXICAN)

In 1531 the ancient Goddess Tonantzin appeared on this day to Juan Diego at the site of her old pagan temple on Tepayak Hill, which had stood undisturbed since the Spanish conquest. According to Juan Diego, Tonantzin said she loved the people and wanted her shrine rebuilt. Her wish was granted. Tonantzin was believed to be the manifestation of the Virgin Mary. Hence, Tonantzin is called the Virgin of Guadalupe, and on this day she is celebrated by Mexican people, who come to her shrine from all over the world. "For I am the Mother of all of you who dwell in this land," said she.* Viva Tonantzin!

December 13
ST. LUCY'S DAY (SWEDISH)

This is the grandest celebration of Lucina as Sun Goddess. Women dress as brides and parade through the streets dispensing cookies and drinks, spreading cheer as the Goddess dispenses the new rays of the sun. The daughter of the house, wearing a candle crown, awakens the family with cakes and song. Young girls in white dresses are most prominent in these celebrations, since the Sun Goddess is a child still. Men dress as elves, Lucy's helpers. If you fly on Swedish airlines on this day, the crew will still perform Lucy's fest for you.

---

*Durbin-Robertson, *Juno Covella*, 248.

December 17
CELEBRATION OF OPS; SATURNALIA (ROMAN)

Saturn and Ops, the Goddess of Plenty, celebrate their blessings today. This was the original gift-giving season, when people gave each other things wrapped in rice paper for Ops, Goddess of Fertility, and dolls representing the people themselves in health and prosperity. Saturn liked partying, with wine and singing. Slaves were given freedom on this day, and every effort was made to return to the Golden Age, when there had been no social ranks. The festival went on for the rest of the month. This custom is the origin of all the carnivals and revels. Some of these carnivals have survived in Austria, Belgium, Germany, France, Spain, Italy, and Hungary.

December 21
WINTER SOLSTICE; SUN REENTERS CAPRICORN

This is the Winter Solstice, the birth of light—a major sabbat for witches, who greet the sun with all-night vigils and dance and sing in the new rays. The sun reenters Capricorn, the sign of the goat. Virgin mothers give birth to their children all around the world: Rhiannon gives birth to the sacred son Pryderi. Isis is rebirthing Horus. Demeter gives birth to her sacred daughter Persephone; the earth goddess gives birth to Dionysus. Amaterasu (Japan) comes out of her cave. These various celebrations of rebirth are the origins of Christmas.

December 23

FOOL'S DAY (EUROPEAN)

Pagan lore tells of the yearly dying and rebirth of the king. On this day in Europe, the town's fool was crowned and seated on the throne, and the real king went into "hiding," a simulated death. Even the mighty had to die in order to be reborn again.

December 24

MOTHER NIGHT (ANGLO-SAXON)

Our pagan Anglo-Saxon ancestors called the night before Christmas the night of the mothers—or Modraniht (Anglo-Saxon for Mother Night). Who were these mysterious mothers, who awed all the world? As in an orchestrated divine act, the great goddesses from all over the world gave birth, and the new world was born.

This is a magical time—a renewed commitment to life has been made by the mothers. Youth is filled with excitement, because after the night of the mothers, their turn is coming. The next day, all the love the mothers celebrated will shower down on the young in the form of presents of magical meaning. These early Anglo-Saxons most likely had a big dinner for each other, where the women of the family visited and got presents ready for the children. All the popular symbols of this season come from pagan times. The Tree of Life, our Christmas tree, we decorate today with round balls and lights. The sweets we hang on it, the gifts we place under it, the entire nativity scene is part of the pagan heritage. Putting the yule log on the fire has Germanic/Scandinavian origins. Yule means "the wheel." Ops is still giving presents as her festival continues. The Star Goddess, the Lady of Nature, rules over the world. Her symbol of the pole star, displayed on top of all Christmas trees, reminds us of our deep memories of her.

December 25

JUVENALIA: DAY OF THE CHILDREN (ROMAN)

On this day, much artistic entertainment—theater, mummers, stories, magical characters (harlequins, fools) in costumes and masks—was provided for the children. Everyone wore their best clothes and ate the best foods. Giving talisman presents that had good luck value—a bell, a lucky hat, a pair of socks for you to wear on your lucky path, toys, warm things to wear during the winter yet to come—were probably the first gifts. There were dances, where youth met, courted each other, and fell in love under the mistletoe. Long before our Anglo-Saxon ancestors had their very first contact with Christianity (a Far Eastern import not indigenous to Europe), they already celebrated Christmas, which for centuries was known as Modraniht, much as we celebrate it today.

December 25

CELEBRATION OF ASTARTE (SEMITIC)

Related to Ishtar of Babylon, starry Astarte, the Great Goddess from the Middle East, dates back to neolithic times. She was the creating, preserving, and destroying power we associate with all the virgin goddesses. Solomon in the Bible worshipped her; maybe that's why the Christians made her into the devil Astoreth and, to make things worse, masculinized her as well. Astarte was called Athtar by the Arabs. In Aramaic, she was Attar-Samayin, the morning star in heaven. To the Canaanites, she was known as Ashtoreth, the celestial ruler, mother of Baalim, mother of all the gods.

December 25

YULE: RETURN OF THE SUN (TEUTONIC)

The figure of Santa Claus has gone through many incarnations, from old god to Christian saint to a major figure in American folklore.

His reindeer testify clearly to his shamanic origins, and his elves are from the fairy traditions of the Old Religion. The Kissing Bough is the mistletoe, magic cast on would-be lovers. Sometimes a girl would sit atop the yule log as it was dragged in; then everybody drank to the health of the girl, who symbolized the sun goddess.

Saturnalia continues during this time.

December 31

HECATE'S DAY (ROMAN)

The year is turning. The flames of the hearth are rekindled. Hestia/Vesta, the Goddess of the Flame, is honored. Build fires in this season, in a fireplace or outside. Light lots of candles to brighten this winter month. Banish fear, raise joy, for your journey around the sun is complete. Give thanks for the rich experiences you have had and renew your hope for another ticket around the sun:

Queen of heaven, Goddess of the Universe,
The One who walked in the terrible chaos
And brought life by the law of love
And out of chaos brought us harmony
And from chaos she has led us by the hand.
Woman of women, Goddess who knows no
equal,
She who decrees the destiny of people,
Highest ruler of the world,
Sovereign of heaven,
Goddess even of those who live in Heaven—
*Hear our prayer!**

---

*"Ishtar," in Stone, *Ancient Mirrors of Womanhood*, 107. Permission to reprint courtesy of Beacon Press.

The December Teaching: The Mystical, Practical Art of Celebration

ONCE UPON A TIME I was asked to conduct the main circle ritual at a gathering in Wisconsin in 1988 for the Developing Dianic Wicca Conference. For two years, about a hundred and fifty women from all over the country had been gathering in Wisconsin to define and develop the tradition of the women's mysteries. One might imagine that a large number of beautiful women could easily perform a wonderful mystical ritual, but it wasn't so. The priestess came prepared with many ideas and offered opportunities for the group to participate in the circle. But the group was not unified yet; the women had just arrived from all over the United States and were not in a mood to reveal themselves.

What causes circles to die—to limp and bog down? Gone are the times when women circled naturally with each other; we are now ignorant or have acquired bad habits. Rule number 1, I found, was to never plan a ritual for a group without the group being part of the planning. When leading a circle ritual, make time beforehand to involve everybody in creating the experience. This will keep the women interested and will give them specific things to do that will liberate them from being passive bystanders. Tell people to gather flowers, bring candles, contribute some of their occult supplies. This will avoid another problem—that of having your own supplies used up, mine often were.

When planning a circle ritual, first find out how big the circle is to be. Everybody should get up and hold hands; then you can see what you have to work with. Make sure the group makes a real circle, if possible, not a potato shape. The difference is that from any point in a real circle, you can see everybody else. This gives people a chance to see themselves for the first time as a group. They need to see who is there; they need to feel it. Does it feel good? Affinities must be allowed to come into play, participants allowed to change places with each other.

From your first to your last request to the group, you as ritualist must project that you are accessible, that you are organically part of the whole, not someone set apart as privileged or divinely "chosen" and therefore better than the rest. You must belong to your function as priestess and nothing else. What do I mean by this? A Goddess priestess, for example, would not position herself apart from the group, sitting on a throne in the middle, or elevated above others' heads. She would position herself as part of the group, thus giving her easy access to talk to the group at any time. I use humor often, because women relax if they can laugh. I call it laughter yoga. Just start a good cackle sometimes; that will break the ice.

Now find out who are the air signs in your group—Gemini, Libra, Aquarius. Charge the air sign women to create their own corner of the universe, to make an altar to the east. This will bring them together; having something in common, all being air signs, they will have their own symbols to draw on. Then do this with all the fire signs—Aries, Sagittarius, Leo; they will create the altar to the south. Water signs—Cancer, Pisces, Scorpio—should work on the corner of the west. The north altar should be created by the earth signs—Taurus, Virgo, Capricorn. Suddenly, the whole group is busy and starting to use their intuitive powers by making altars, arranging flowers, pouring water into chalices, making things look beautiful, talking to each other, trusting each other. The middle of the altar for the Goddess herself should be created by all the women after they have created their special corner of the universe. You would be surprised how quickly beautiful altars are built by different women. The experience of creating sacred space together is already trancelike; it is an unusual activity, for centuries forbidden and punished with death. Witches have returned to worship the life force again. Now the women dress up, putting on their ritual finery. Crowns are made of flowers, grasses, and branches. Some don real silver crowns and silver bracelets;

others wear beads and gems. Transformation is already taking place.

A circle is like a layered cake. Every layer is followed by the next layer, each higher than the one before. Energy is built the same way; the first layer of energy is forming the circle. It is important that we don't fudge on raising power. Power is what the Goddess is all about. The very energy of life is the goddess's power, and that force must be channeled into the circle in great fluid streams. This invisible energy becomes visible when everyone holds hands and the group starts swaying unconsciously, first just a little, then full waves that involve all participants, bodies moving gently by the power of the flow of the goddess energy.

The next step of raising energy must be even higher, like the next layer of cake. Humming is the traditional Dianic power-raising technique. You vibrate the skull by letting your vocal cords rub together gently. Check the top of your head; is it vibrating? Keep humming for about three to five minutes to balance the electricity in your blood. When the Dianics started attending mixed pagan festivals and attracted priestesses from all traditions, women quickly learned humming and introduced the technique in their own covens.

After the humming has taken the circle into a deeper meditative mode, that is when you call in the corners of the universe, that is when you raise your voice loud and clear and address the forces in nature—the air, the fire, the water, the earth. Calling the powers of the universe can also be done communally. All the women who belong to a particular corner, according to the zodiac, can call it in, using all the imagination they have. They can call individually, they can call communally, they can add to each other's invocations, they can make noises to underscore them. The only thing not allowed is to drop the energy. The energy must keep rising, no matter what happens. If it is allowed to drop, the circle is lost. You have to start all over again. One good way to make sure the energy doesn't drop is to keep humming gently underneath all the other invocations.

Let's say you have done what you needed to do, you called in the appropriate goddesses and elements of air, fire, water, and earth, and the circle has been closed. Here is the center of the magic: What is your purpose, what is this circle for? Magic of the Goddess should not be used just to make you feel good or because it's groovy to be in the magical circle. Power must be used; you called it in, you asked it to be present, now you must send it somewhere. This isn't so hard, since you have already agreed on this before you started, as part of the preparation for the circle work. I offer world peace or an end to child abuse, sexism, and violence as valid goals.

Imagine the Goddess actually floating overhead, composed of all the emanations of the women's bioplasma, our bodies' vibrations. She is now waiting for you to relate to her. Offer the chalice to the Goddess, with the invocation to the Star Goddess.* This is my favorite prayer. It always evokes the awe of the Goddess, makes us think about immortality, lifts our hopes, and makes us wise. But whatever sacred text you use, this is the moment in the circle when it is good to get reverential. If the group knows this prayer, it is most powerful to recite it in unison. It sends shivers up your spine, it can be so moving.

After a pause, the humming continues, low and steady, to support the energy rising. This is the part when individuals can come to the Goddess, addressing her as they would their own mother, and ask for things in their lives—health, wealth, wisdom, cures, solutions. We usually do this by stepping into the circle and lighting our candle while we speak. Other women hum and pay attention. We usually go around the circle at least once and light all the candles on the altar.

We have now arrived at the high point of the circle. If there was a chill in the air before, now there is none of it left. Our body temperature as well as the room or space around us is sizzling hot with candlelight and energy. Now is the time to chant and sing Goddess songs and, eventually, when the time is right, to dance around the altar at least three times for good luck so that all that has been asked of the Goddess is blessed. My favorite chant is "The Goddess is alive! Magic is afoot!"

Each woman affirms the Goddess: "The Goddess is alive!" And each time the group chants back, "Magic is afoot!" After the affirmation of the goddess, each woman substitutes her own name to affirm her connection to the divine. "Zsuzsanna is alive! Magic is afoot!" This raises even more energy. You must be careful; not just any chant or song will do; it must go with the existing energy level. Don't bring down the group with a slow song now; save it for later when you are grounding the energy. A priestess must have a varied repertoire of songs and chants.

Finally, everyone holds hands and encircles the altar. The lit candles burn low now, the last request has been made, and

---

*Z. Budapest, *The Holy Book of Women's Mysteries* (Oakland, Calif.: Wingbow, 1989), 125.

the dance is in progress. Move gracefully and joyously in the circle dance. When it is finished, it is time to ground the energy. It has been a popular practice to ground the energy by banging on the dusty floor, kissing the ground, or making other ground-oriented gestures. I prefer to only kiss the earth in nature—and I don't mean sidewalks. To ground, the ancients simply settled down to a feast. Food is the most natural way to ground. If food is not available (as it always should be), use breathing to ground. Inhale the energy as if through a straw, store it in your body, and tell yourself that this space will live on inside you—all you have to do is to breathe to get to it. I also use communal applause to ground. We applaud each other and the experience. It is an excellent way to calm down from a ritual. With food itself, there are rituals that continue the good feelings and blessings. We usually feed each other the first bite and first sip of water, saying, "May you never hunger! May you never thirst!" Only after we have fed somebody else, do we ourselves start eating. It reinforces the feeling of being one; to share foods and think of somebody else first is what is done at sacred meals.

Finally, when the energy is about to slip away but just before it does, all should rise again and together thank the power, the Goddess, for having visited us with her presence. Just as we had lots of enthusiastic participation calling in the four corners of the universe, the same energy is now evoked to thank them. I always like to throw a flower in each direction—a daisy or a rose, whatever is available—as a true hail and farewell. It just makes a classy exit. I like to think the Goddess appreciates a fine touch.

I also use closing songs that I compose myself for a good ending after a good gathering. The ending is as important as the beginning, if not more so.

May Artemis protect you
And Hera provide you
And the woman soul within you
Guide your way home.
Merry meet and merry part
And merry meet again!

The women now collect their valuables from the altar— their candles (they can finish burning them on their home altars), jewels, cloths, whatever they contributed to the building of the altars. In this way, the women also gain insight into the magic they have created; they remember putting things up and now taking

them down. It was the magic of the goddess, but somehow it was the women the magic was created by. It's a good lesson to ponder. When all is said and done, drive home safely.

A good ritual stays with you for weeks, giving you energy. Little moments pop into your mind from the evening. You remember things that happened, how you felt, and how you feel now. Two women from our last full moon celebration remembered how they saw a white emanation of the Goddess in the middle of the circle all during our prayers. I remembered how smoothly the energy flowed and how I lost the sense of time; it was 1:30 A.M. when we stopped, and it felt as if it were only 10:00 P.M. When you enter the space between the worlds, such as a magic circle, your sense of time goes first. The best remembrance is when the spells come in, one by one, and you can see how what you asked for was granted. Ultimately, that is the proof of a good ritual: Did it work?

Feel what the group needs. Can you channel the communal will? Can you enhance the state of feelings? Can you create a ritual that fits precisely the moment and the people? All I do is feel. It comes in, like a song on the radio. It comes to me exactly what's needed—even in what order. But it is a lot of work. It is a lot of risk, staying open like that, trusting what's to happen. I never think "What if I don't get the next move? What if I don't receive the ritual through my priestessing/channeling?" There was one time when I went blank, when nothing seemed to come in, but then we used this silence. The silence taught us a lot more than we knew before. It rested all of us—total silence.

Rituals, as I have suggested in this book, barely touch the surface of the knowledge and breadth and width that this spiritual endeavor requires. I would like to see women take the skills of managing communal energy more to heart and increase the trust in the unexpected. Theater and skills of improvisation must be blended into ritual work, or we drown ourselves in trivia and boredom. Ritual leaders—dress up more, use your tools, don't just keep them in the house. The psyches of women are hungry for the ancient archetypes; encourage the women who have it in them to lead. Exercise your own self-knowledge, recognize your limits, and recognize your own strengths. This will make you the priestess the Goddess needs you to be; none of us can do it all nor do we need to do it all; that is why we have each other. And that is good.

BIBLIOGRAPHY

Adler, Margo. *Drawing Down the Moon*. New York: Harper & Row, 1987.

Allen, Richard Hinckley. *Star Names: Their Lore and Meaning*. New York: Dover, 1963. (Originally published 1899.)

Arguelles, Jose A. *The Transformative Vision*. Boulder: Shambala, 1975.

Atwater, Donald. *The Penguin Dictionary of Saints*. 2nd ed. Harmondsworth, England: Penguin, 1985.

Bailey, Alice A. *A Treatise on White Magic*. New York: Lucis, 1974.

The Beltane Papers (1984–88). (*Beltane Papers*, P.O. Box 8, Clear Lake, WA 98235)

Berger, Pamela. *The Goddess Obscured: Transformation of the Grain Protectress from Goddess to Saint*. Boston: Beacon Press, 1985.

Better Homes and Gardens Heritage Cookbook. New York: Meredith Corporation, 1975.

Blavatsky, H. P. *An Abridgement to the Secret Doctrine*. Wheaton, Ill.: Theosophical Publishing House, 1973a.

———. *Isis Unveiled*. Wheaton, Ill.: Theosophical Publishing House, 1973b.

Blofeld, John. *Compassion Yoga: The Mystical Cult of Kwan Yin*. London: Allen Unwin Paperbacks, 1977.

Bodde, Derk. *Festivals in Classical China: New Year and Other Annual Observances During the Han Dynasty, 206 B.C.–A.D. 220*. Princeton, N.J.: Princeton University Press, 1975.

Bradley, Marion Zimmer. *The Mists of Avalon*. New York: Knopf, 1983.

Budapest, Z. E. *The Holy Book of Women's Mysteries*. Oakland, Calif.: Wingbow, 1989.

Budge, E. A. Wallis. *The Egyptian Book of the Dead*. New York: Dover, 1967.

Calendar of Irish Folk Customs, 1984. Belfast, Ireland: Appletree Press, 1983.

Carlyon, Richard. *A Guide to the Gods*. London: Heinemann/Quixote, 1981.

Cassella, Dolores. *A World of Breads*. Port Washington, N.Y.: David White, 1977.

Christ, Carol P. *Diving Deep and Surfacing: Women Writers on Spiritual Quest*. Boston: Beacon Press, 1980.

Clark, Ella E. *Indian Legends of the Pacific Northwest*. Berkeley: University of California Press, 1953.

Collins, June McCormick. *Valley of the Spirits: The Upper Skagit Indians of Western Washington*. Seattle: University of Washington Press, 1980.

Deramer, Percy, Ralph Vaughan Williams, and Martin Shaw. *The Oxford Book of Carols*. New York: Oxford University Press, 1975. (Originally published 1928.)

Downing, Christine. *The Goddess: Mythological Images of the Feminine*. New York: Crossroads, 1981.

Durdin-Robertson, Lawrence. *Juno Covella: Perpetual Calendar of the Fellowship of Isis*. Enniscorthy, Ireland: Cesara, 1982.

Ehrenreich, Barbara, and Deirdre English. *Witches, Midwives, and Nurses: A History of Women Healers*. Old Westbury, N.Y.: Feminist Press, 1973.

Engwall's Journal: A Newsletter for Coffee Connoisseurs (1987). (*Engwall's Journal*, Letter Drop, 120 Brighton Road, P.O. Box 5221, Clifton, NJ 07015)

Estrada, Alvaro. *Maria Sabina: Her Life and Chants*, translated by Henry Munn. Santa Barbara, Calif.: Ross-Erikson, 1981.

Faron, L. C. *Hawks of the Sun*. Pittsburgh: University of Pittsburgh Press, 1964.

———. *The Mapuche Indians of Chile*. New York: Holt, Rinehart & Winston, 1972.

Friedrich, Paul. *The Meaning of Aphrodite*. Chicago: University of Chicago Press, 1978.

Gimbutas, Marija. *Goddesses and Gods of Old Europe, 6500–3500 B.C.: Myths and Cult Images*. Berkeley: University of California Press, 1982.

Goddesses and Their Offspring: Nineteenth- and Twentieth-Century Eastern European Embroideries. 1986 exhibit catalog. Binghamton, N.Y.: Roberson Center for the Arts and Sciences, 1986.

Goldenberg, Naomi R. *Changing of the Gods: Feminism and the End of Traditional Religions.* Boston: Beacon Press, 1979.

Graves, Robert. *The Greek Myths.* Vols. 1 and 2. Harmondsworth, England: Penguin, 1983.

———. *The White Goddess.* New York: Farrar, Straus & Giroux, 1966. (Originally published 1948.)

Greenberg, Florence. *Florence Greenberg's Jewish Cookbook.* Secaucus, N.J.: Chartwell Books, 1980.

Grieve, M. *A Modern Herbal.* 2 vols. New York: Dover, 1971.

Griffin, Susan. *Women and Nature: The Roaring Inside Her.* New York: Harper & Row, 1978.

Grimal, Pierre, ed. *Larousse World Mythology.* London: Paul Hamlyn, 1965.

Guren, Denise, and Nealy Gillette. *The Ovulation Method: Cycles of Fertility.* Bellingham, Wash.: Ovulation Teachers Association, 1984.

Haich, Elizabeth. *Initiation.* Palo Alto, Calif.: Seed Center, 1974.

Hall, Nor. *The Moon and the Virgin: Reflections on the Archetypical Feminine.* New York: Harper & Row, 1980.

Harding, M. Esther. *Woman's Mysteries: Ancient and Modern.* New York: Harper & Row, 1971.

Harlan, William. *The Horizon Cookbook and Illustrated History of Eating and Drinking Through the Ages.* New York: American Heritage/Doubleday, 1968.

Harrison, Jane Ellen. *Prolegomena to the Study of Greek Religion.* New York: Meridian, 1955.

Harrison, Kenneth. *The Framework of Anglo-Saxon History to A.D. 900.* Cambridge, England: Cambridge University Press, 1976.

Harvey, Youngsook Kim. "Possession Sickness and Woman Shamans in Korea." In *Unspoken Worlds,* edited by Falk and Gross. New York: Harper & Row, 1980.

———. *Six Korean Women: The Socialization of Shamans.* St. Paul, Minn.: West, 1979.

Hendricks, Rhoda A. *Mythologies of the World: A Concise Encyclopedia.* New York: McGraw-Hill, 1979.

Hickey, Elizabeth. *The Legend of Tara.* Dundalk, Ireland: Dundalgan Press, 1982.

Hope, Murry. *The Way of Cartouche.* New York: St. Martin's Press, 1985.

Hultkrantz, Ake. "The Religion of the Goddess in North America." In *The Book of the Goddess, Past and Present,* edited by Carl Olson. New York: Crossroad, 1985.

Iglehart, Hallie. *Womanspirit: A Guide to Women's Wisdom.* New York: Harper & Row, 1983.

Jobes, Gertrude, and James Jobes. *Outer Space: Myths, Name Meanings, Calendars.* New York: Scarecrow Press, 1964.

Kavasch, Barrie. *Native Harvests: Recipes and Botanicals of the American Indian.* New York: Random House/First Vintage Books, 1979.

Kimball, Yeffe, and Jean Anderson. *The Art of American Indian Cooking.* New York: Doubleday, 1965.

Kovi, Paul. *Transylvanian Cuisine.* New York: Crown, 1985.

Krieg, Saul. *The Alpha and Omega of Greek Cooking.* New York: Macmillan, 1973.

Krupp, E. C. *Echoes of the Ancient Skies: The Astronomy of Lost Civilizations.* New York: New American Library, 1983.

Lurker, Manfred. *The Gods and Symbols of Ancient Egypt,* translated by Barbara Cumming. New York: Thames and Hudson, 1980.

Metropolitan Museum of Art/Los Angeles County Museum of Art. *From the Lands of the Scythians: Ancient Treasures from the Museums of the U.S.S.R., 3000 B.C. to 100 B.C.* 1975 exhibit catalog. New York/Los Angeles, 1975.

Mikalson, Jon. *The Sacred and Civil Calendar of the Athenian Year.* Princeton, N.J.: Princeton University Press, 1975.

Monaghan, Patricia. *The Book of Goddesses and Heroines.* New York: Dutton, 1981.

Murphy, John. *Traditional Irish Recipes.* Handscribed by Margaret Batt. Belfast, Ireland: Appletree Press, 1980.

Nowak, Margaret, and Stephen Durrant. *The Tale of the Nisan Shamaness: A Manch Folk Epic.* Seattle: University of Washington Press, 1977.

Octava: Newsletter for the Eight Feasts, TBPs (1986–). (*Octava,* P.O. Box 8, Clear Lake, WA 98235)

Ouei, Mimie. *The Art of Chinese Cooking*. New York: Random House, 1960.

Palmer, Martin, ed. *T'ung Shu: The Ancient Chinese Almanac*. Boston: Shambala, 1986.

Passmore, Nancy F. W. et al. *The Lunar Calendar: Dedicated to the Goddess in Her Many Guises*. Boston: Luna Press.

Piercy, Marge. *The Moon Is Always Female*. New York: Random House, 1980.

———. *Woman on the Edge of Time*. New York: Knopf, 1976.

Potts, Billie. *Witches Heal: Lesbian Herbal Self-Sufficiency*. Bearsville, N.Y.: Hecuba's Daughters, 1981.

Rich, Adrienne. *Of Woman Born: Motherhood as Experience and Institution*. New York: Bantam, 1977.

Roberts, Jane. *The Nature of Personal Reality*. Englewood Cliffs, N.J.: Prentice-Hall, 1974.

Robinson, Herbert Spencer, and Knox Wilson. *Myths and Legends of All Nations*. Totowa, N.J.: Littlefield, Adams, 1976.

Rudhyar, Diane. *The Lunation Cycle*. New York: Shambala, 1971.

Sanday, Peggy Reeves. *Female Power and Male Dominance: On the Origins of Sexual Inequalities*. Cambridge, England: Cambridge University Press, 1981.

Santa Maria, Jack. *Indian Sweet Cookery*. Boulder: Shambala, 1980.

Sojourner, Sabrina. "From the House of Yemanja: The Goddess Heritage of Black Women." In *The Politics of Women's Spirituality*, edited by Charlene Spretnak. Garden City, N.Y.: Anchor Press/Doubleday, 1982.

Spicer, Dorothy Gladys. *The Book of Festivals*. New York: Woman's Press, 1937.

Spretnak, Charlene. *Lost Goddesses of Early Greece*. Berkeley, Calif.: Moon Books, 1978.

———. *The Politics of Women's Spirituality*. Garden City, N.Y.: Anchor Press/Doubleday, 1982.

Starhawk. *The Spiral Dance*. New York: Harper & Row, 1979.

Stein, Diane. *The Kwan Yin Book of Changes*. St. Paul, Minn.: Llewellyn, 1986.

Stewart, Katie, and Pamela Michael. *Wild Blackberry Cobbler and Other Old-Fashioned Recipes*. Salem, N.H.: Salem House, 1984.

Stone, Merlin. *Ancient Mirrors of Womanhood: Our Goddess and Heroine Heritage*. Boston: Beacon Press, [1979] 1984.

The Time-Life Holiday Cookbook. New York: Time-Life Books, 1976.

Tun Li-ch'en. *Annual Customs and Festivals in Peking*, translated by Derk Bodde. Peiping: Henri Vetch, 1936. (Originally published 1900.)

Walker, Barbara G. *The Woman's Encyclopedia of Myths and Secrets*. San Francisco: Harper & Row, 1983.

Wasson, R. Gordon. *Maria Sabina and Her Mazatec Velada*. New York: Harcourt Brace Jovanovich, 1974.

Zimmerman, J. E. *Dictionary of Classical Mythology*. Toronto: Bantam, 1980.

INDEX

witches' broom, 94
witches' girdles, 14
witches' sabbat, 14–17, 55
Witch Queen, 224
witch trial, 229–30
Wives' Feasts, 30
Wolf, Kate, 170
wolves, 22, 32
women: creativity of, 123; as
     cultivators, 33; middle-
     aged, 190; protection of,
     115–16; as rulers, 144;
     sexuality of, 75
Women's Day, international,
     52–53

women's rights: festival of,
     206–7; first convention,
     143
Women's Spirituality
     Movement, 14–19
Womyn's Music Festival,
     Michigan, 164–73
wood betony, 199, 221
World War II, 86
wormwood (Artemisia), 92–93
wrens, 117

Yakima tribe root festival, 82
yellow candles, 29, 100–101,
     192, 221

yellow color, 100, 157, 192
yellow dock, 158
Yemaya, 124
yerba maté, 179–80
yew tree, 199
Yggdrasil, 137
young creatures, goddess of,
     95
Yule, 238, 242
yule log, 241, 242

Zeus, 54–55, 133
zircon, 235
zoni, 10

About the Author

Zsuzsanna Emese Budapest was born in Budapest, Hungary, during a big winter storm on January 30, 1940. Her mother, Masika Szilagyi, was a medium and a practicing witch who supported herself and her daughter with her art, as a sculptress. Masika's themes always celebrated the Triple Goddess and the Fates, and Zsuzsanna ("Z") grew up respecting and appreciating Mother Nature as a god. The poverty of postwar Europe and political oppression under the Russian occupation made Z fiercely political, so when the Hungarian Revolution broke out in 1956, she took her destiny into her own hands and became one of those sixty-five thousand political refugees who left the country, mostly young workers and students like herself. She finished high school in Innsbruck, graduated from a bilingual gymnasium, and won a scholarship to the University of Vienna where she studied languages.

Z emigrated to the United States in 1959, became a student at the University of Chicago, married, and gave birth to two sons. In Chicago she studied with Second City, an improvisational theatrical school, the only one in the country at that time. Her family's spiritual tradition, however, started seeping back into her life, and she practiced solo worship of the Goddess at her home altar (in her backyard). When she entered her Saturn cycle at the age of thirty, she became involved with the women's liberation movement in Los Angeles and became an activist herself, staffing the Women's Center there for many years.

There she recognized a need for a spiritual dimension so far lacking in the feminist movement and started the women's spirituality movement. She founded the Susan B. Anthony Coven Number 1, the first feminist witches' coven, which became the role model for thousands of other spiritual groups being born and spreading across the nation. She wrote *The Holy Book of Women's Mysteries* (Wingbow Publishers, 1989) (originally published in 1975 as *The Feminist Book of Lights and Shadows*), which served as the first hands-on book to lead women into their own spiritual/Goddess heritage.

Z was arrested in 1975 for reading Tarot cards to an undercover policewoman; she lost the trial but won the issue, and the law against psychics was struck down nine years later. Z has led rituals, lectured, taught classes, given workshops, written articles tirelessly, and published in hundreds of women's newpapers across the country. She has powerfully influenced many of the future teachers and writers about the Goddess.

Today Z lives in the San Francisco Bay Area, traveling a lot, giving workshops and lectures, but always making time to smell the roses. She is the star of her own cable TV show called "13th Heaven" and acts as the director of the Women's Spirituality Forum, a nonprofit organization sponsoring a monthly lecture series in the Bay Area about the Goddess, spirituality retreats, and annual spiral dances on Halloween. Z's business address is c/o Women's Spirituality Forum, P.O. Box 11363, Oakland, California 94611.